The Sinners

Colors by Val Staples

CRIMINAL VOL. 5: THE SINNERS. Contains material originally published in magazine form as CRIMINAL: The Sinners #1-5. First printing 2010. ISBN# 978-0-7851-3229-5. Published by MARVEL WORLDWIDE, INC., a subsidiary of MARVEL ENTERTAINMENT, LLC. OFFICE OF PUBLICATION: 417 5th Avenue, New York, NY 10016.

$15.99 per copy in the U.S. (GST #R127032852) in the direct market; Canadian Agreement #40668537.

Printed in the U.S.A.

10 9 8 7 6 5 4 3 2 1

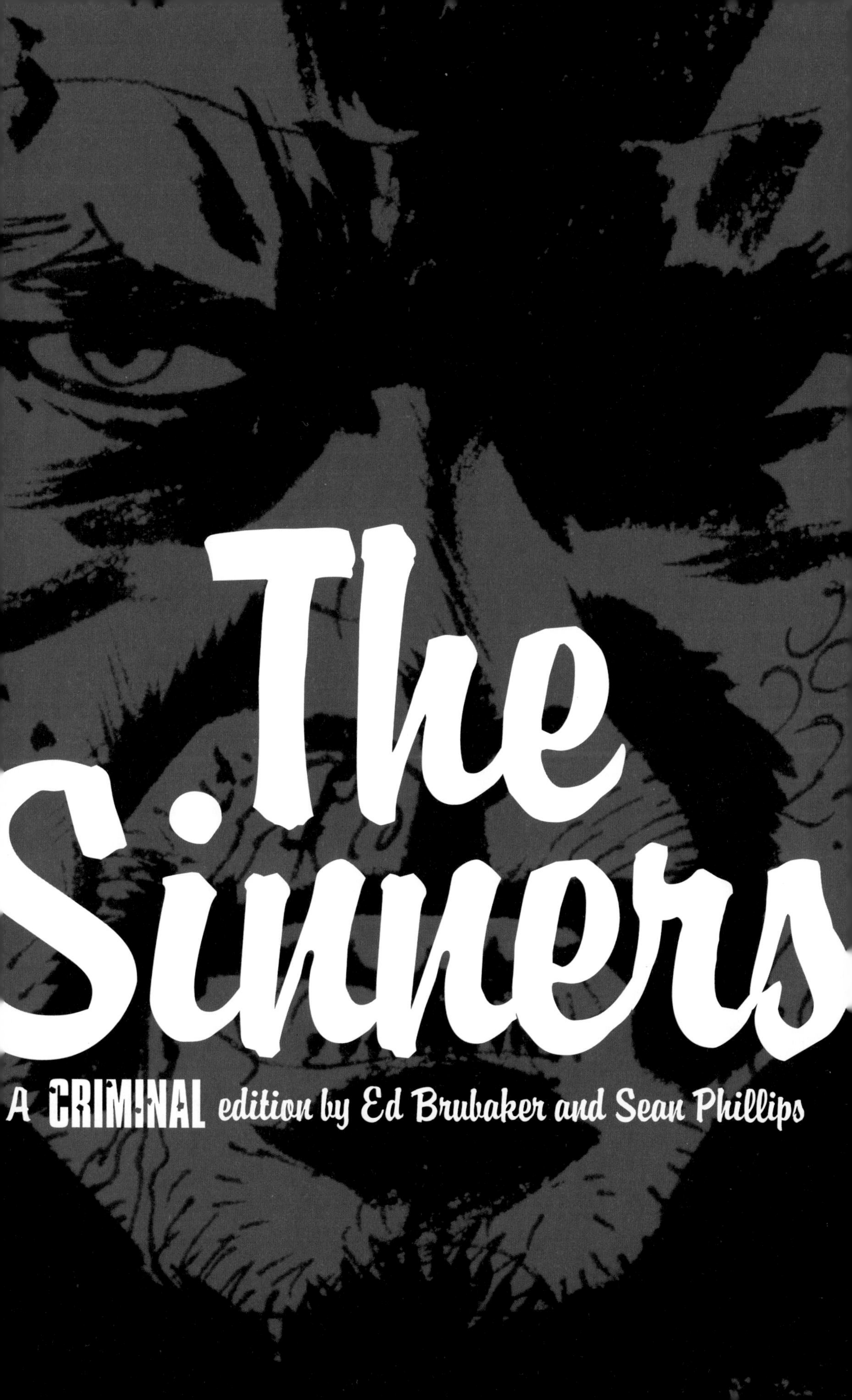

The Sinners

A CRIMINAL edition by Ed Brubaker and Sean Phillips

Introduction

"Tracy Lawless was becoming the worst hitman in the world…"

Who's going to stop reading there? Who is not going to be compelled to find out just what's happening to Lawless? Is he losing his nerve or growing a conscience? And how would any of that square with his employer, especially when Tracy is slipping a length to said employer's wife? Add in the fact that Lawless is a deserter with a detective on his tail and you have a story claustrophobic enough to leave anyone gasping for breath.

And the thing is: that's not even the half of it. Not even close.

Welcome to the New Noir, in the capable hands of its pre-eminent creators and facilitators, writer Ed Brubaker and artist Sean Phillips. Welcome to moral dilemmas, wrong roads taken, friendships sullied and misdemeanours past, present and forthcoming.

But what exactly *is* "noir"? No one seems able to agree. The critic Ian Ousby says that it 'eludes definition', but he is able to point to some of its requisites: 'tough detectives, brutal cops, mobsters, small-time criminals, crazed killers, men on the run, *femmes fatales* and (from the mid-1940s) war-tortured veterans playing out their destinies in confined interiors and the anonymous streets of the city. Their characteristic inner state is confusion, fear or obsession, and their characteristic relationship with others is intrigue or betrayal. The characteristic outcome is defeat…'

Read 'The Sinners', then come back and look at that list again. All present and correct. But what lifts Brubaker and Phillips above the herd is their particular genius. Brubaker knows what makes a good, tense crime story, but he adds layers and texture. His characters rise above the two-dimensional; they seem real to us, so that we can imagine their stories happening in reality. Phillips is a master of light and shade. He gives Lawless heft without allowing him to appear superhuman. He captures pain, loneliness, rage and despair with breathtaking economy.

There's a line in Raymond Chandler's 'The Big Sleep' where his private eye, Philip Marlowe, ruminates on the plot he's embroiled in: 'knights had no meaning in this game; it wasn't a game for knights'. Yet Lawless can't help behaving like a knight - albeit one whose armour is tarnished beyond hope. He attempts to 'rescue' damsels while fighting off 'dragons' (whether they be vigilantes or Triad mobsters). He has a personal code of honour. He feels that there is some sort of grail at the end of his quest, even though he has no sense of what it might comprise.

And we're rooting for him.

We don't want him to lose.

But we know he must lose. It's one of the rules of the game.

Then again, as Lawless himself might agree, rules are there to be broken….

Ian Rankin

Ian Rankin is the author of the internationally-acclaimed 'Inspector Rebus' series of novels. His first graphic novel, 'Dark Entries', was published in 2009.

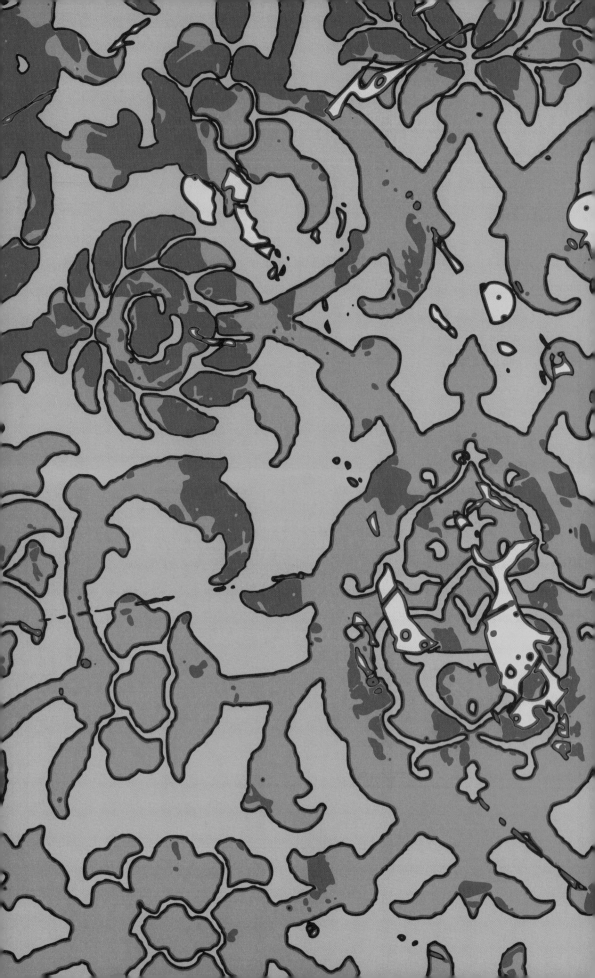

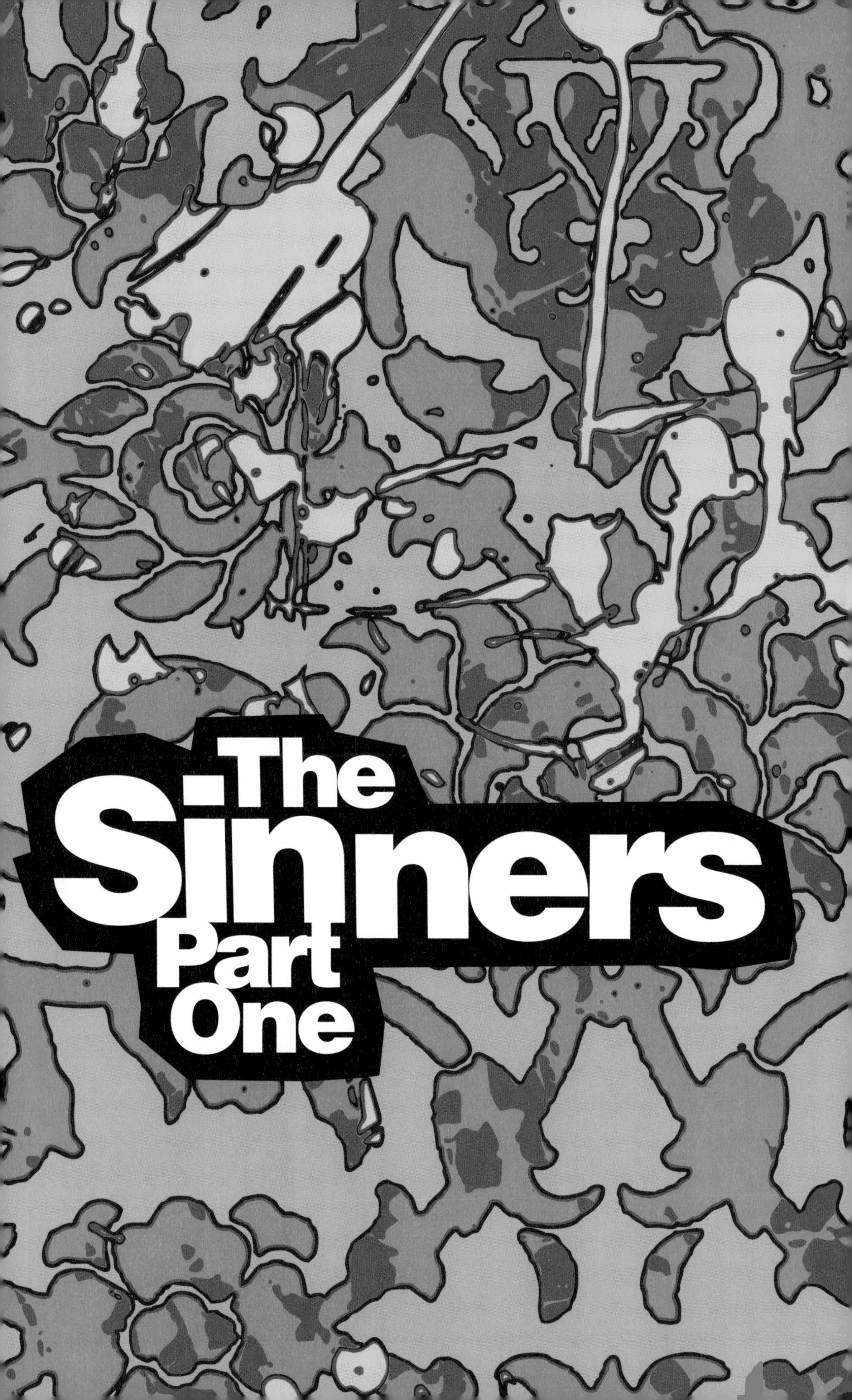
The
Sinners
Part
One

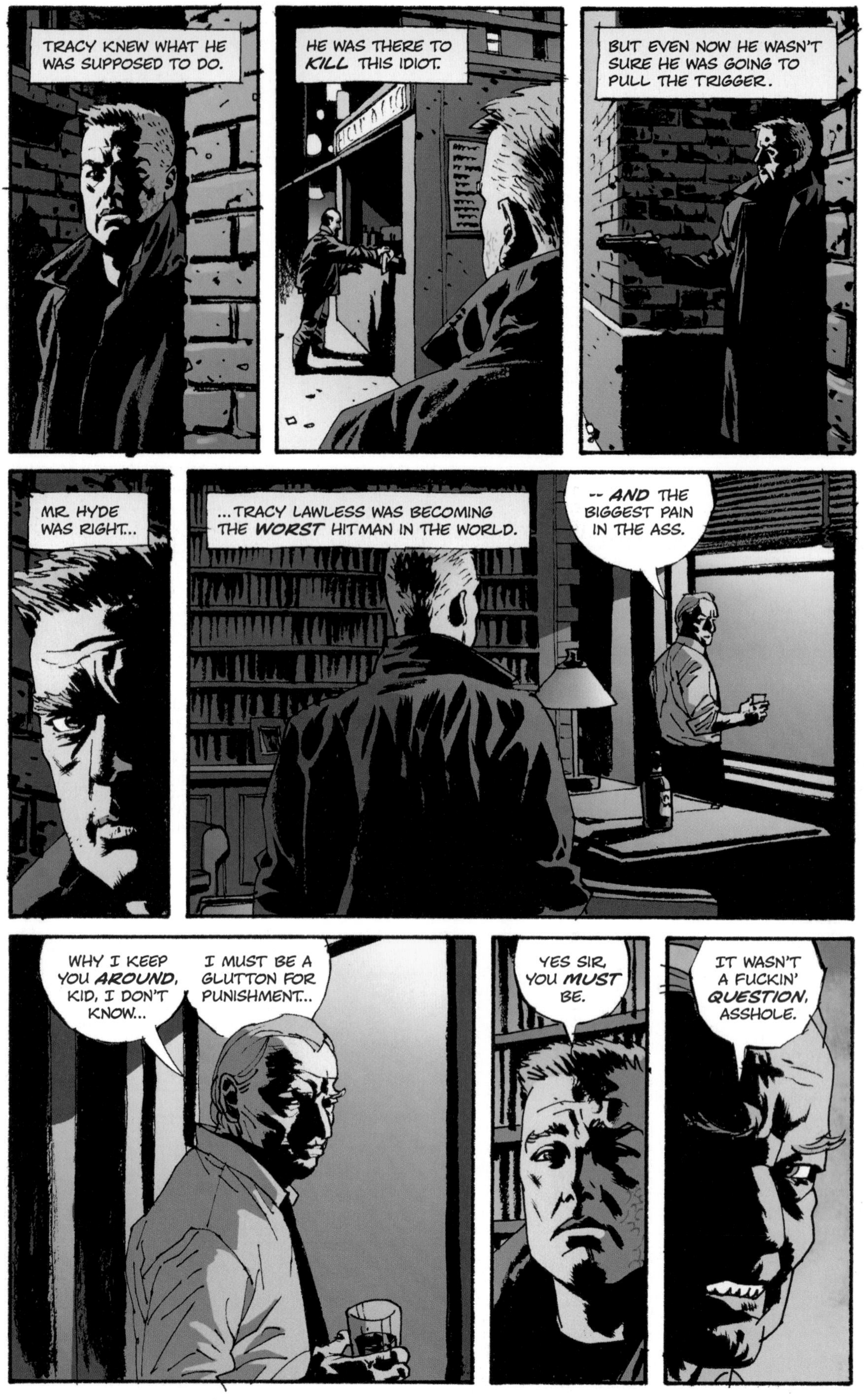
TRACY KNEW WHAT HE WAS SUPPOSED TO DO.
HE WAS THERE TO KILL THIS IDIOT.
BUT EVEN NOW HE WASN'T SURE HE WAS GOING TO PULL THE TRIGGER.
MR. HYDE WAS RIGHT...
...TRACY LAWLESS WAS BECOMING THE WORST HITMAN IN THE WORLD.
-- AND THE BIGGEST PAIN IN THE ASS.
WHY I KEEP YOU AROUND, KID, I DON'T KNOW...
I MUST BE A GLUTTON FOR PUNISHMENT...
YES SIR, YOU MUST BE.
IT WASN'T A FUCKIN' QUESTION, ASSHOLE.

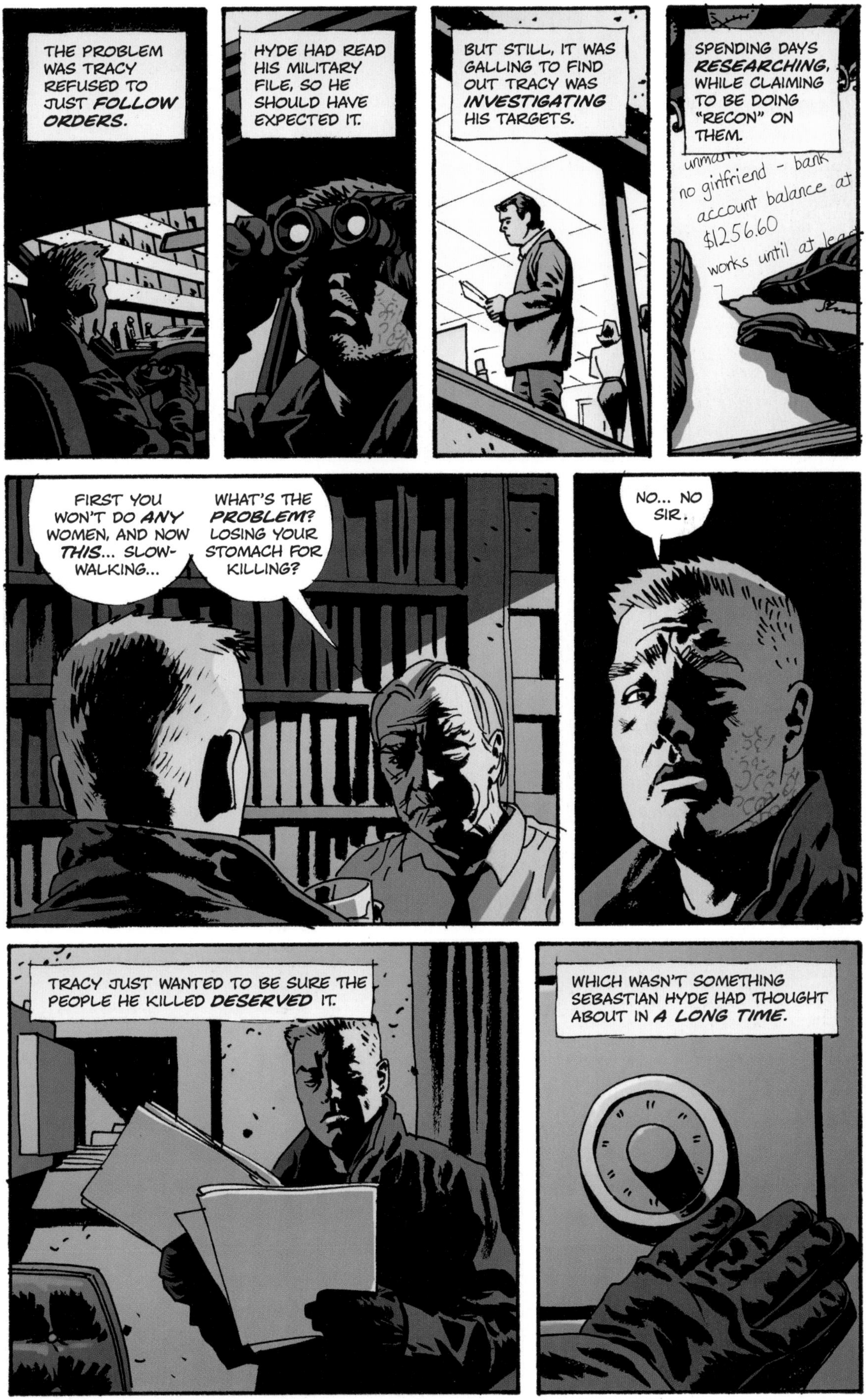
THE PROBLEM WAS TRACY REFUSED TO JUST **FOLLOW ORDERS.**
HYDE HAD READ HIS MILITARY FILE, SO HE SHOULD HAVE EXPECTED IT.
BUT STILL, IT WAS GALLING TO FIND OUT TRACY WAS ***INVESTIGATING*** HIS TARGETS.
SPENDING DAYS ***RESEARCHING,*** WHILE CLAIMING TO BE DOING "RECON" ON THEM.
no girlfriend - bank
account balance at
$1256.60
works until at
FIRST YOU WON'T DO ***ANY*** WOMEN, AND NOW ***THIS***... SLOW-WALKING...
WHAT'S THE ***PROBLEM?*** LOSING YOUR STOMACH FOR KILLING?
NO... NO SIR.
TRACY JUST WANTED TO BE SURE THE PEOPLE HE KILLED ***DESERVED*** IT.
WHICH WASN'T SOMETHING SEBASTIAN HYDE HAD THOUGHT ABOUT IN ***A LONG TIME.***

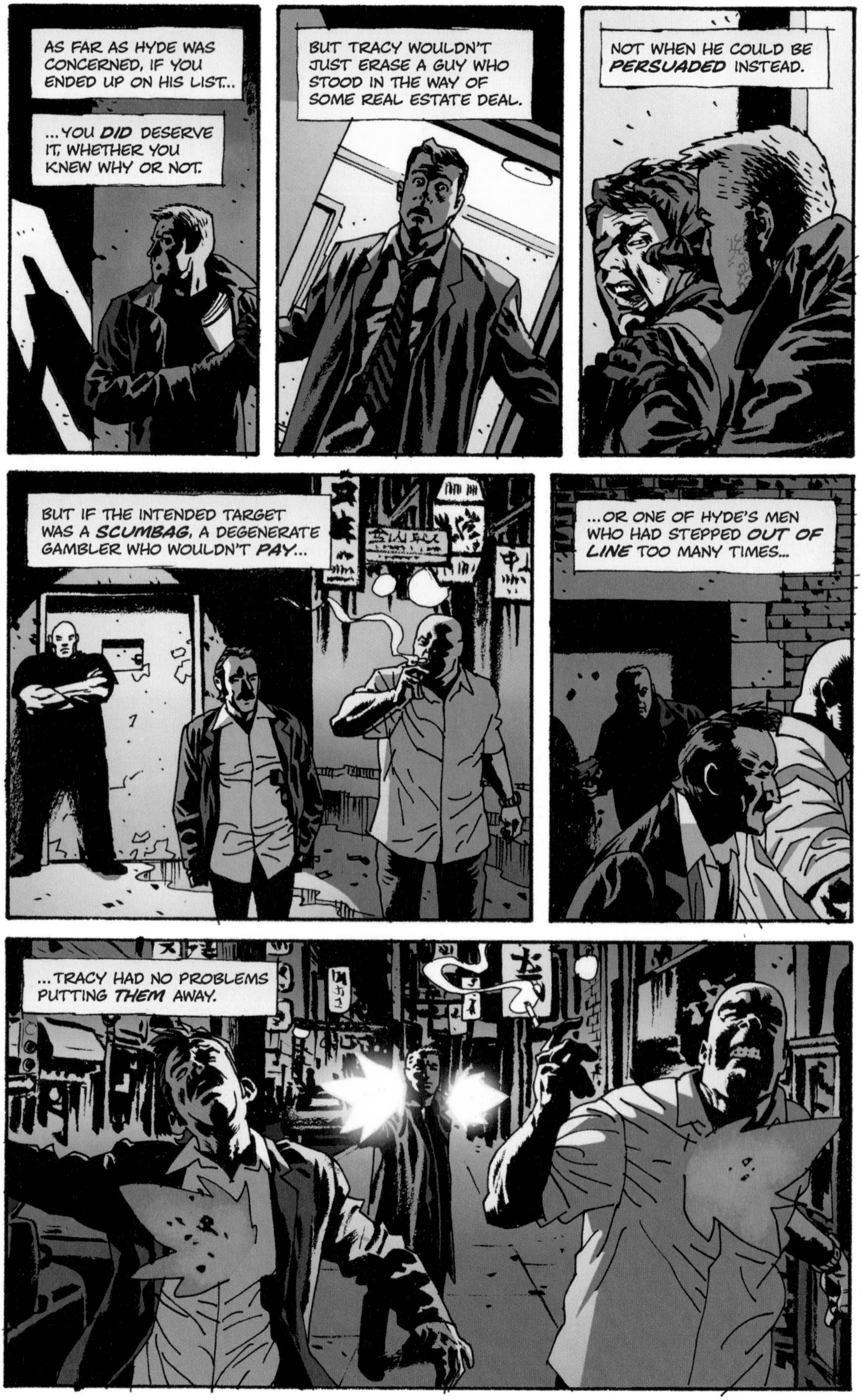
AS FAR AS HYDE WAS CONCERNED, IF YOU ENDED UP ON HIS LIST...
...YOU DID DESERVE IT, WHETHER YOU KNEW WHY OR NOT.
BUT TRACY WOULDN'T JUST ERASE A GUY WHO STOOD IN THE WAY OF SOME REAL ESTATE DEAL.
NOT WHEN HE COULD BE PERSUADED INSTEAD.
BUT IF THE INTENDED TARGET WAS A SCUMBAG, A DEGENERATE GAMBLER WHO WOULDN'T PAY...
...OR ONE OF HYDE'S MEN WHO HAD STEPPED OUT OF LINE TOO MANY TIMES...
...TRACY HAD NO PROBLEMS PUTTING THEM AWAY.

BUT A GUY LIKE THIS... NICK THE HOTDOG VENDOR.

HE WAS RIGHT ON THE EDGE.

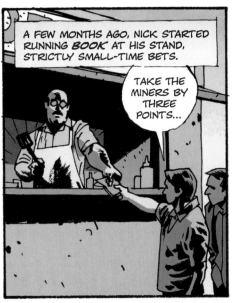

A FEW MONTHS AGO, NICK STARTED RUNNING *BOOK* AT HIS STAND, STRICTLY SMALL-TIME BETS.

TAKE THE MINERS BY THREE POINTS...

AND WHEN WORD GOT BACK TO *HYDE*, NICK HAD BEEN STUPID...

TELL YOUR BOSS TO COME SEE ME *HIMSELF*, HE WANTS SOME'A *MY* CABBAGE...

FUCKHEAD...

DID BEING STUPID AND DISRESPECTFUL EARN A GUY *DEATH?* OVER A FEW GRAND?

TRACY WASN'T SURE.

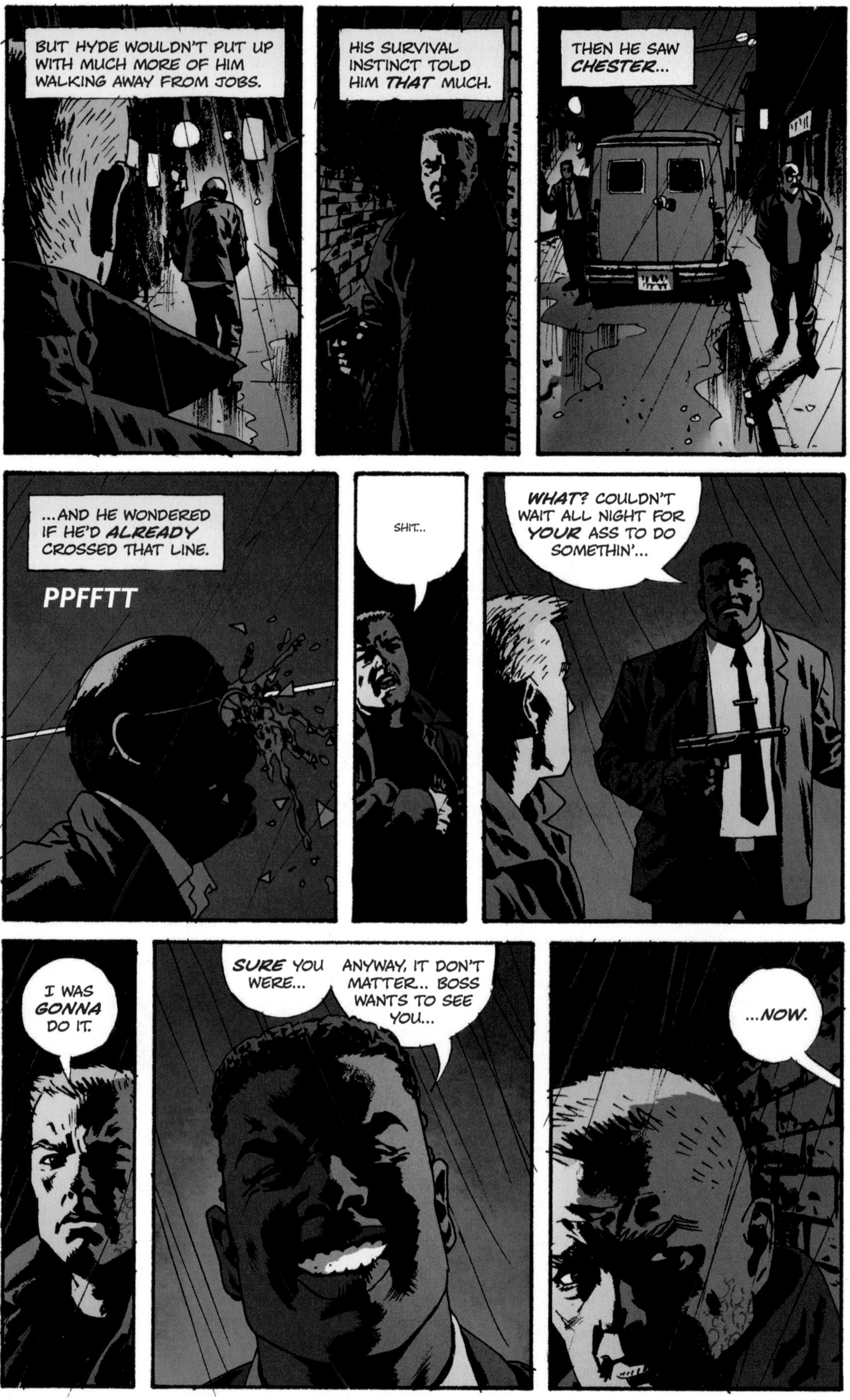

BUT HYDE WOULDN'T PUT UP WITH MUCH MORE OF HIM WALKING AWAY FROM JOBS.
HIS SURVIVAL INSTINCT TOLD HIM *THAT* MUCH.
THEN HE SAW *CHESTER*...
...AND HE WONDERED IF HE'D *ALREADY* CROSSED THAT LINE.
PPFFTT
SHIT...
WHAT? COULDN'T WAIT ALL NIGHT FOR *YOUR* ASS TO DO SOMETHIN'...
I WAS *GONNA* DO IT.
SURE YOU WERE...
ANYWAY, IT DON'T MATTER... BOSS WANTS TO SEE YOU...
...*NOW*.

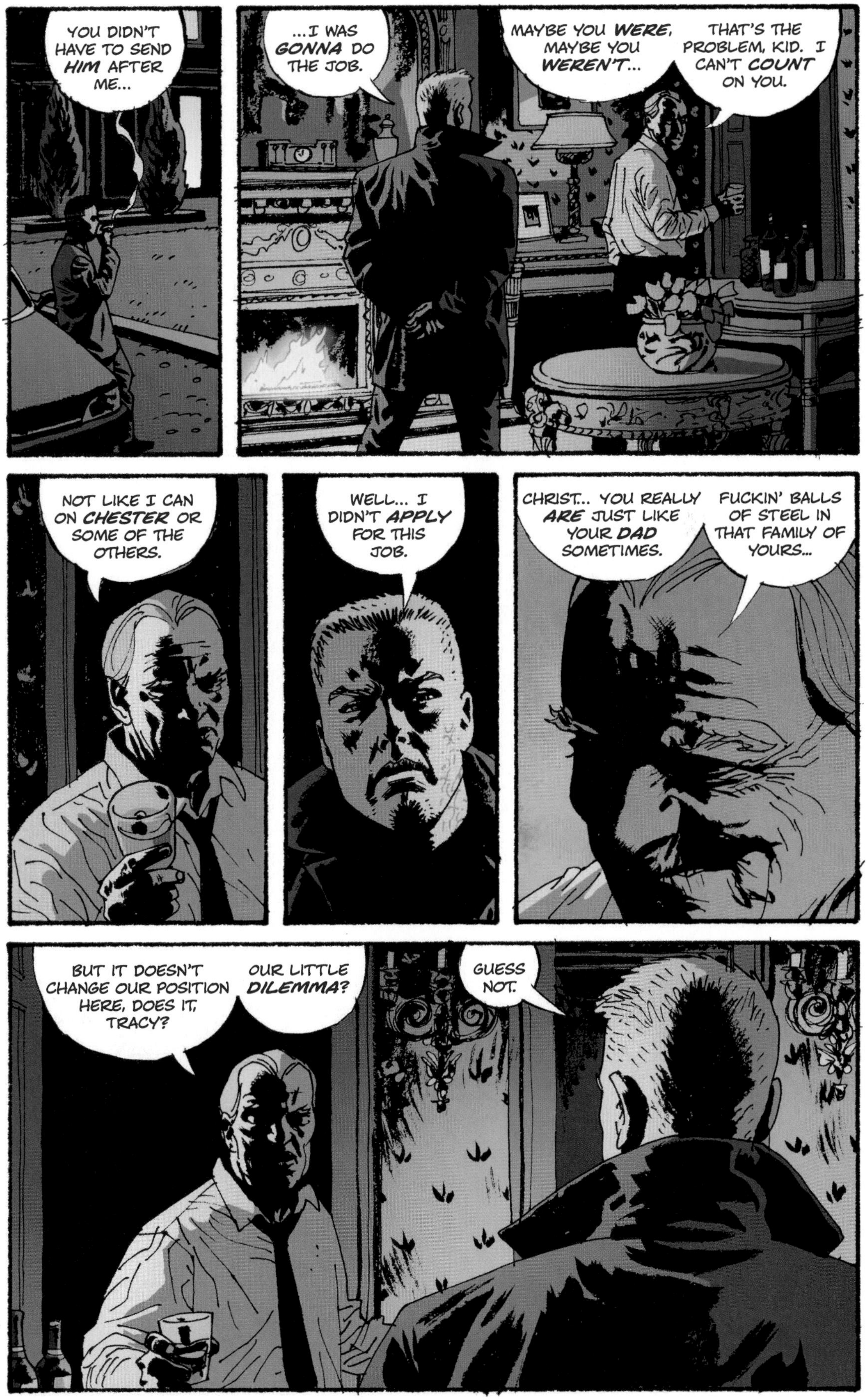
YOU DIDN'T HAVE TO SEND HIM AFTER ME...
...I WAS GONNA DO THE JOB.
MAYBE YOU WERE, MAYBE YOU WEREN'T...
THAT'S THE PROBLEM, KID. I CAN'T COUNT ON YOU.
NOT LIKE I CAN ON CHESTER OR SOME OF THE OTHERS.
WELL... I DIDN'T APPLY FOR THIS JOB.
CHRIST... YOU REALLY ARE JUST LIKE YOUR DAD SOMETIMES.
FUCKIN' BALLS OF STEEL IN THAT FAMILY OF YOURS...
BUT IT DOESN'T CHANGE OUR POSITION HERE, DOES IT, TRACY?
OUR LITTLE DILEMMA?
GUESS NOT.

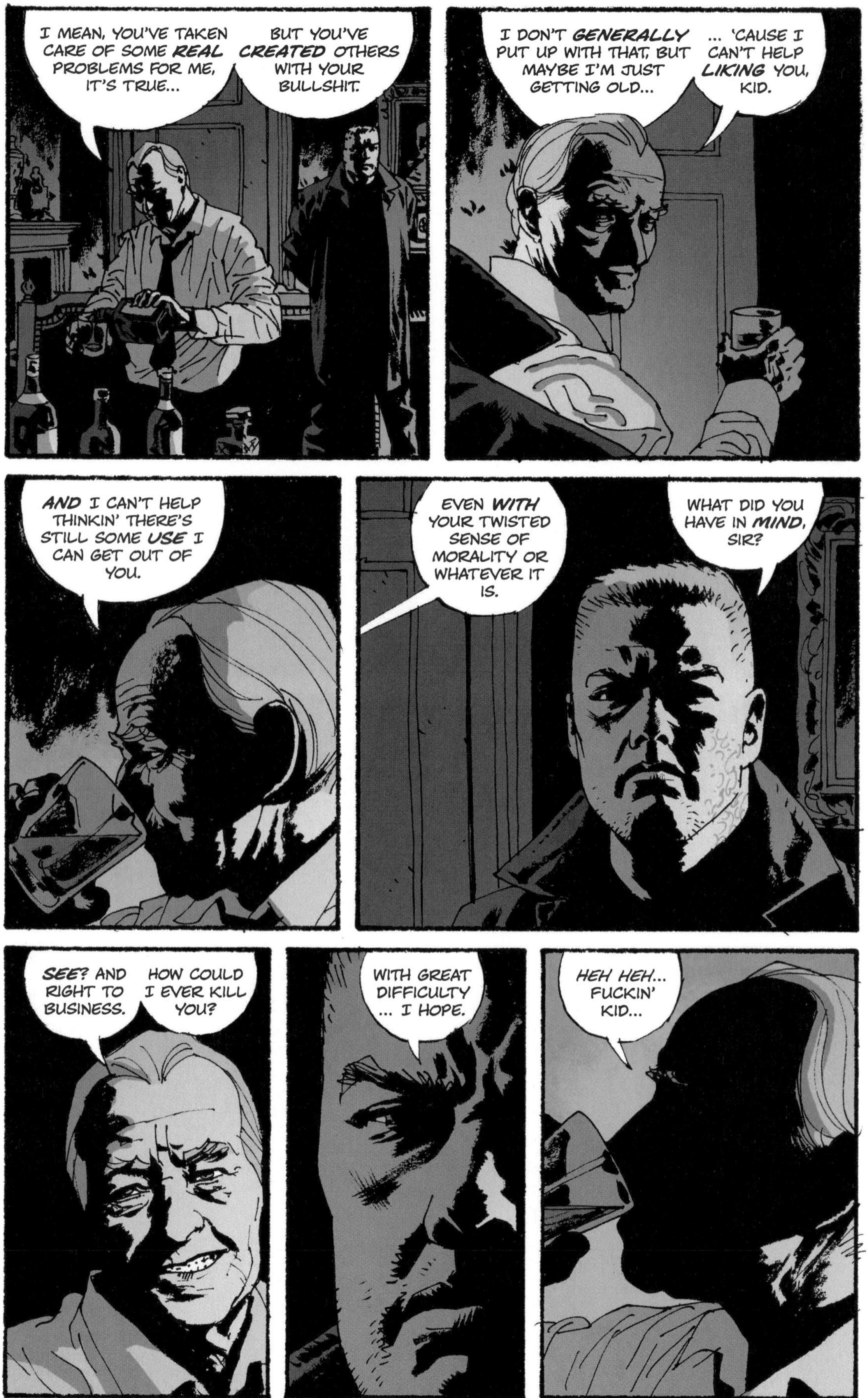
I MEAN, YOU'VE TAKEN CARE OF SOME REAL PROBLEMS FOR ME, IT'S TRUE...
BUT YOU'VE CREATED OTHERS WITH YOUR BULLSHIT.
I DON'T GENERALLY PUT UP WITH THAT, BUT MAYBE I'M JUST GETTING OLD...
... 'CAUSE I CAN'T HELP LIKING YOU, KID.
AND I CAN'T HELP THINKIN' THERE'S STILL SOME USE I CAN GET OUT OF YOU.
EVEN WITH YOUR TWISTED SENSE OF MORALITY OR WHATEVER IT IS.
WHAT DID YOU HAVE IN MIND, SIR?
SEE? AND RIGHT TO BUSINESS.
HOW COULD I EVER KILL YOU?
WITH GREAT DIFFICULTY ... I HOPE.
HEH HEH... FUCKIN' KID...

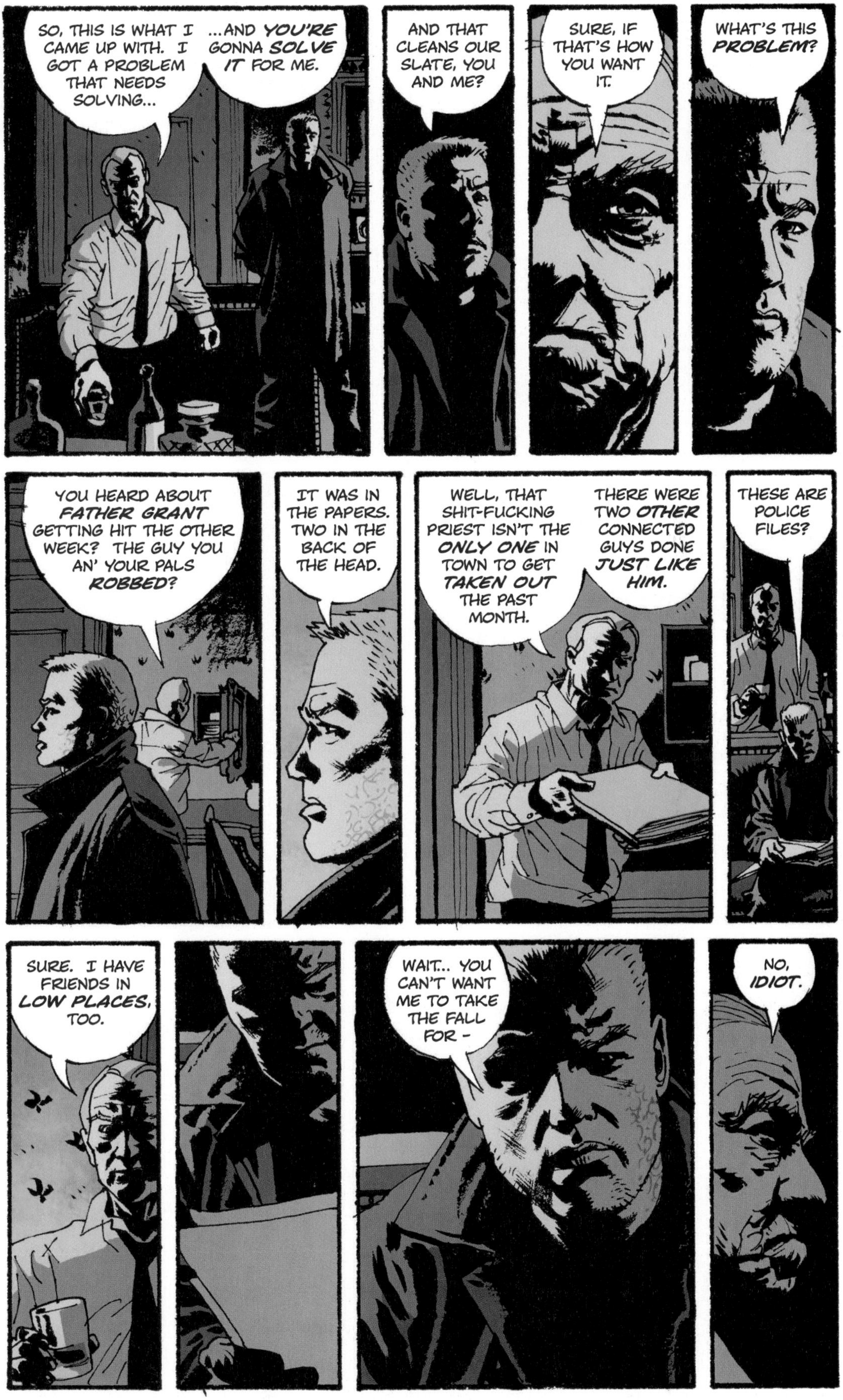
SO, THIS IS WHAT I CAME UP WITH. I GOT A PROBLEM THAT NEEDS SOLVING...
...AND YOU'RE GONNA SOLVE IT FOR ME.
AND THAT CLEANS OUR SLATE, YOU AND ME?
SURE, IF THAT'S HOW YOU WANT IT.
WHAT'S THIS PROBLEM?
YOU HEARD ABOUT FATHER GRANT GETTING HIT THE OTHER WEEK? THE GUY YOU AN' YOUR PALS ROBBED?
IT WAS IN THE PAPERS. TWO IN THE BACK OF THE HEAD.
WELL, THAT SHIT-FUCKING PRIEST ISN'T THE ONLY ONE IN TOWN TO GET TAKEN OUT THE PAST MONTH.
THERE WERE TWO OTHER CONNECTED GUYS DONE JUST LIKE HIM.
THESE ARE POLICE FILES?
SURE. I HAVE FRIENDS IN LOW PLACES, TOO.
WAIT... YOU CAN'T WANT ME TO TAKE THE FALL FOR -
NO, IDIOT.

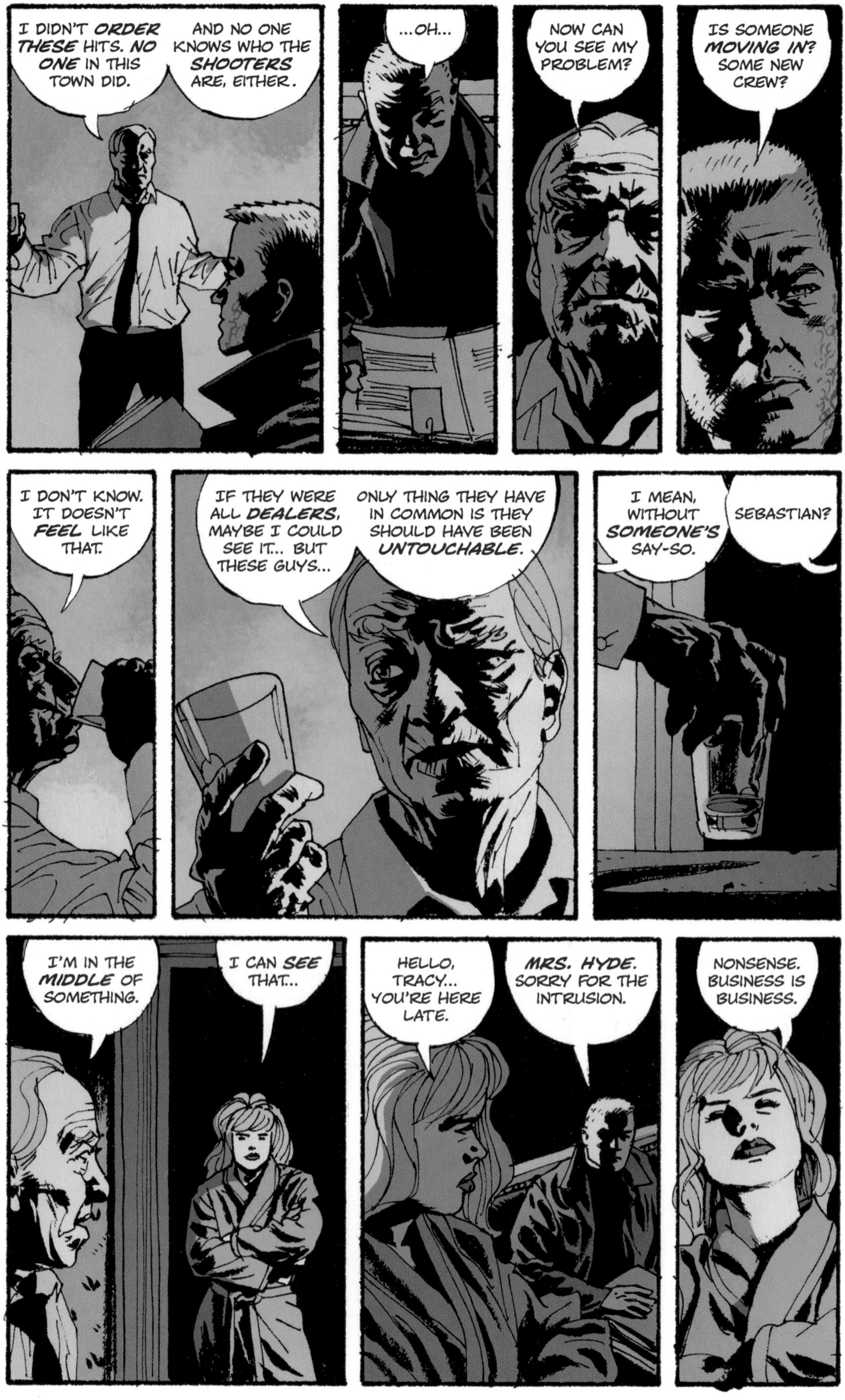
I DIDN'T ORDER THESE HITS. NO ONE IN THIS TOWN DID.
AND NO ONE KNOWS WHO THE SHOOTERS ARE, EITHER.
...OH...
NOW CAN YOU SEE MY PROBLEM?
IS SOMEONE MOVING IN? SOME NEW CREW?
I DON'T KNOW. IT DOESN'T FEEL LIKE THAT.
IF THEY WERE ALL DEALERS, MAYBE I COULD SEE IT... BUT THESE GUYS...
ONLY THING THEY HAVE IN COMMON IS THEY SHOULD HAVE BEEN UNTOUCHABLE.
I MEAN, WITHOUT SOMEONE'S SAY-SO.
SEBASTIAN?
I'M IN THE MIDDLE OF SOMETHING.
I CAN SEE THAT...
HELLO, TRACY... YOU'RE HERE LATE.
MRS. HYDE. SORRY FOR THE INTRUSION.
NONSENSE. BUSINESS IS BUSINESS.

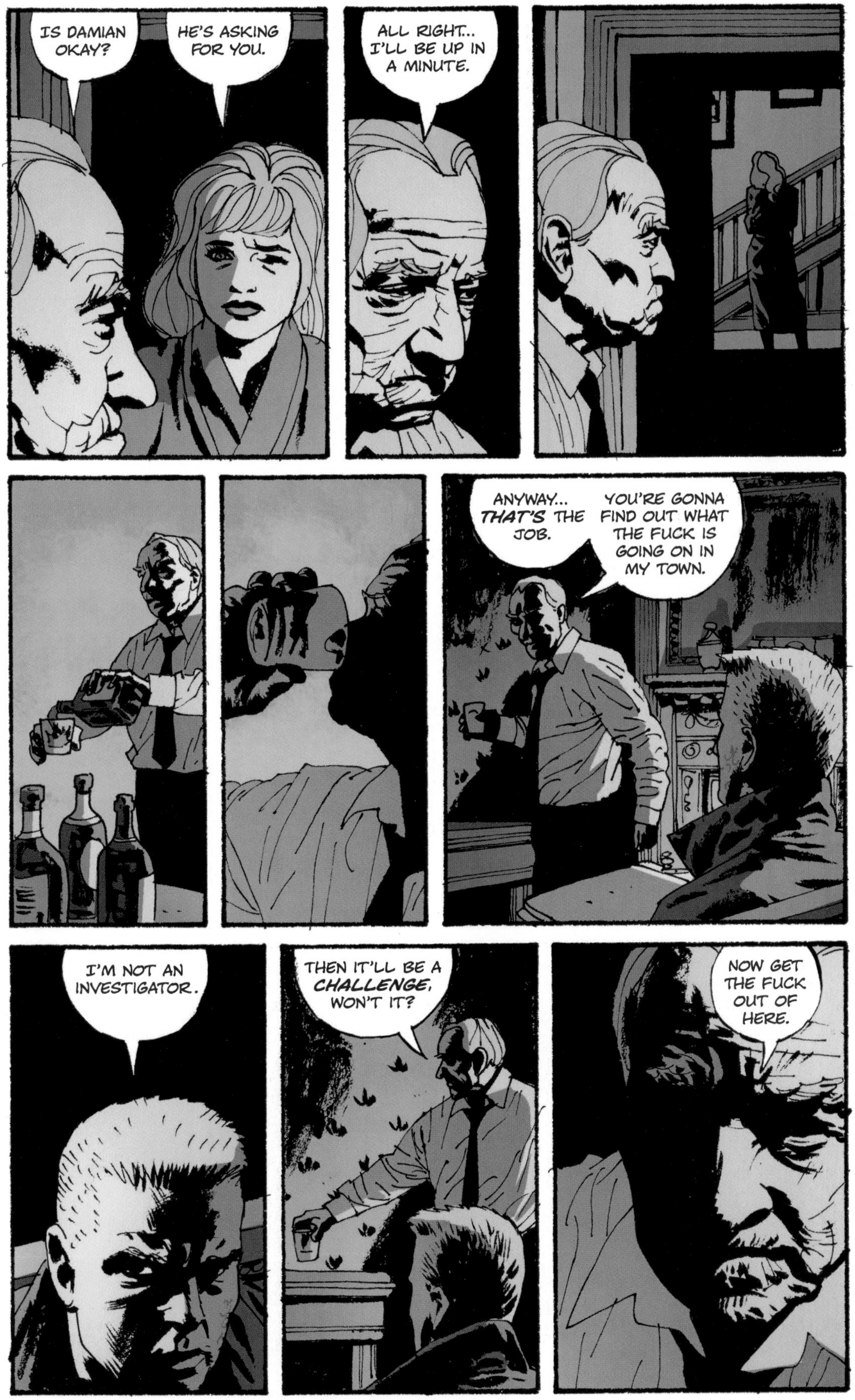
IS DAMIAN OKAY?
HE'S ASKING FOR YOU.
ALL RIGHT... I'LL BE UP IN A MINUTE.
ANYWAY... THAT'S THE JOB.
YOU'RE GONNA FIND OUT WHAT THE FUCK IS GOING ON IN MY TOWN.
I'M NOT AN INVESTIGATOR.
THEN IT'LL BE A CHALLENGE, WON'T IT?
NOW GET THE FUCK OUT OF HERE.

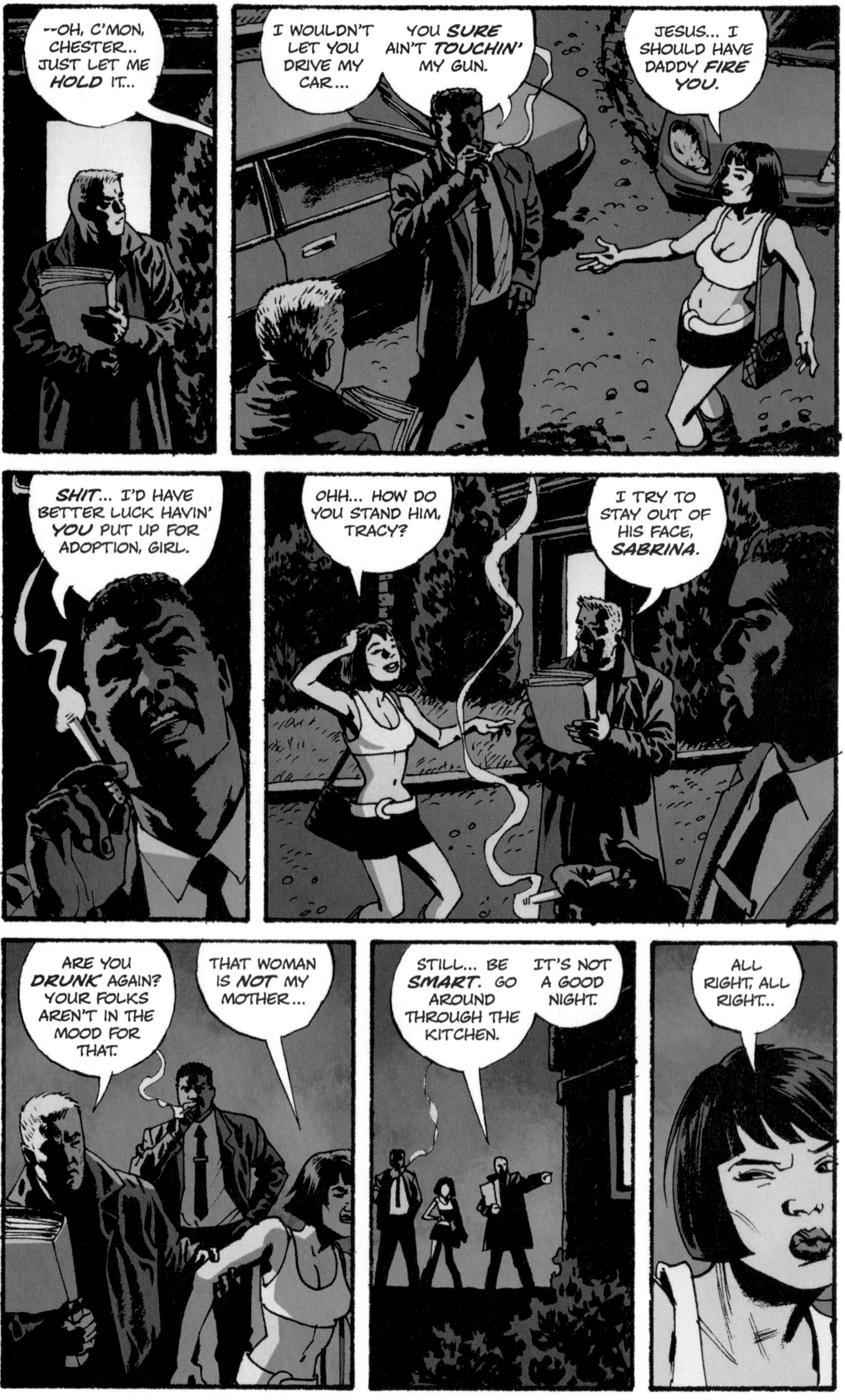
--OH, C'MON, CHESTER.. JUST LET ME HOLD IT...
I WOULDN'T LET YOU DRIVE MY CAR...
YOU SURE AIN'T TOUCHIN' MY GUN.
JESUS... I SHOULD HAVE DADDY FIRE YOU.
SHIT... I'D HAVE BETTER LUCK HAVIN' YOU PUT UP FOR ADOPTION, GIRL.
OHH... HOW DO YOU STAND HIM, TRACY?
I TRY TO STAY OUT OF HIS FACE, SABRINA.
ARE YOU DRUNK AGAIN? YOUR FOLKS AREN'T IN THE MOOD FOR THAT.
THAT WOMAN IS NOT MY MOTHER...
STILL... BE SMART. GO AROUND THROUGH THE KITCHEN.
IT'S NOT A GOOD NIGHT.
ALL RIGHT, ALL RIGHT...

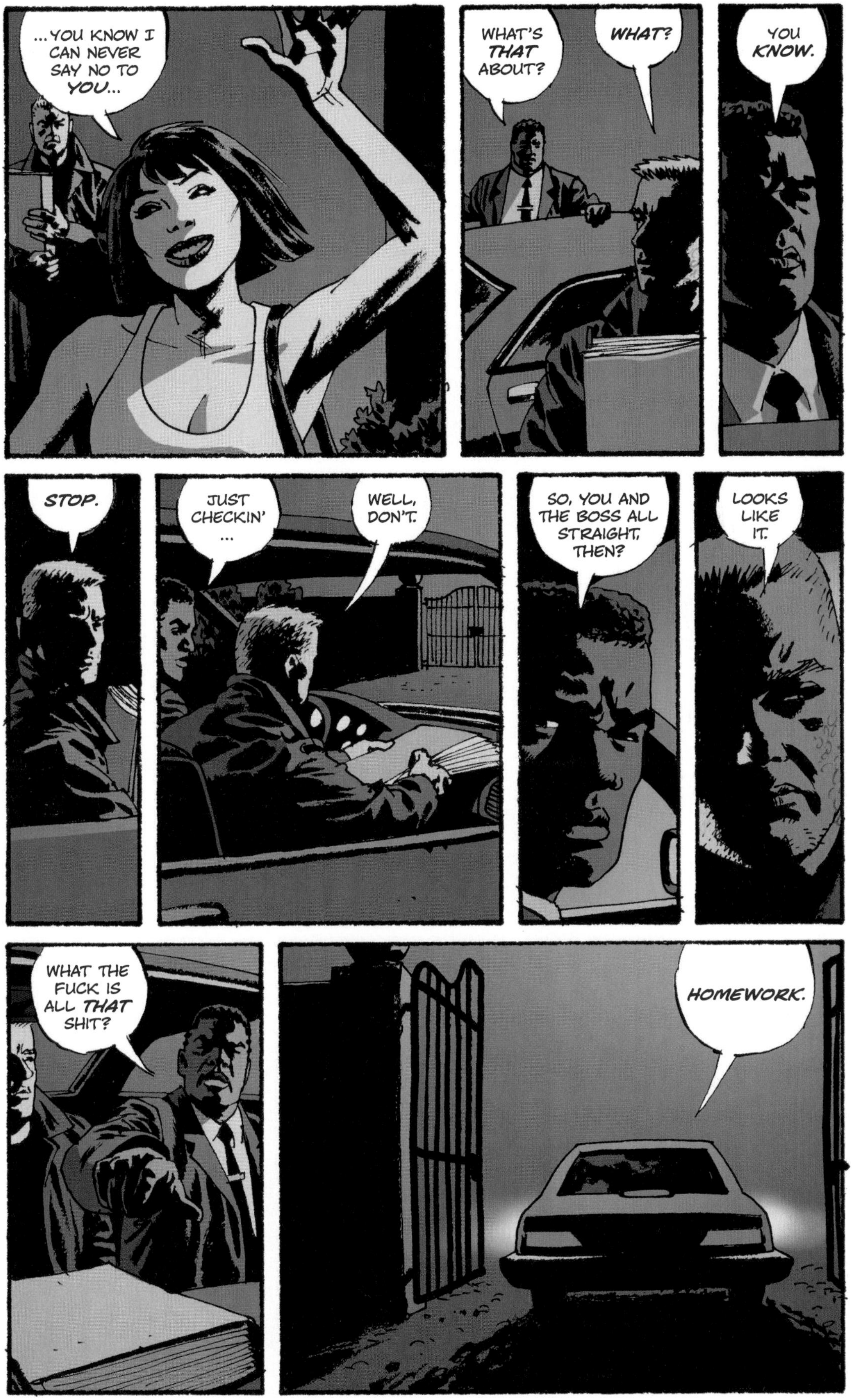
...YOU KNOW I CAN NEVER SAY NO TO YOU...
WHAT'S THAT ABOUT?
WHAT?
YOU KNOW.
STOP.
JUST CHECKIN' ...
WELL, DON'T.
SO, YOU AND THE BOSS ALL STRAIGHT, THEN?
LOOKS LIKE IT.
WHAT THE FUCK IS ALL THAT SHIT?
HOMEWORK.

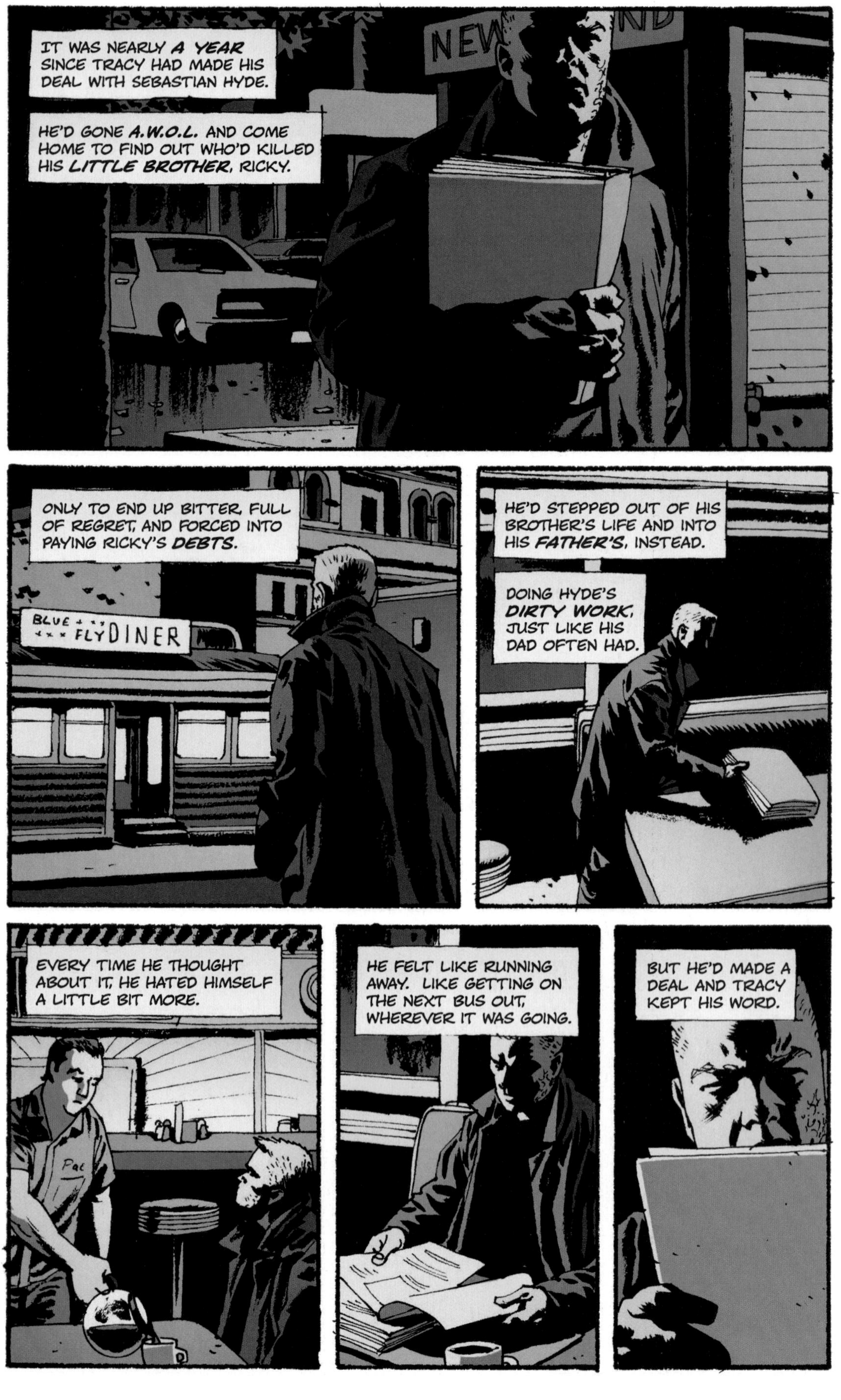
IT WAS NEARLY A YEAR SINCE TRACY HAD MADE HIS DEAL WITH SEBASTIAN HYDE.
HE'D GONE A.W.O.L. AND COME HOME TO FIND OUT WHO'D KILLED HIS LITTLE BROTHER, RICKY.
NEW
ONLY TO END UP BITTER, FULL OF REGRET, AND FORCED INTO PAYING RICKY'S DEBTS.
BLUE FLY DINER
HE'D STEPPED OUT OF HIS BROTHER'S LIFE AND INTO HIS FATHER'S, INSTEAD.
DOING HYDE'S DIRTY WORK, JUST LIKE HIS DAD OFTEN HAD.
EVERY TIME HE THOUGHT ABOUT IT, HE HATED HIMSELF A LITTLE BIT MORE.
Pat
HE FELT LIKE RUNNING AWAY. LIKE GETTING ON THE NEXT BUS OUT, WHEREVER IT WAS GOING.
BUT HE'D MADE A DEAL AND TRACY KEPT HIS WORD.

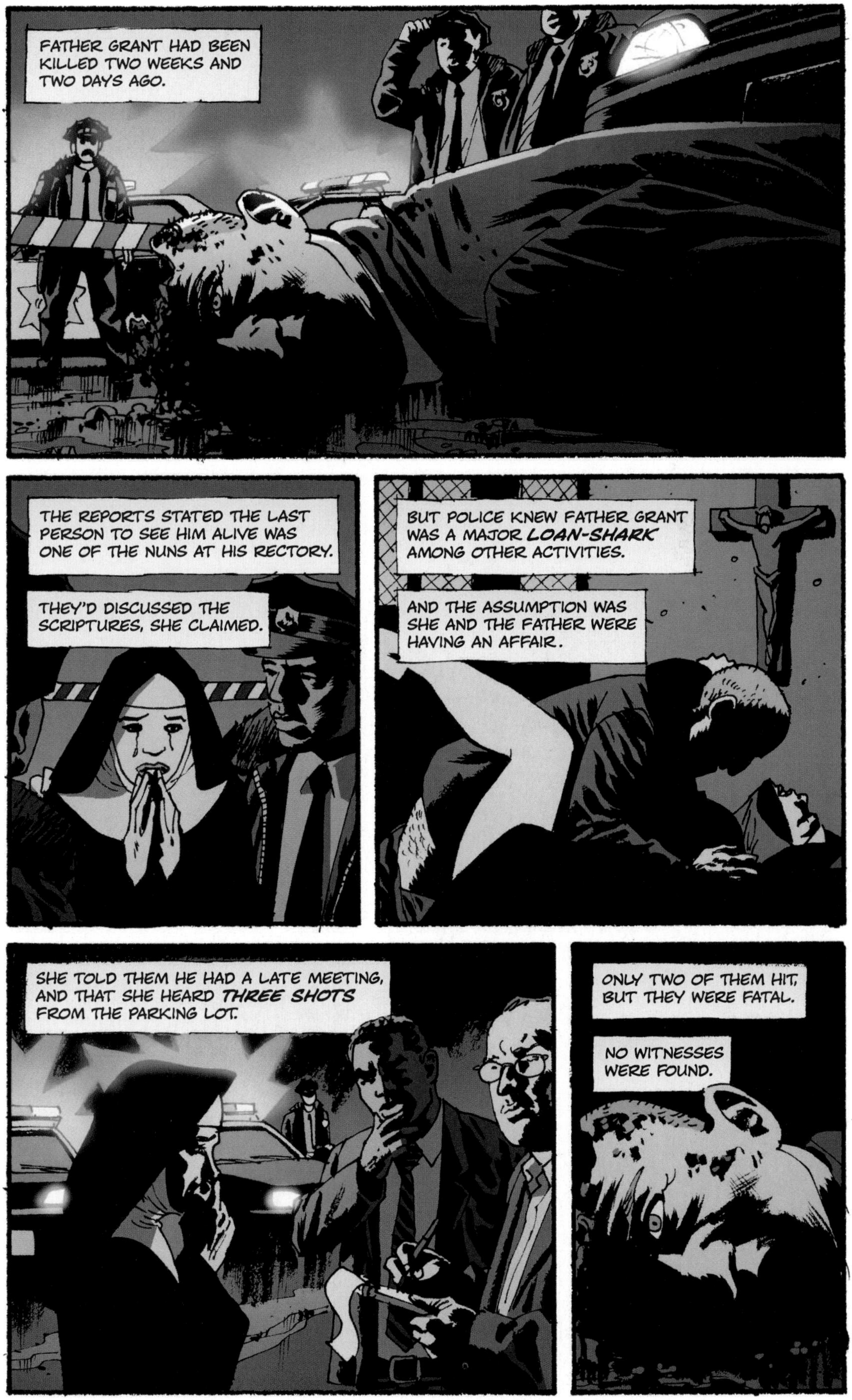
FATHER GRANT HAD BEEN KILLED TWO WEEKS AND TWO DAYS AGO.
THE REPORTS STATED THE LAST PERSON TO SEE HIM ALIVE WAS ONE OF THE NUNS AT HIS RECTORY.
THEY'D DISCUSSED THE SCRIPTURES, SHE CLAIMED.
BUT POLICE KNEW FATHER GRANT WAS A MAJOR LOAN-SHARK AMONG OTHER ACTIVITIES.
AND THE ASSUMPTION WAS SHE AND THE FATHER WERE HAVING AN AFFAIR.
SHE TOLD THEM HE HAD A LATE MEETING, AND THAT SHE HEARD THREE SHOTS FROM THE PARKING LOT.
ONLY TWO OF THEM HIT, BUT THEY WERE FATAL.
NO WITNESSES WERE FOUND.

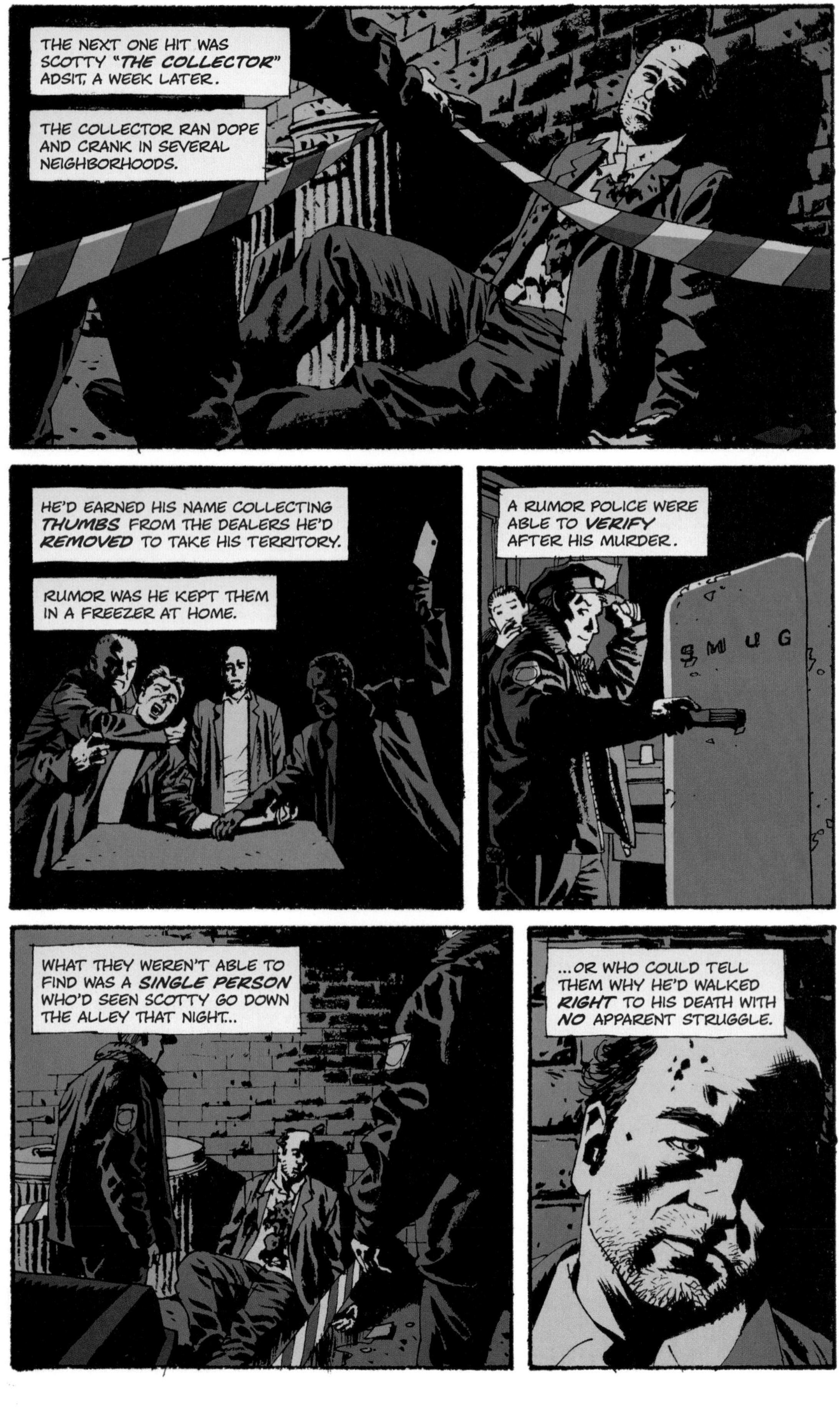
THE NEXT ONE HIT WAS SCOTTY "THE COLLECTOR" ADSIT, A WEEK LATER.
THE COLLECTOR RAN DOPE AND CRANK IN SEVERAL NEIGHBORHOODS.
HE'D EARNED HIS NAME COLLECTING THUMBS FROM THE DEALERS HE'D REMOVED TO TAKE HIS TERRITORY.
RUMOR WAS HE KEPT THEM IN A FREEZER AT HOME.
A RUMOR POLICE WERE ABLE TO VERIFY AFTER HIS MURDER.
SMUG
WHAT THEY WEREN'T ABLE TO FIND WAS A SINGLE PERSON WHO'D SEEN SCOTTY GO DOWN THE ALLEY THAT NIGHT...
...OR WHO COULD TELL THEM WHY HE'D WALKED RIGHT TO HIS DEATH WITH NO APPARENT STRUGGLE.

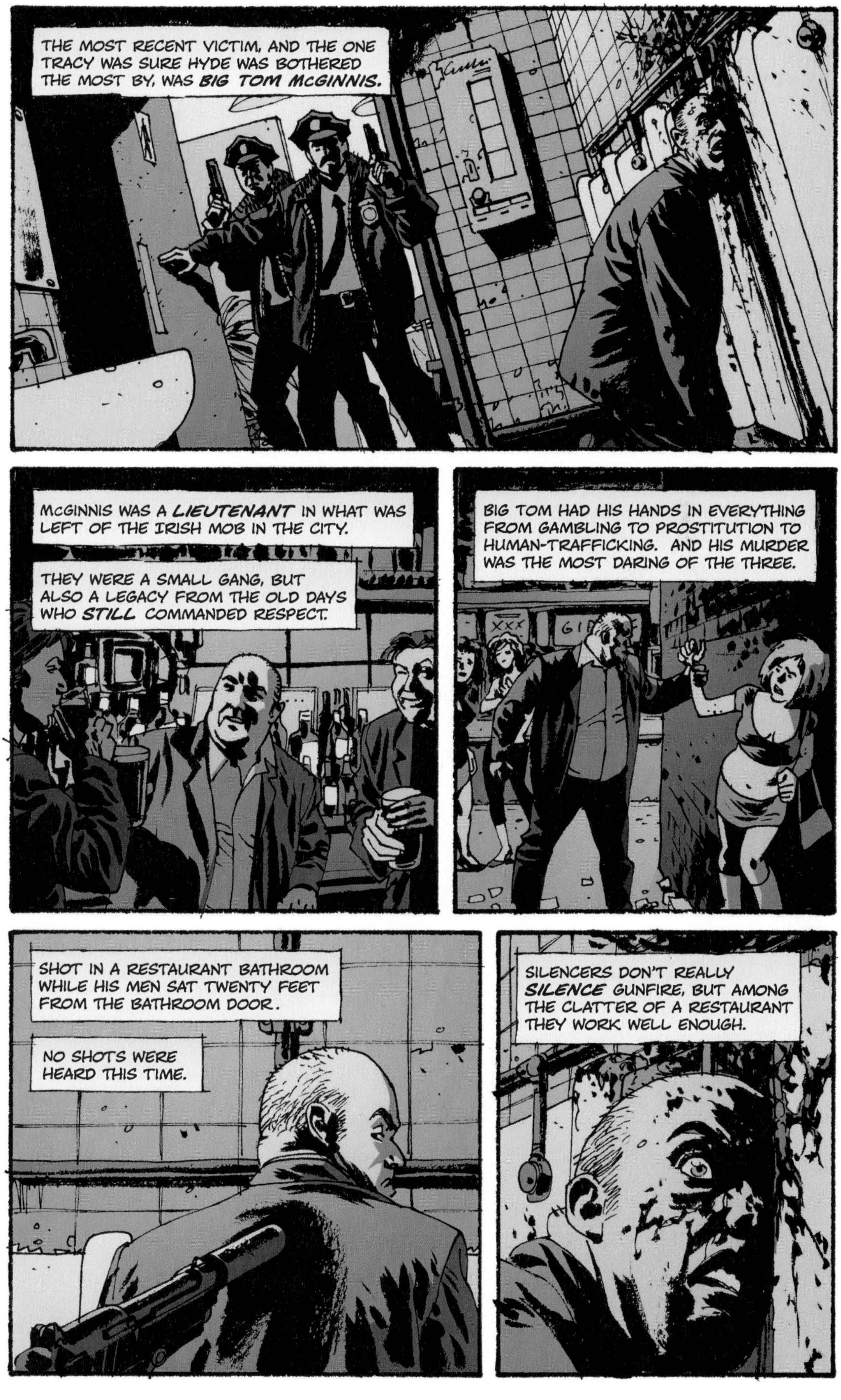
THE MOST RECENT VICTIM, AND THE ONE TRACY WAS SURE HYDE WAS BOTHERED THE MOST BY, WAS BIG TOM McGINNIS.
McGINNIS WAS A LIEUTENANT IN WHAT WAS LEFT OF THE IRISH MOB IN THE CITY.
THEY WERE A SMALL GANG, BUT ALSO A LEGACY FROM THE OLD DAYS WHO STILL COMMANDED RESPECT.
BIG TOM HAD HIS HANDS IN EVERYTHING FROM GAMBLING TO PROSTITUTION TO HUMAN-TRAFFICKING. AND HIS MURDER WAS THE MOST DARING OF THE THREE.
SHOT IN A RESTAURANT BATHROOM WHILE HIS MEN SAT TWENTY FEET FROM THE BATHROOM DOOR.
NO SHOTS WERE HEARD THIS TIME.
SILENCERS DON'T REALLY SILENCE GUNFIRE, BUT AMONG THE CLATTER OF A RESTAURANT THEY WORK WELL ENOUGH.

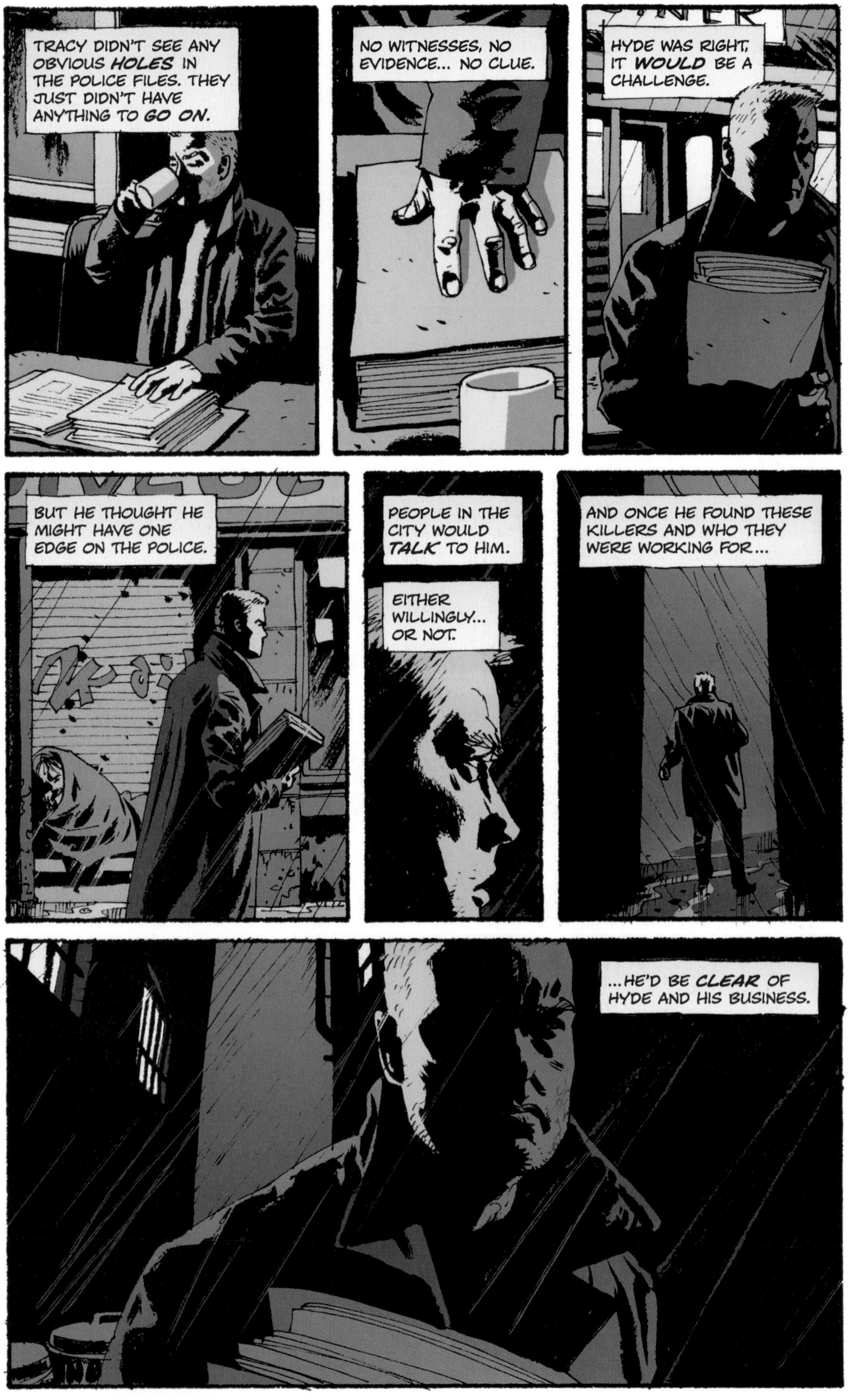
TRACY DIDN'T SEE ANY OBVIOUS HOLES IN THE POLICE FILES. THEY JUST DIDN'T HAVE ANYTHING TO GO ON.
NO WITNESSES, NO EVIDENCE... NO CLUE.
HYDE WAS RIGHT, IT WOULD BE A CHALLENGE.
BUT HE THOUGHT HE MIGHT HAVE ONE EDGE ON THE POLICE.
PEOPLE IN THE CITY WOULD TALK TO HIM.
EITHER WILLINGLY... OR NOT.
AND ONCE HE FOUND THESE KILLERS AND WHO THEY WERE WORKING FOR...
...HE'D BE CLEAR OF HYDE AND HIS BUSINESS.

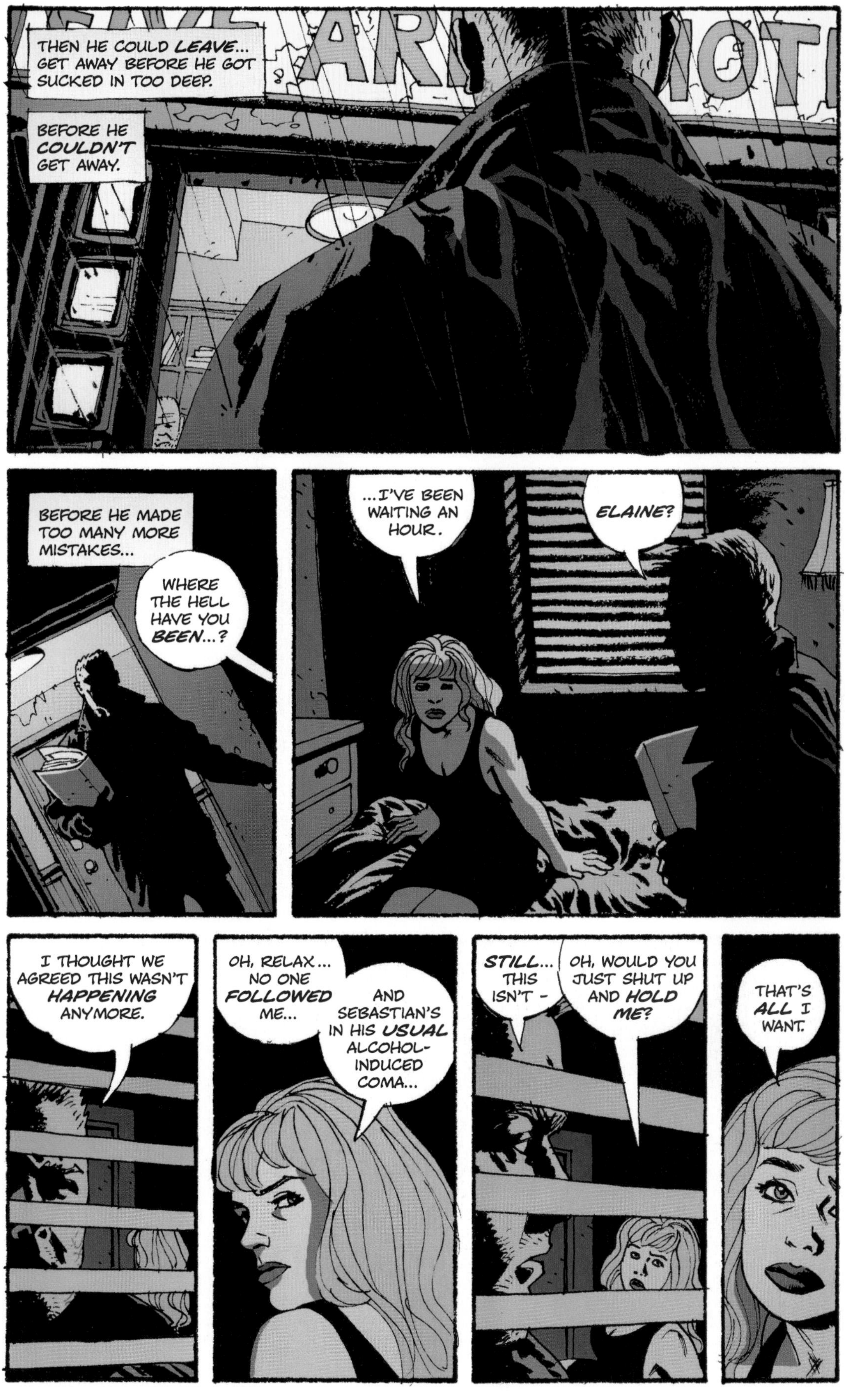
THEN HE COULD LEAVE... GET AWAY BEFORE HE GOT SUCKED IN TOO DEEP.
BEFORE HE COULDN'T GET AWAY.
BEFORE HE MADE TOO MANY MORE MISTAKES...
WHERE THE HELL HAVE YOU BEEN...?
...I'VE BEEN WAITING AN HOUR.
ELAINE?
I THOUGHT WE AGREED THIS WASN'T HAPPENING ANYMORE.
OH, RELAX... NO ONE FOLLOWED ME...
AND SEBASTIAN'S IN HIS USUAL ALCOHOL-INDUCED COMA...
STILL... THIS ISN'T -
OH, WOULD YOU JUST SHUT UP AND HOLD ME?
THAT'S ALL I WANT.

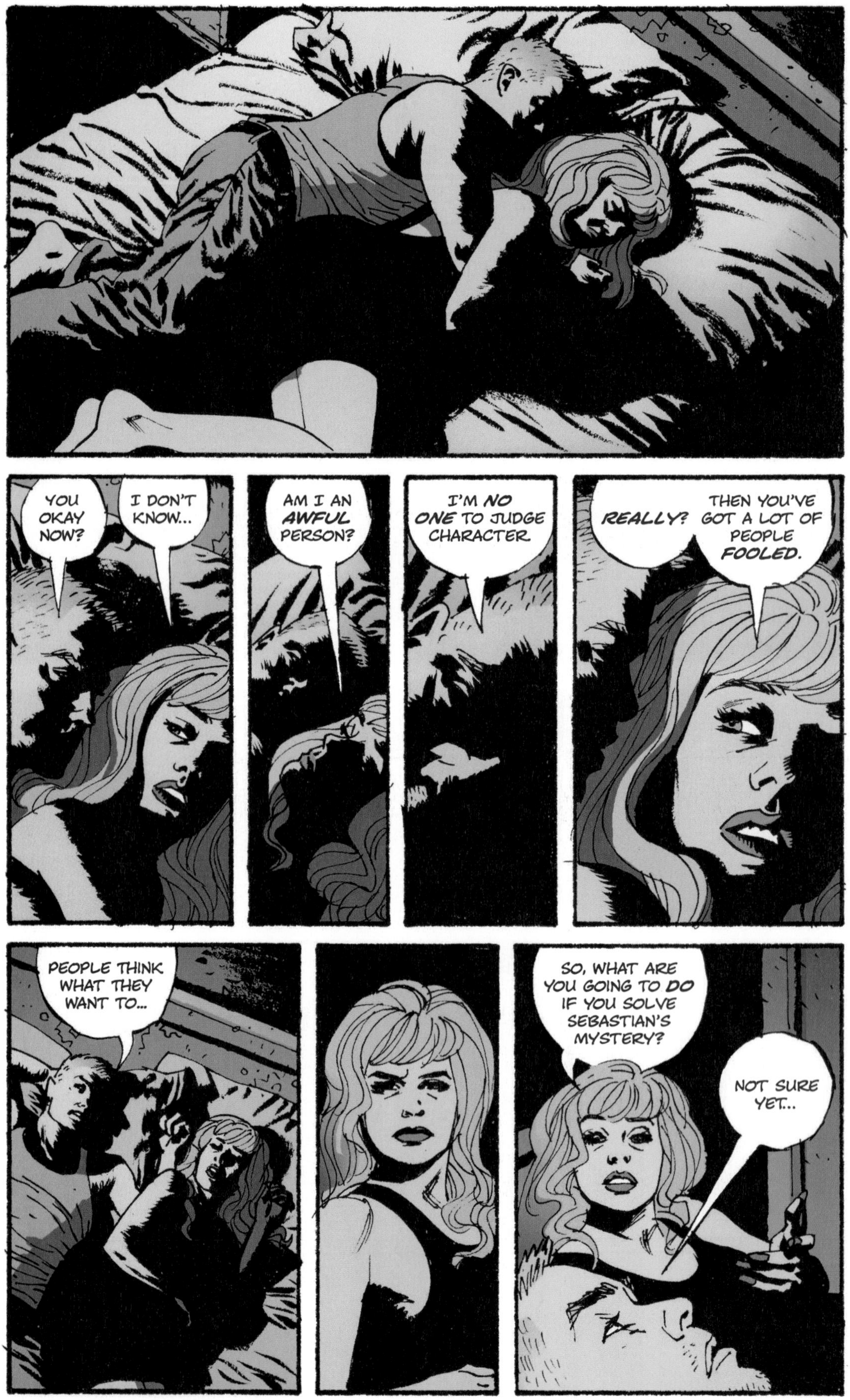
YOU OKAY NOW?
I DON'T KNOW...
AM I AN AWFUL PERSON?
I'M NO ONE TO JUDGE CHARACTER
REALLY?
THEN YOU'VE GOT A LOT OF PEOPLE FOOLED.
PEOPLE THINK WHAT THEY WANT TO...
SO, WHAT ARE YOU GOING TO DO IF YOU SOLVE SEBASTIAN'S MYSTERY?
NOT SURE YET...

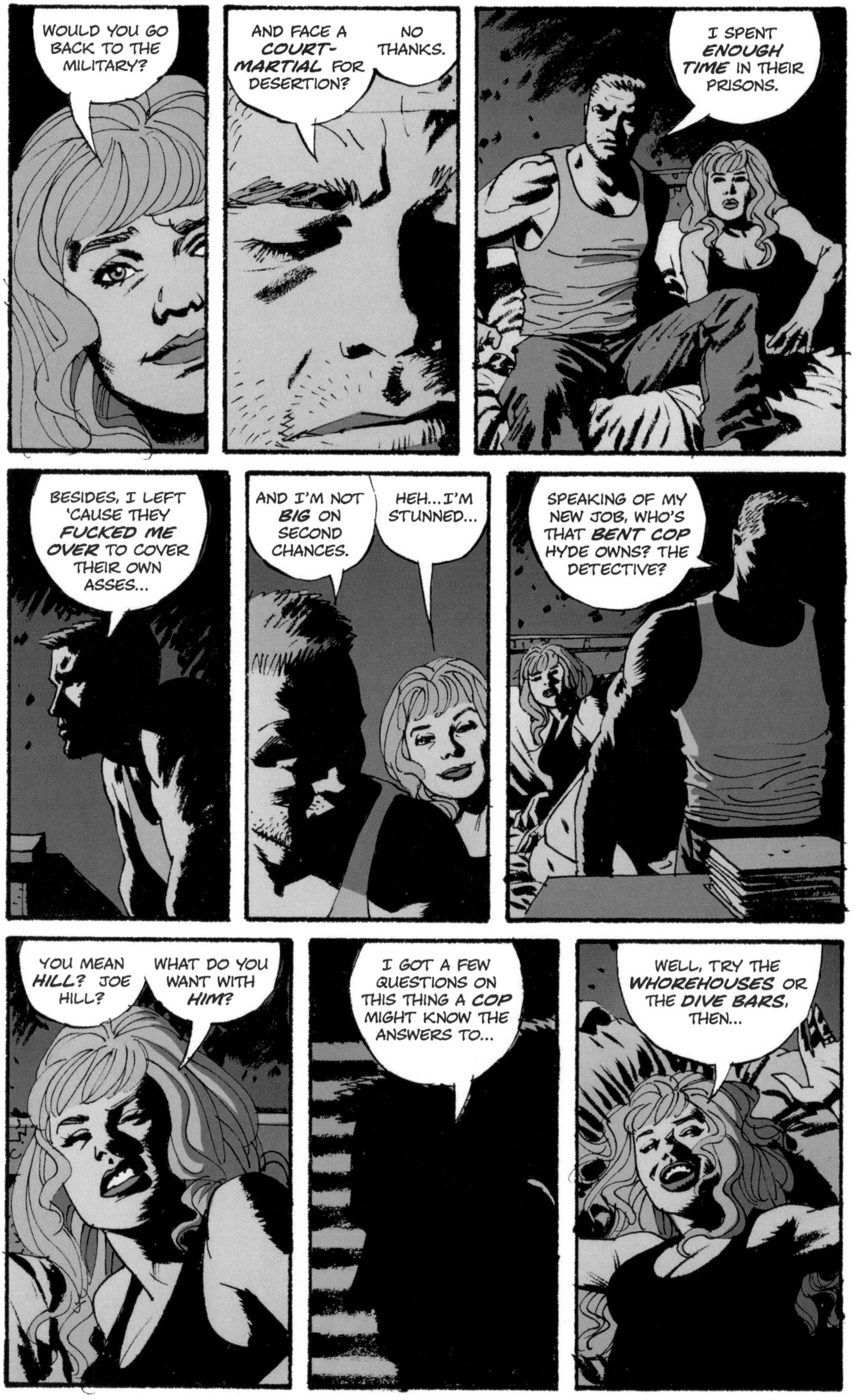
WOULD YOU GO BACK TO THE MILITARY?
AND FACE A *COURT-MARTIAL* FOR DESERTION?
NO THANKS.
I SPENT *ENOUGH TIME* IN THEIR PRISONS.
BESIDES, I LEFT 'CAUSE THEY *FUCKED ME OVER* TO COVER THEIR OWN ASSES...
AND I'M NOT *BIG* ON SECOND CHANCES.
HEH...I'M STUNNED...
SPEAKING OF MY NEW JOB, WHO'S THAT *BENT COP* HYDE OWNS? THE DETECTIVE?
YOU MEAN *HILL?* JOE HILL?
WHAT DO YOU WANT WITH *HIM?*
I GOT A FEW QUESTIONS ON THIS THING A *COP* MIGHT KNOW THE ANSWERS TO...
WELL, TRY THE *WHOREHOUSES* OR THE *DIVE BARS,* THEN...

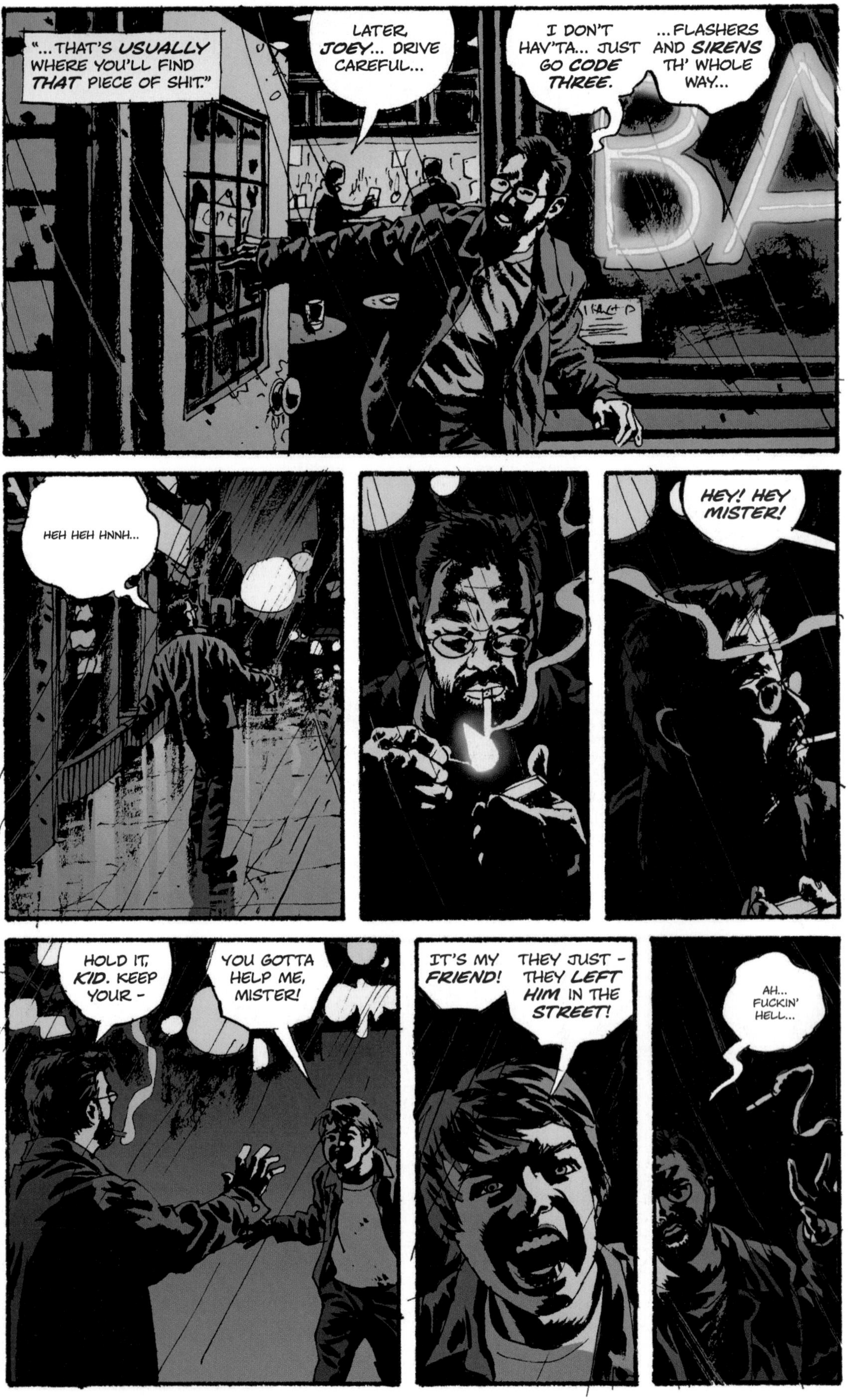
"...THAT'S USUALLY WHERE YOU'LL FIND THAT PIECE OF SHIT."
LATER, JOEY... DRIVE CAREFUL...
I DON'T HAV'TA... JUST GO CODE THREE.
...FLASHERS AND SIRENS TH' WHOLE WAY...
HEH HEH HNNH...
HEY! HEY MISTER!
HOLD IT, KID. KEEP YOUR -
YOU GOTTA HELP ME, MISTER!
IT'S MY FRIEND!
THEY JUST - THEY LEFT HIM IN THE STREET!
AH... FUCKIN' HELL...

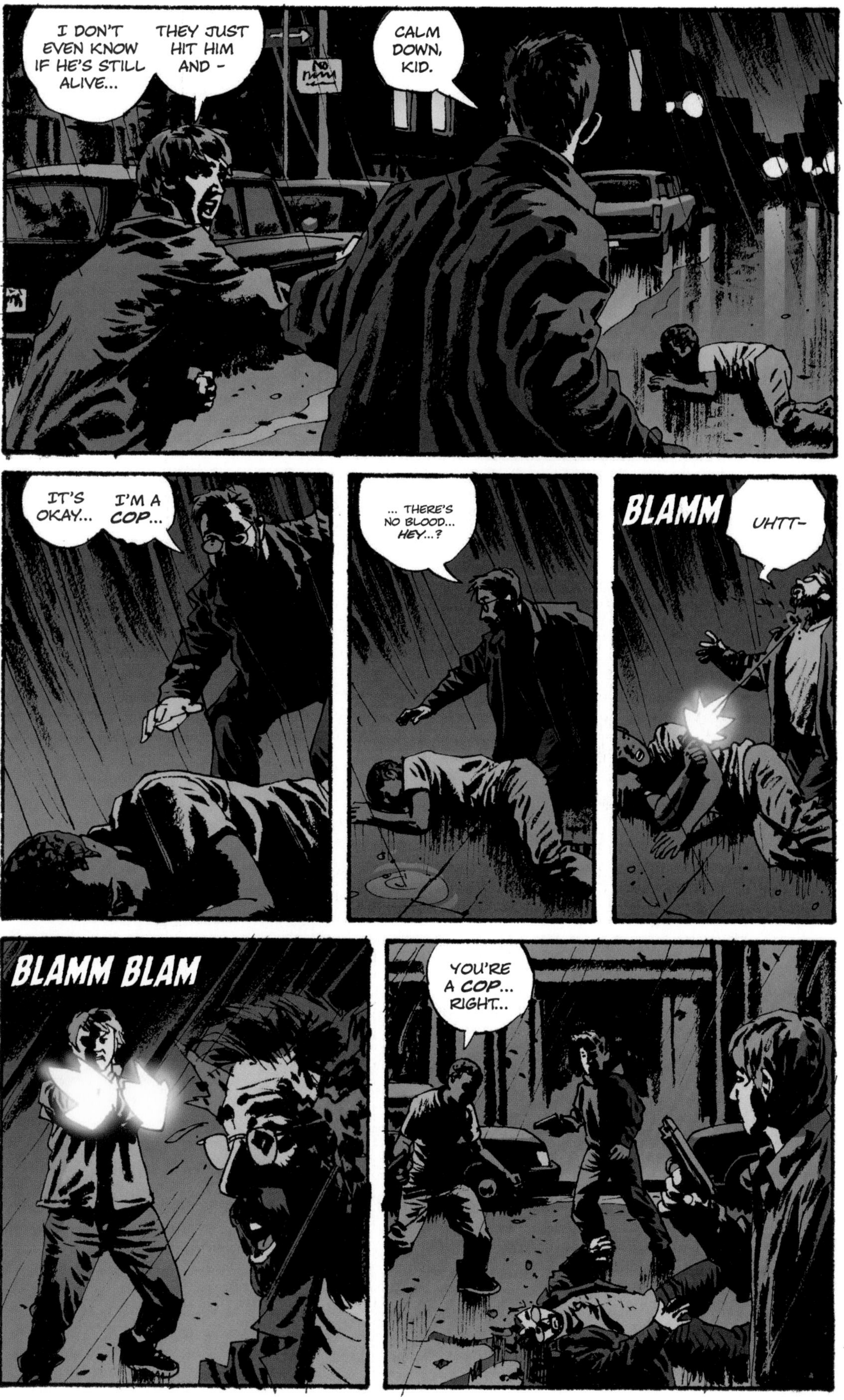
I DON'T EVEN KNOW IF HE'S STILL ALIVE...
THEY JUST HIT HIM AND -
CALM DOWN, KID.
IT'S OKAY...
I'M A COP...
... THERE'S NO BLOOD... HEY...?
BLAMM
UHTT-
BLAMM BLAM
YOU'RE A COP... RIGHT...

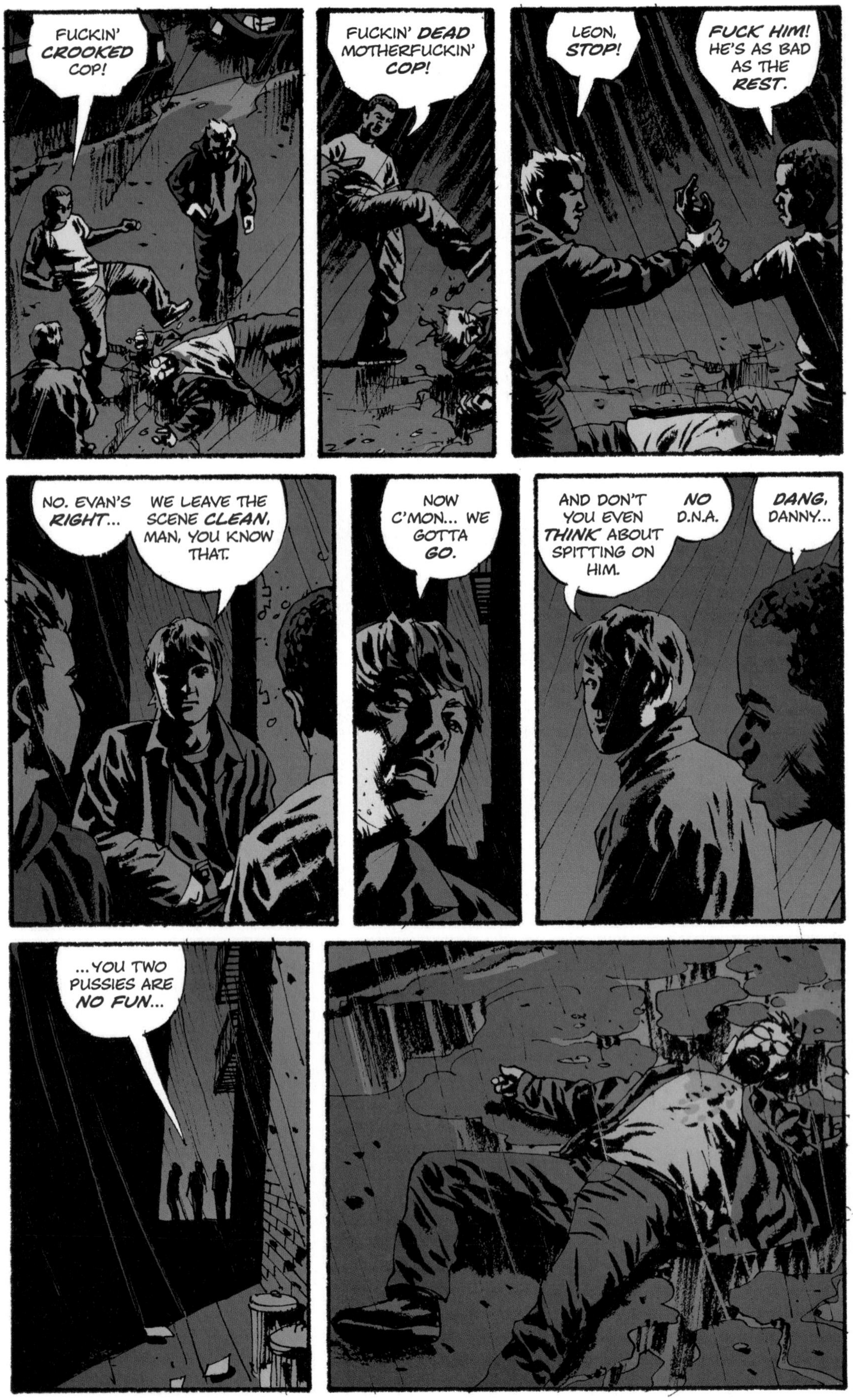
FUCKIN' CROOKED COP!
FUCKIN' DEAD MOTHERFUCKIN' COP!
LEON, STOP!
FUCK HIM! HE'S AS BAD AS THE REST.
NO. EVAN'S RIGHT...
WE LEAVE THE SCENE CLEAN, MAN, YOU KNOW THAT.
NOW C'MON... WE GOTTA GO.
AND DON'T YOU EVEN THINK ABOUT SPITTING ON HIM.
NO D.N.A.
DANG, DANNY...
...YOU TWO PUSSIES ARE NO FUN...

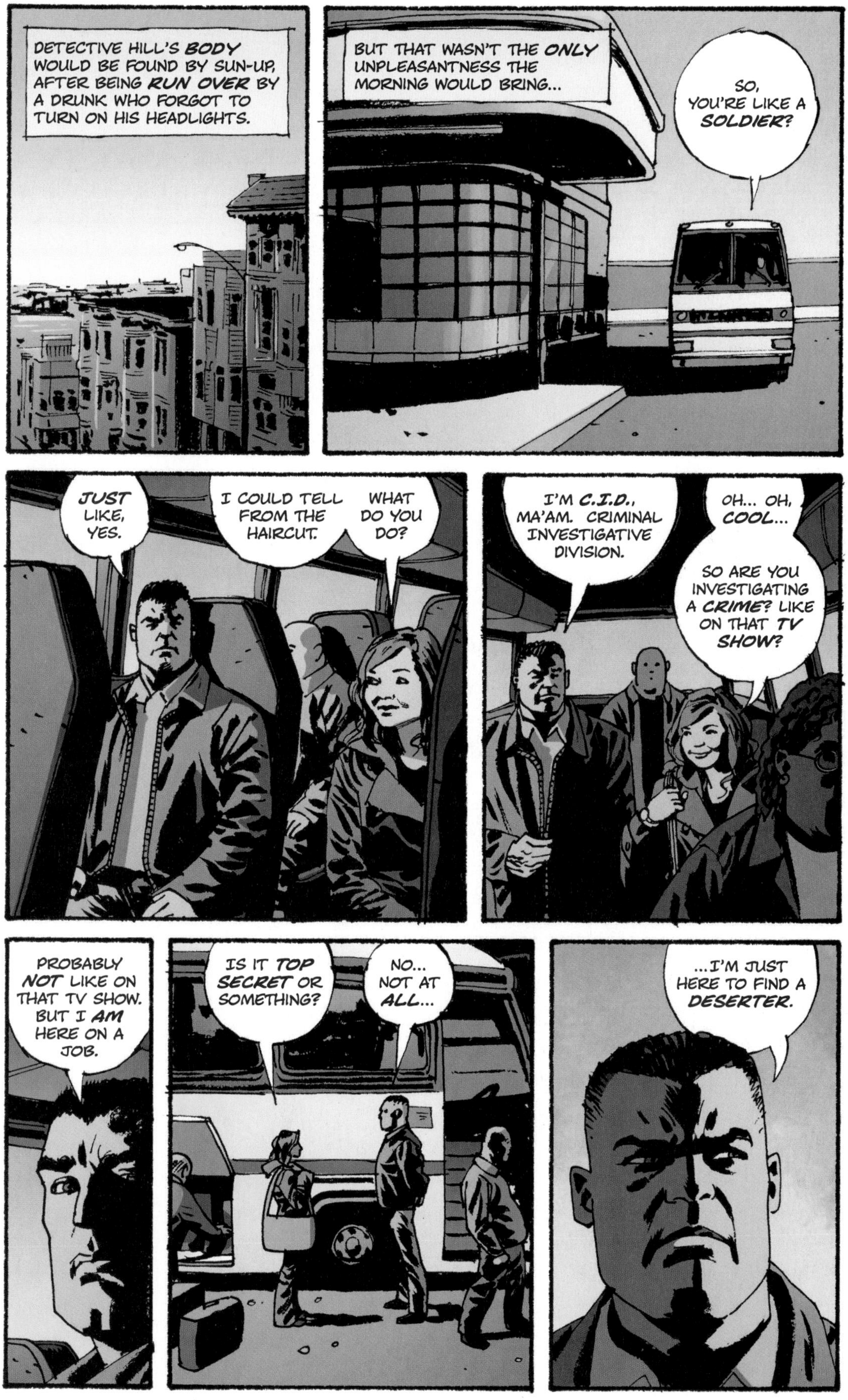
DETECTIVE HILL'S BODY WOULD BE FOUND BY SUN-UP, AFTER BEING RUN OVER BY A DRUNK WHO FORGOT TO TURN ON HIS HEADLIGHTS.
BUT THAT WASN'T THE ONLY UNPLEASANTNESS THE MORNING WOULD BRING...
SO, YOU'RE LIKE A SOLDIER?
JUST LIKE, YES.
I COULD TELL FROM THE HAIRCUT.
WHAT DO YOU DO?
I'M C.I.D., MA'AM. CRIMINAL INVESTIGATIVE DIVISION.
OH... OH, COOL...
SO ARE YOU INVESTIGATING A CRIME? LIKE ON THAT TV SHOW?
PROBABLY NOT LIKE ON THAT TV SHOW. BUT I AM HERE ON A JOB.
IS IT TOP SECRET OR SOMETHING?
NO... NOT AT ALL...
...I'M JUST HERE TO FIND A DESERTER.

The Sinners
Part Two

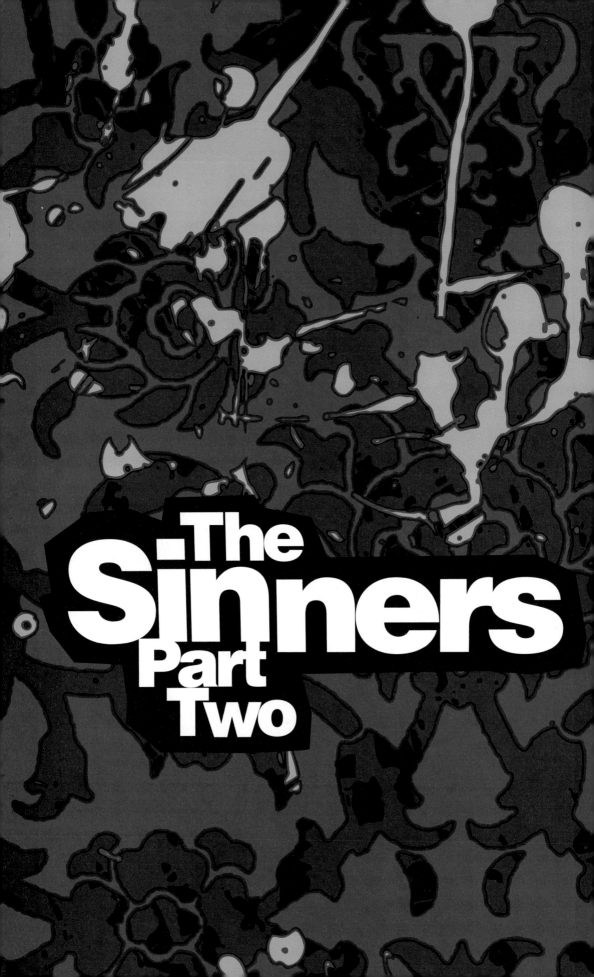

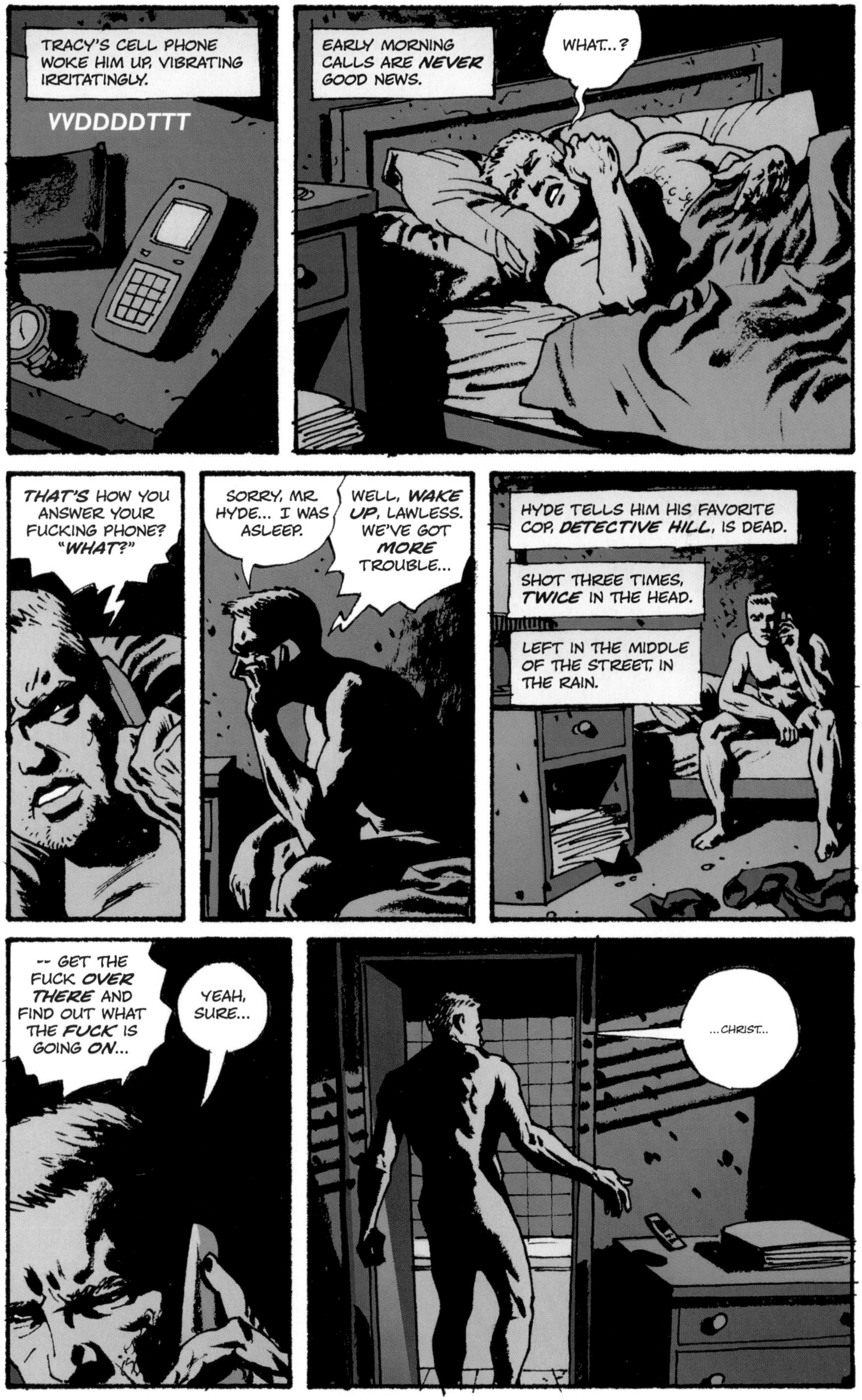

TRACY'S CELL PHONE WOKE HIM UP, VIBRATING IRRITATINGLY.
VVDDDDTTT
EARLY MORNING CALLS ARE NEVER GOOD NEWS.
WHAT...?
THAT'S HOW YOU ANSWER YOUR FUCKING PHONE? "WHAT?"
SORRY, MR HYDE... I WAS ASLEEP.
WELL, WAKE UP, LAWLESS. WE'VE GOT MORE TROUBLE...
HYDE TELLS HIM HIS FAVORITE COP, DETECTIVE HILL, IS DEAD.
SHOT THREE TIMES, TWICE IN THE HEAD.
LEFT IN THE MIDDLE OF THE STREET, IN THE RAIN.
-- GET THE FUCK OVER THERE AND FIND OUT WHAT THE FUCK IS GOING ON...
YEAH, SURE...
...CHRIST...

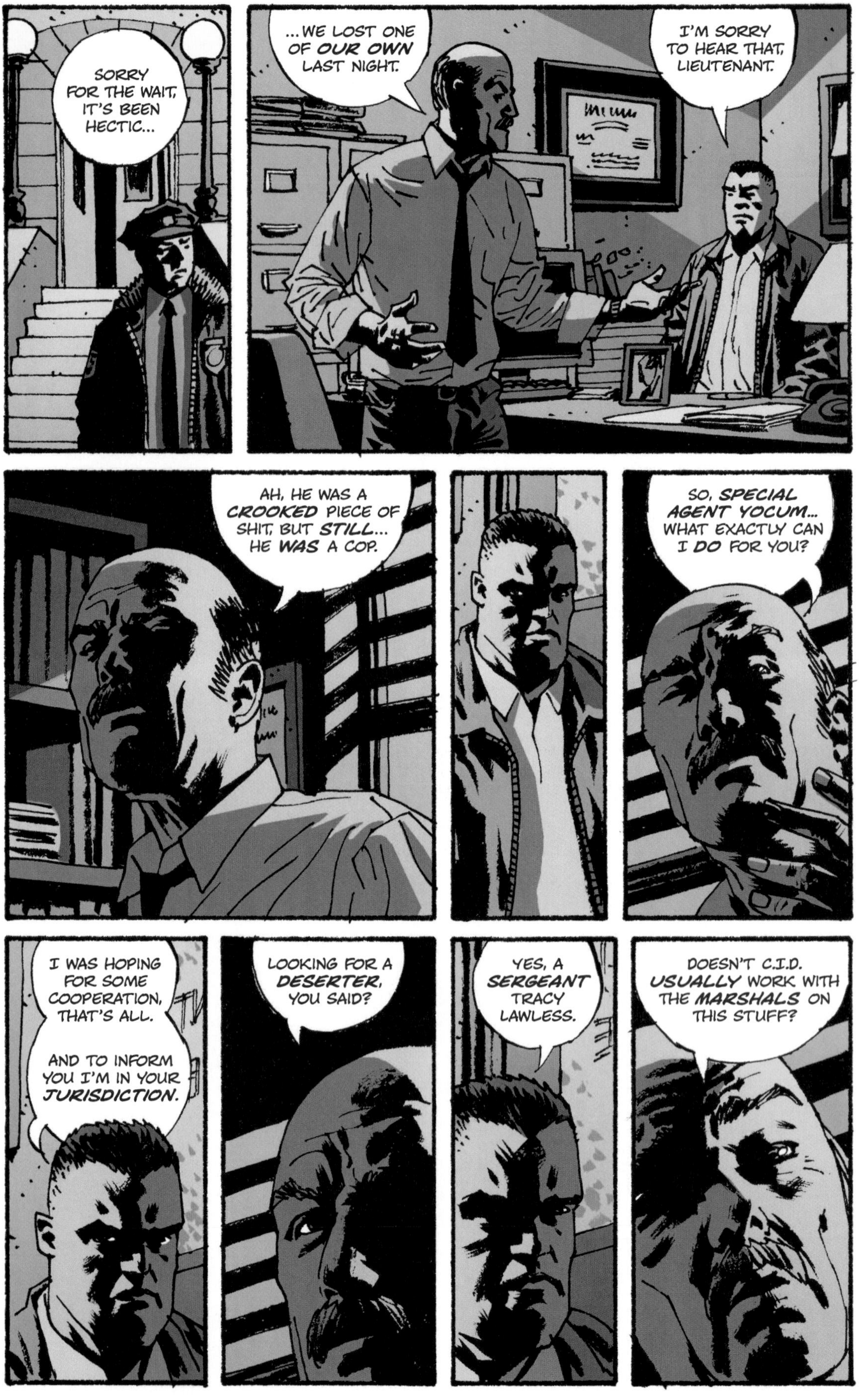
SORRY FOR THE WAIT, IT'S BEEN HECTIC...
...WE LOST ONE OF OUR OWN LAST NIGHT.
I'M SORRY TO HEAR THAT, LIEUTENANT.
AH, HE WAS A CROOKED PIECE OF SHIT, BUT STILL... HE WAS A COP.
SO, SPECIAL AGENT YOCUM... WHAT EXACTLY CAN I DO FOR YOU?
I WAS HOPING FOR SOME COOPERATION, THAT'S ALL.
AND TO INFORM YOU I'M IN YOUR JURISDICTION.
LOOKING FOR A DESERTER, YOU SAID?
YES, A SERGEANT TRACY LAWLESS.
DOESN'T C.I.D. USUALLY WORK WITH THE MARSHALS ON THIS STUFF?

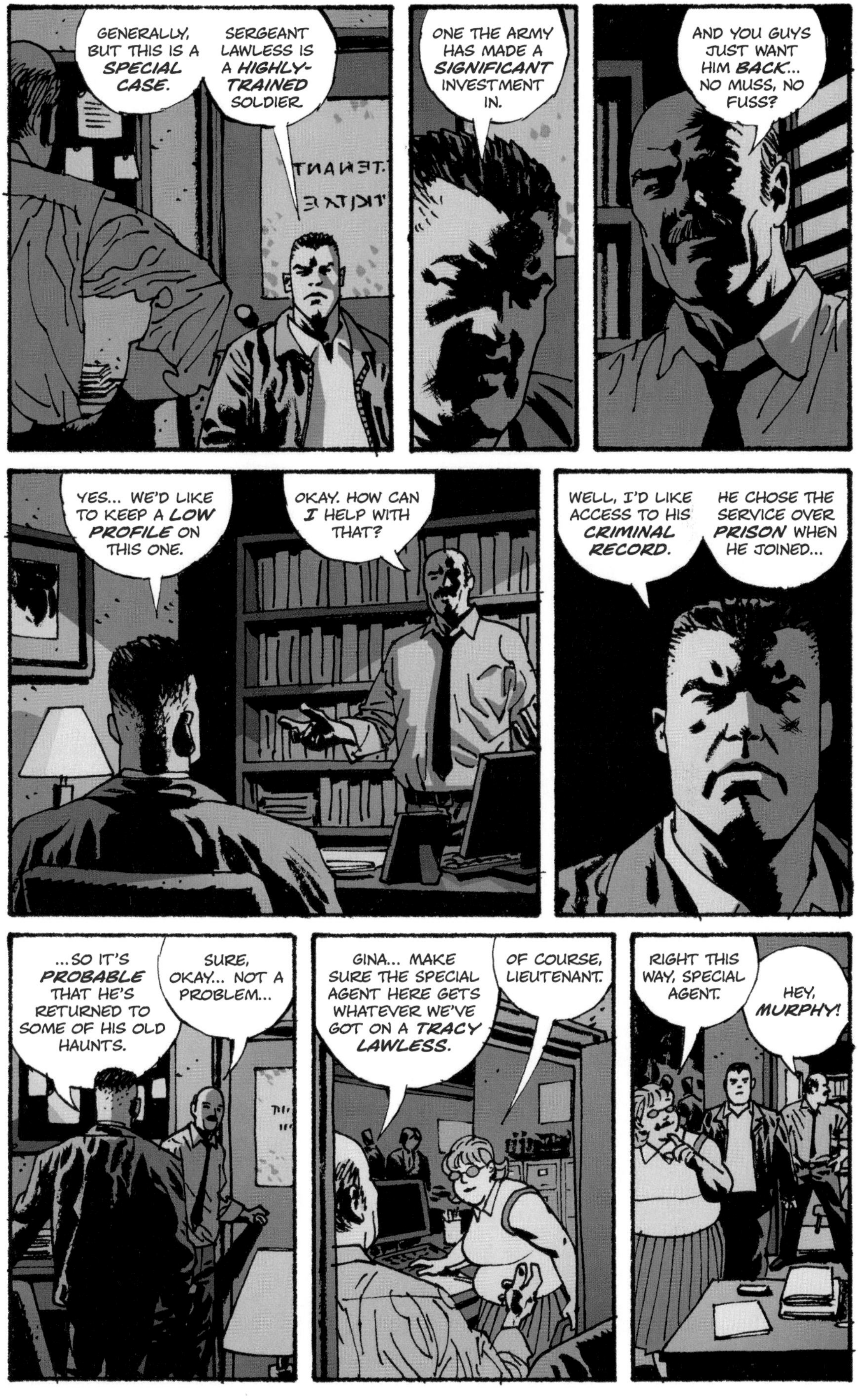
GENERALLY, BUT THIS IS A SPECIAL CASE.
SERGEANT LAWLESS IS A HIGHLY-TRAINED SOLDIER.
ONE THE ARMY HAS MADE A SIGNIFICANT INVESTMENT IN.
AND YOU GUYS JUST WANT HIM BACK... NO MUSS, NO FUSS?
YES... WE'D LIKE TO KEEP A LOW PROFILE ON THIS ONE.
OKAY. HOW CAN I HELP WITH THAT?
WELL, I'D LIKE ACCESS TO HIS CRIMINAL RECORD.
HE CHOSE THE SERVICE OVER PRISON WHEN HE JOINED...
...SO IT'S PROBABLE THAT HE'S RETURNED TO SOME OF HIS OLD HAUNTS.
SURE, OKAY... NOT A PROBLEM...
GINA... MAKE SURE THE SPECIAL AGENT HERE GETS WHATEVER WE'VE GOT ON A TRACY LAWLESS.
OF COURSE, LIEUTENANT.
RIGHT THIS WAY, SPECIAL AGENT.
HEY, MURPHY!

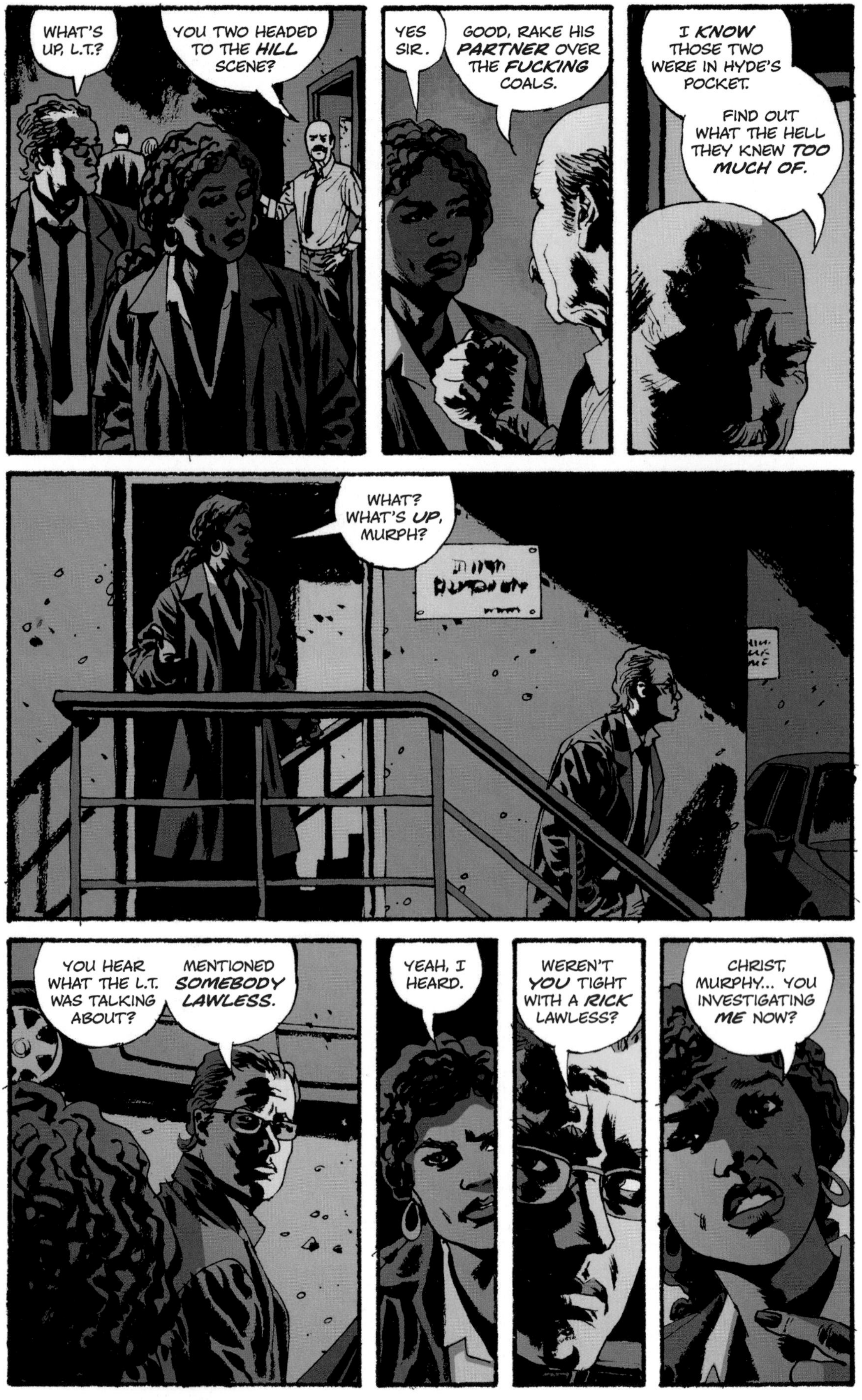
WHAT'S UP, L.T.?
YOU TWO HEADED TO THE HILL SCENE?
YES SIR.
GOOD, RAKE HIS PARTNER OVER THE FUCKING COALS.
I KNOW THOSE TWO WERE IN HYDE'S POCKET.
FIND OUT WHAT THE HELL THEY KNEW TOO MUCH OF.
WHAT? WHAT'S UP, MURPH?
YOU HEAR WHAT THE L.T. WAS TALKING ABOUT?
MENTIONED SOMEBODY LAWLESS.
YEAH, I HEARD.
WEREN'T YOU TIGHT WITH A RICK LAWLESS?
CHRIST, MURPHY... YOU INVESTIGATING ME NOW?

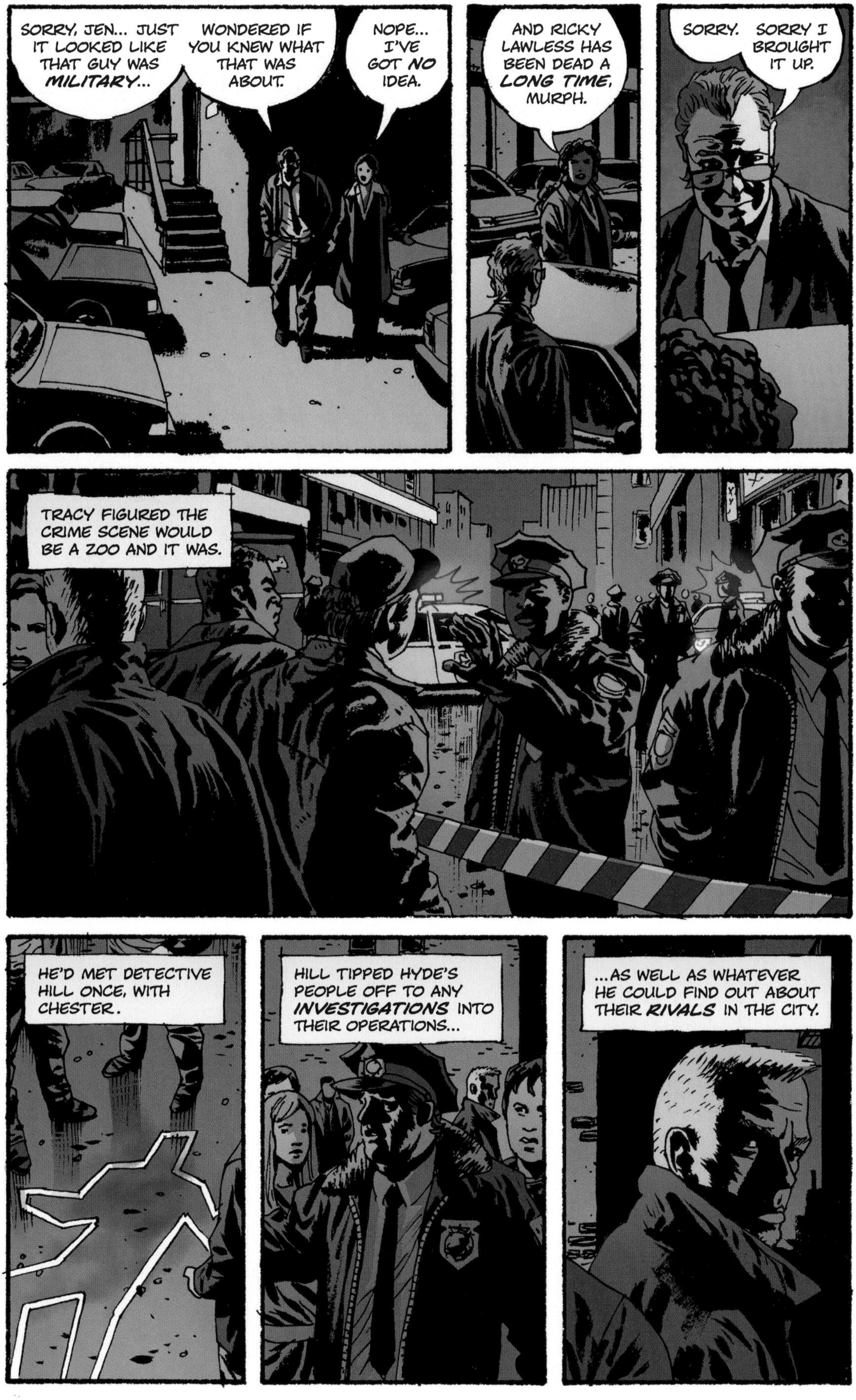
SORRY, JEN... JUST IT LOOKED LIKE THAT GUY WAS *MILITARY*...
WONDERED IF YOU KNEW WHAT THAT WAS ABOUT.
NOPE... I'VE GOT *NO* IDEA.
AND RICKY LAWLESS HAS BEEN DEAD A *LONG TIME*, MURPH.
SORRY.
SORRY I BROUGHT IT UP.
TRACY FIGURED THE CRIME SCENE WOULD BE A ZOO AND IT WAS.
HE'D MET DETECTIVE HILL ONCE, WITH CHESTER.
HILL TIPPED HYDE'S PEOPLE OFF TO ANY *INVESTIGATIONS* INTO THEIR OPERATIONS...
...AS WELL AS WHATEVER HE COULD FIND OUT ABOUT THEIR *RIVALS* IN THE CITY.

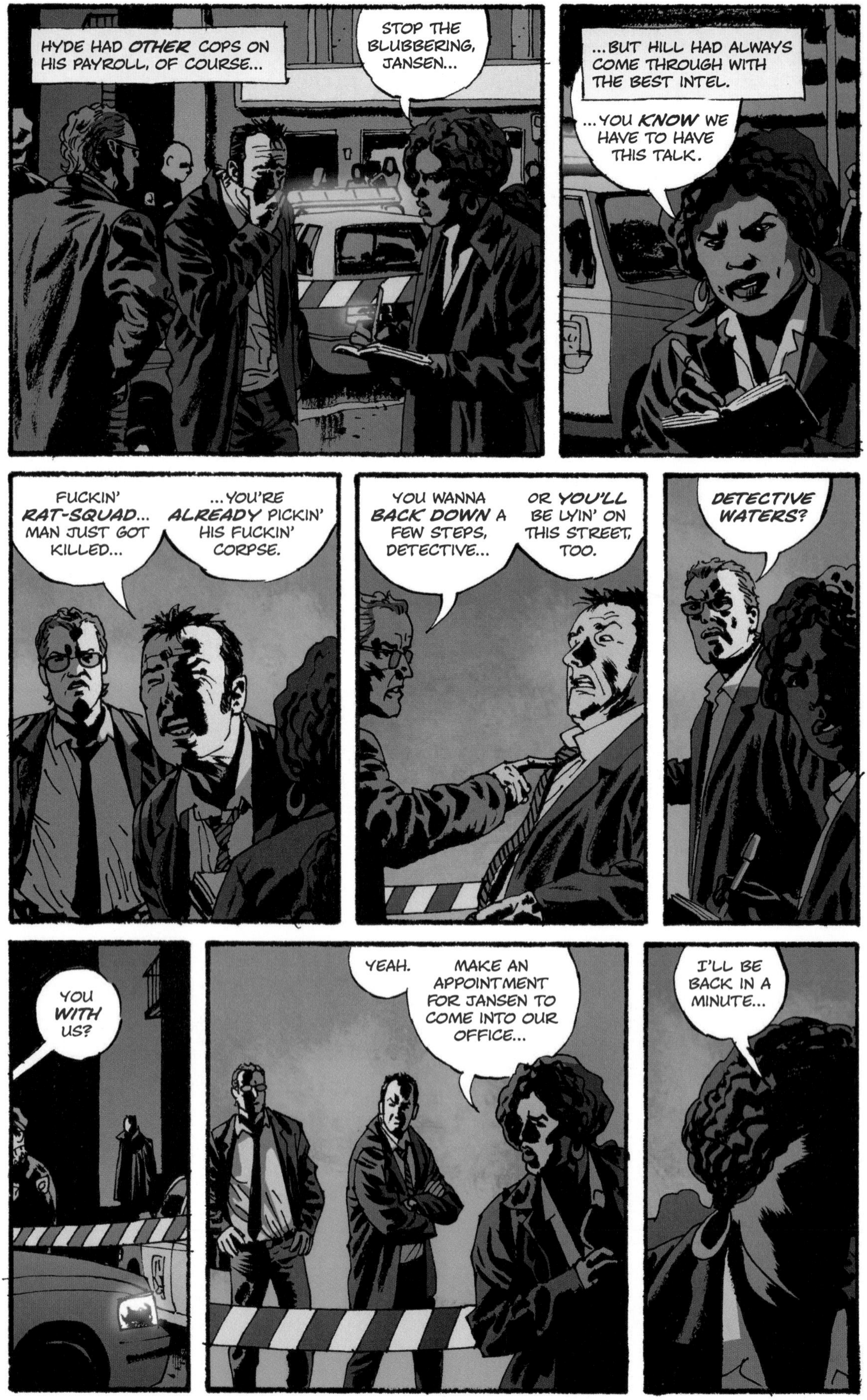
HYDE HAD OTHER COPS ON HIS PAYROLL, OF COURSE...
STOP THE BLUBBERING, JANSEN...
...BUT HILL HAD ALWAYS COME THROUGH WITH THE BEST INTEL.
...YOU KNOW WE HAVE TO HAVE THIS TALK.
FUCKIN' RAT-SQUAD... MAN JUST GOT KILLED...
...YOU'RE ALREADY PICKIN' HIS FUCKIN' CORPSE.
YOU WANNA BACK DOWN A FEW STEPS, DETECTIVE...
OR YOU'LL BE LYIN' ON THIS STREET, TOO.
DETECTIVE WATERS?
YOU WITH US?
YEAH.
MAKE AN APPOINTMENT FOR JANSEN TO COME INTO OUR OFFICE...
I'LL BE BACK IN A MINUTE...

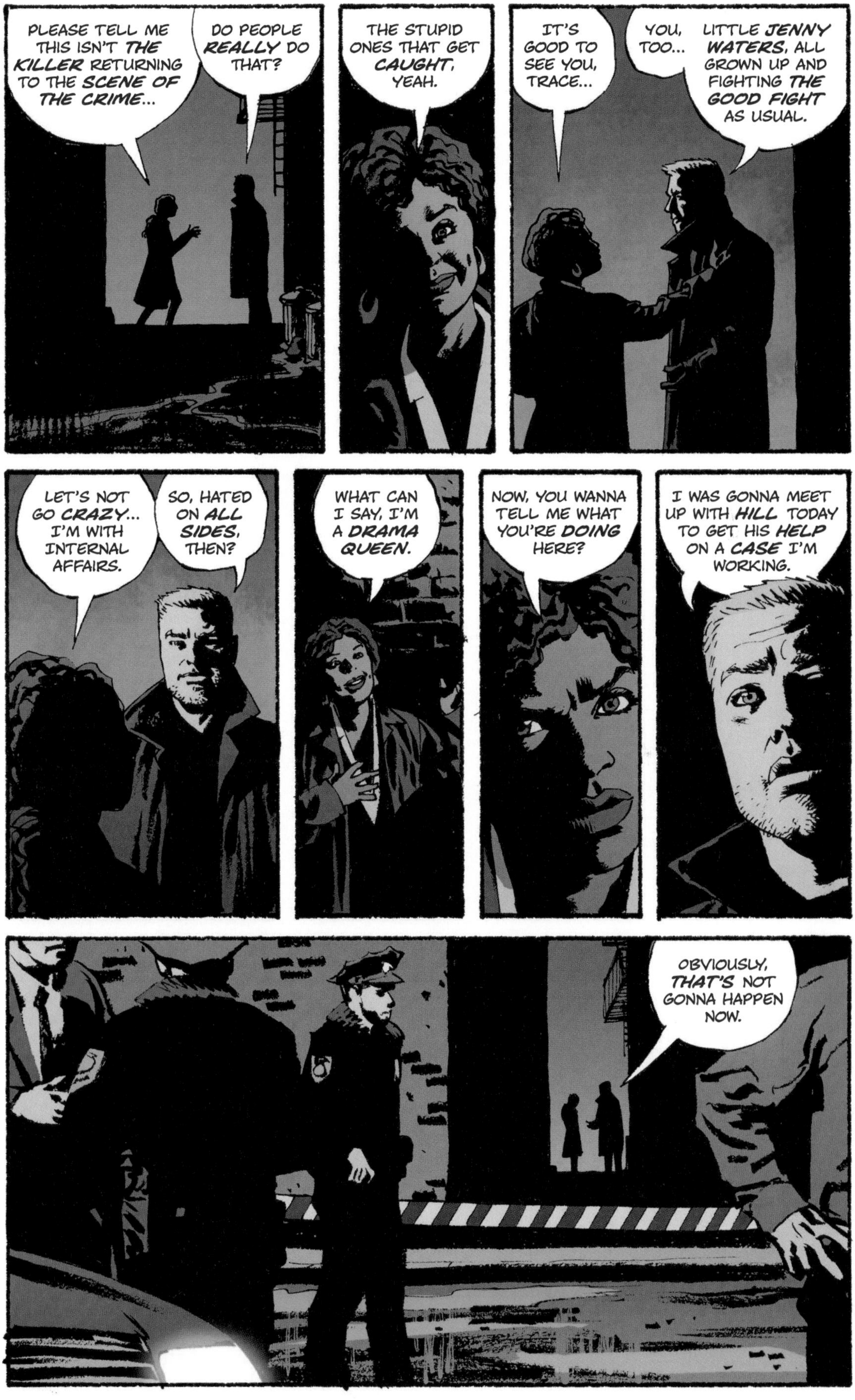

PLEASE TELL ME THIS ISN'T THE KILLER RETURNING TO THE SCENE OF THE CRIME...
DO PEOPLE REALLY DO THAT?
THE STUPID ONES THAT GET CAUGHT, YEAH.
IT'S GOOD TO SEE YOU, TRACE...
YOU, TOO...
LITTLE JENNY WATERS, ALL GROWN UP AND FIGHTING THE GOOD FIGHT AS USUAL.
LET'S NOT GO CRAZY... I'M WITH INTERNAL AFFAIRS.
SO, HATED ON ALL SIDES, THEN?
WHAT CAN I SAY, I'M A DRAMA QUEEN.
NOW, YOU WANNA TELL ME WHAT YOU'RE DOING HERE?
I WAS GONNA MEET UP WITH HILL TODAY TO GET HIS HELP ON A CASE I'M WORKING.
OBVIOUSLY, THAT'S NOT GONNA HAPPEN NOW.

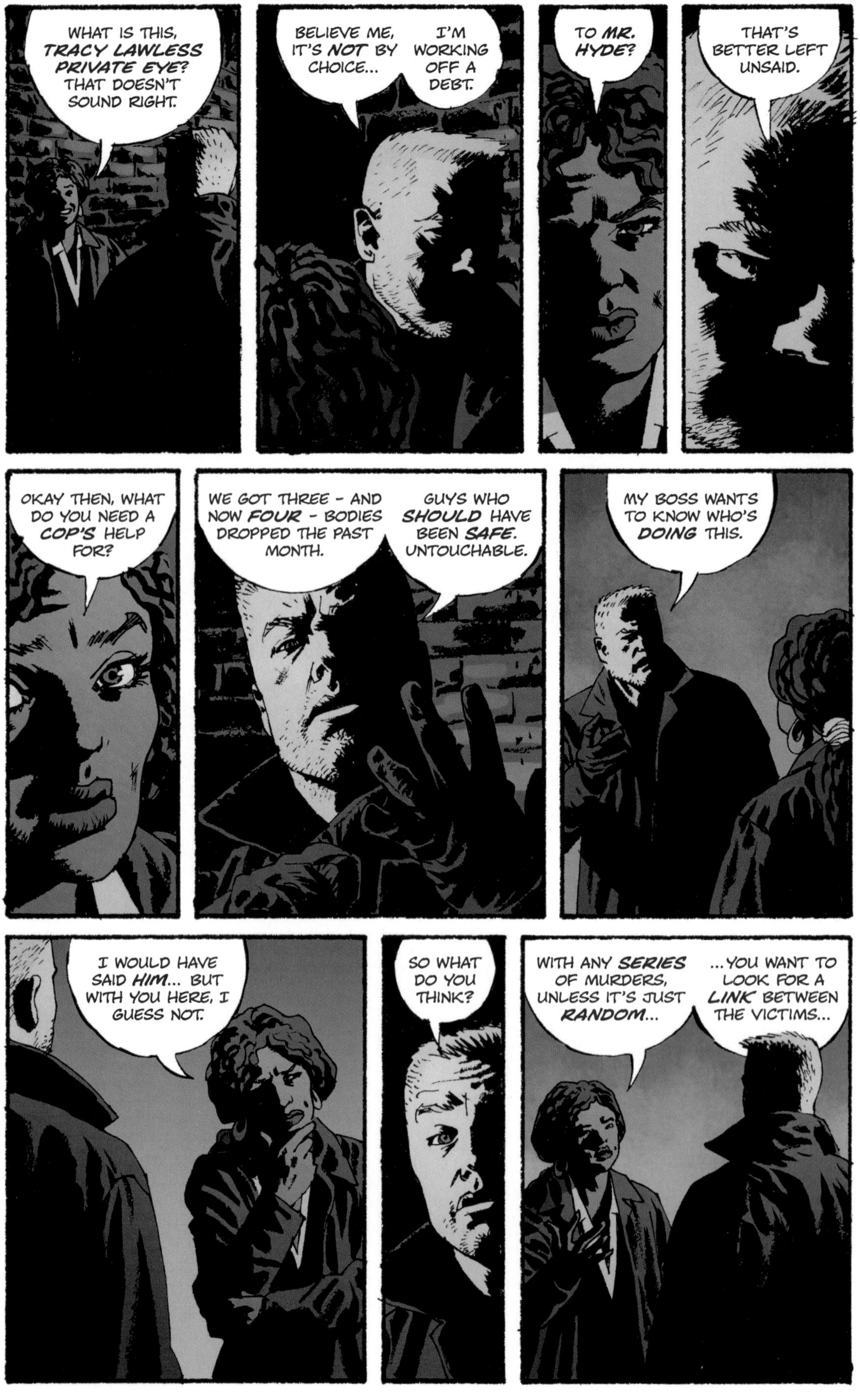
WHAT IS THIS, TRACY LAWLESS PRIVATE EYE? THAT DOESN'T SOUND RIGHT.
BELIEVE ME, IT'S NOT BY CHOICE...
I'M WORKING OFF A DEBT.
TO MR. HYDE?
THAT'S BETTER LEFT UNSAID.
OKAY THEN, WHAT DO YOU NEED A COP'S HELP FOR?
WE GOT THREE - AND NOW FOUR - BODIES DROPPED THE PAST MONTH.
GUYS WHO SHOULD HAVE BEEN SAFE. UNTOUCHABLE.
MY BOSS WANTS TO KNOW WHO'S DOING THIS.
I WOULD HAVE SAID HIM... BUT WITH YOU HERE, I GUESS NOT.
SO WHAT DO YOU THINK?
WITH ANY SERIES OF MURDERS, UNLESS IT'S JUST RANDOM...
...YOU WANT TO LOOK FOR A LINK BETWEEN THE VICTIMS...

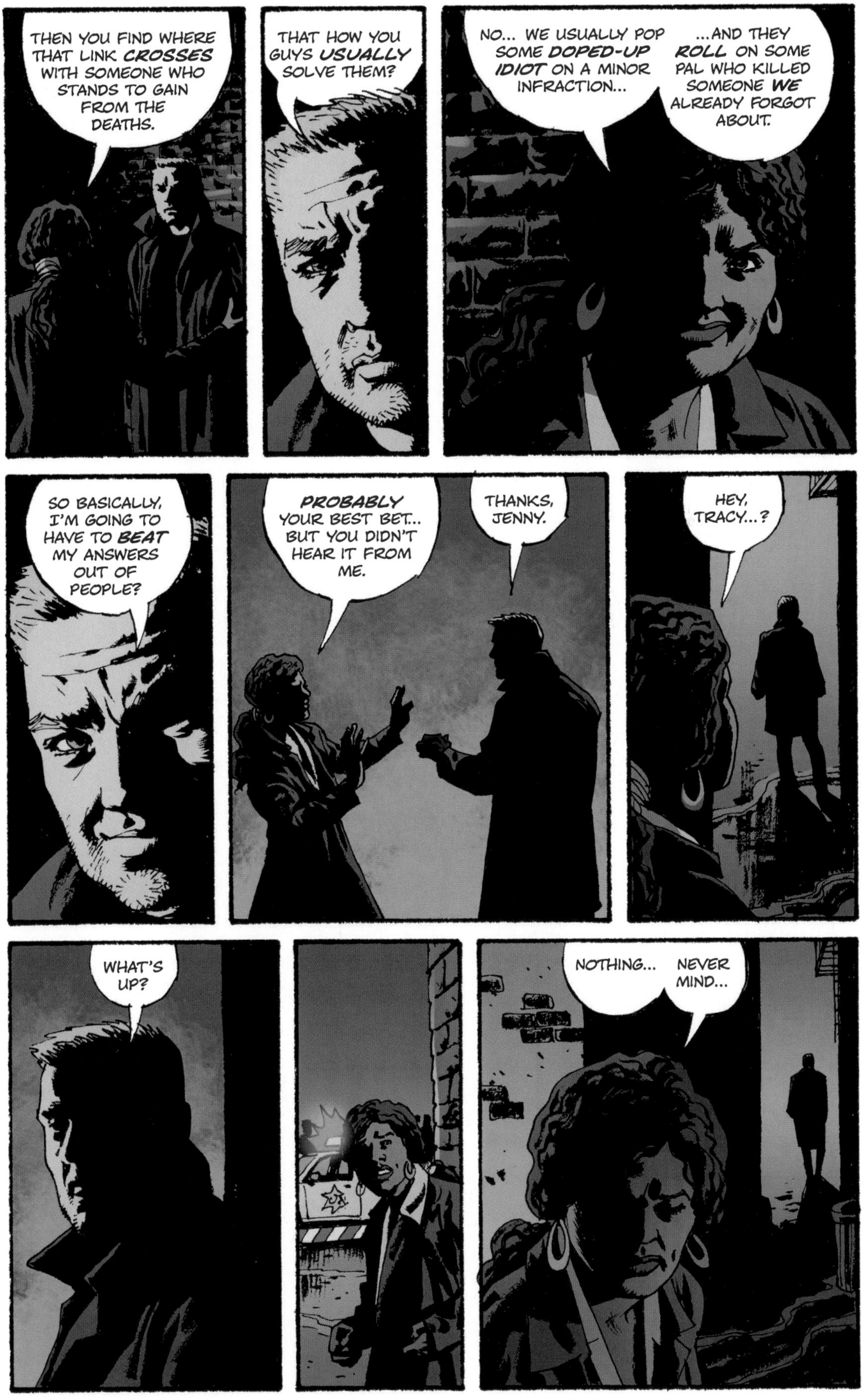
THEN YOU FIND WHERE THAT LINK CROSSES WITH SOMEONE WHO STANDS TO GAIN FROM THE DEATHS.
THAT HOW YOU GUYS USUALLY SOLVE THEM?
NO... WE USUALLY POP SOME DOPED-UP IDIOT ON A MINOR INFRACTION...
...AND THEY ROLL ON SOME PAL WHO KILLED SOMEONE WE ALREADY FORGOT ABOUT.
SO BASICALLY, I'M GOING TO HAVE TO BEAT MY ANSWERS OUT OF PEOPLE?
PROBABLY YOUR BEST BET... BUT YOU DIDN'T HEAR IT FROM ME.
THANKS, JENNY.
HEY, TRACY...?
WHAT'S UP?
NOTHING... NEVER MIND...

HE SPENT THE REST OF THE DAY WATCHING *THE COLLECTOR'S* CORNERS AND THINKING ABOUT WHAT DETECTIVE WATERS HAD SAID.

IF SOMEONE NEW WAS TRYING TO *TAKE OVER* ADSIT'S TERRITORY...

...THEY WERE EITHER WAITING UNTIL *THE STORM* BLEW OVER...

...OR THEY WERE BETTER AT *HIDING* THAN ANYONE TRACY HAS SEEN SINCE *AFGHANISTAN*, AT LEAST.

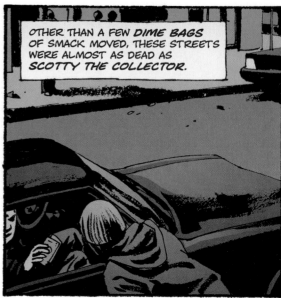

OTHER THAN A FEW *DIME BAGS* OF SMACK MOVED, THESE STREETS WERE ALMOST AS DEAD AS *SCOTTY THE COLLECTOR.*

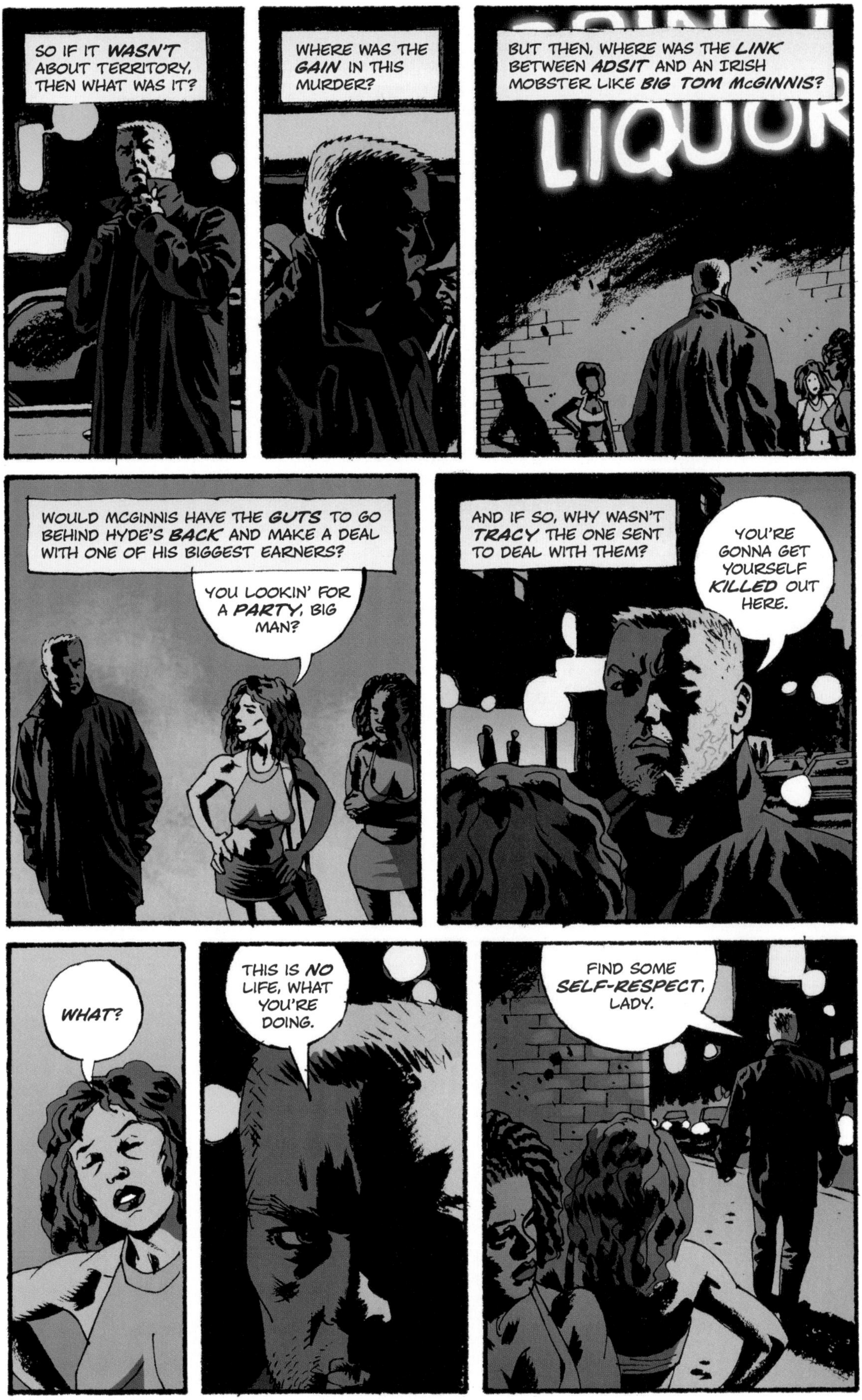
SO IF IT WASN'T ABOUT TERRITORY, THEN WHAT WAS IT?
WHERE WAS THE GAIN IN THIS MURDER?
BUT THEN, WHERE WAS THE LINK BETWEEN ADSIT AND AN IRISH MOBSTER LIKE BIG TOM McGINNIS?
LIQUOR
WOULD MCGINNIS HAVE THE GUTS TO GO BEHIND HYDE'S BACK AND MAKE A DEAL WITH ONE OF HIS BIGGEST EARNERS?
YOU LOOKIN' FOR A PARTY, BIG MAN?
AND IF SO, WHY WASN'T TRACY THE ONE SENT TO DEAL WITH THEM?
YOU'RE GONNA GET YOURSELF KILLED OUT HERE.
WHAT?
THIS IS NO LIFE, WHAT YOU'RE DOING.
FIND SOME SELF-RESPECT, LADY.

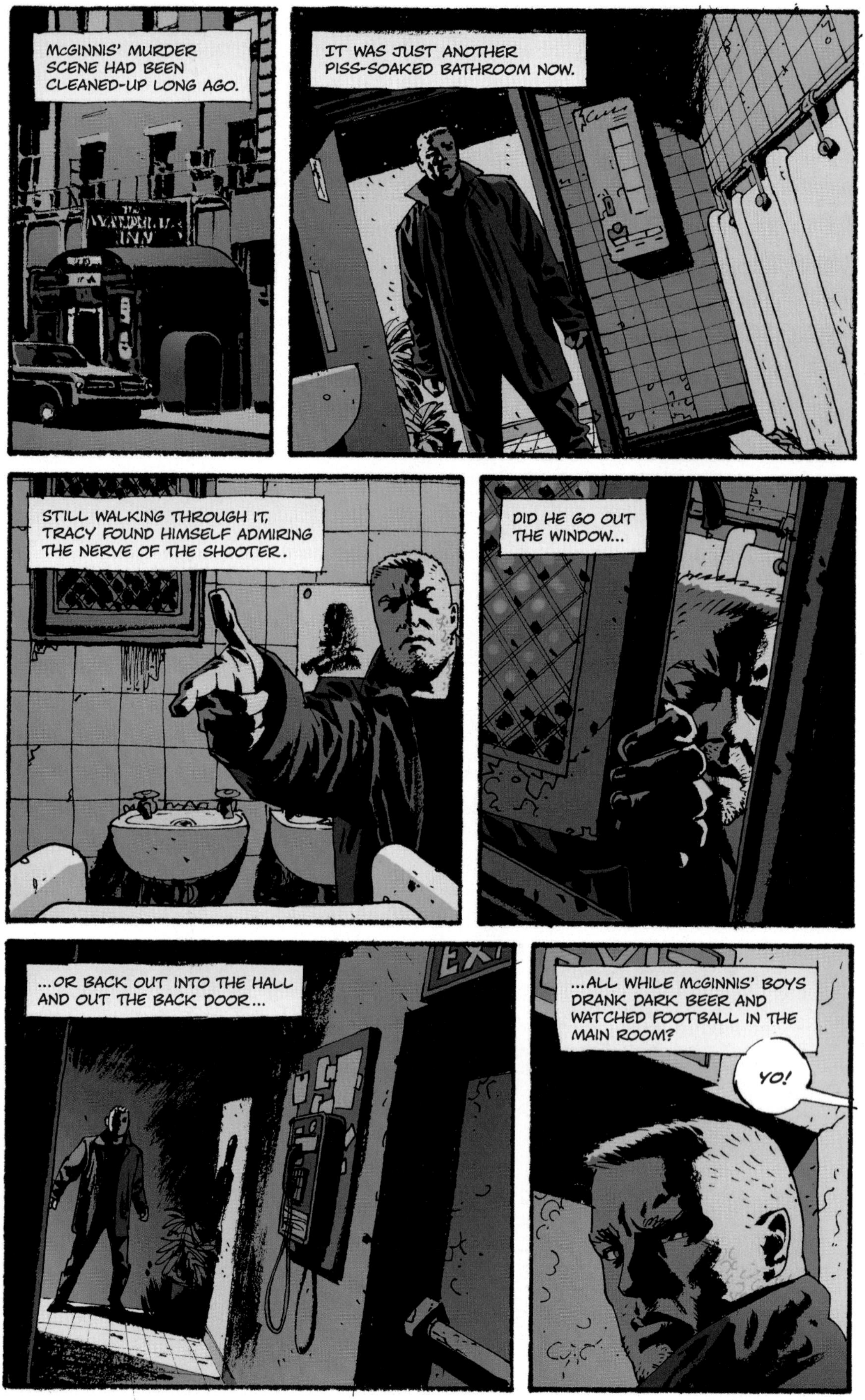
McGINNIS' MURDER SCENE HAD BEEN CLEANED-UP LONG AGO.
IT WAS JUST ANOTHER PISS-SOAKED BATHROOM NOW.
STILL WALKING THROUGH IT, TRACY FOUND HIMSELF ADMIRING THE NERVE OF THE SHOOTER.
DID HE GO OUT THE WINDOW...
...OR BACK OUT INTO THE HALL AND OUT THE BACK DOOR...
...ALL WHILE McGINNIS' BOYS DRANK DARK BEER AND WATCHED FOOTBALL IN THE MAIN ROOM?
YO!

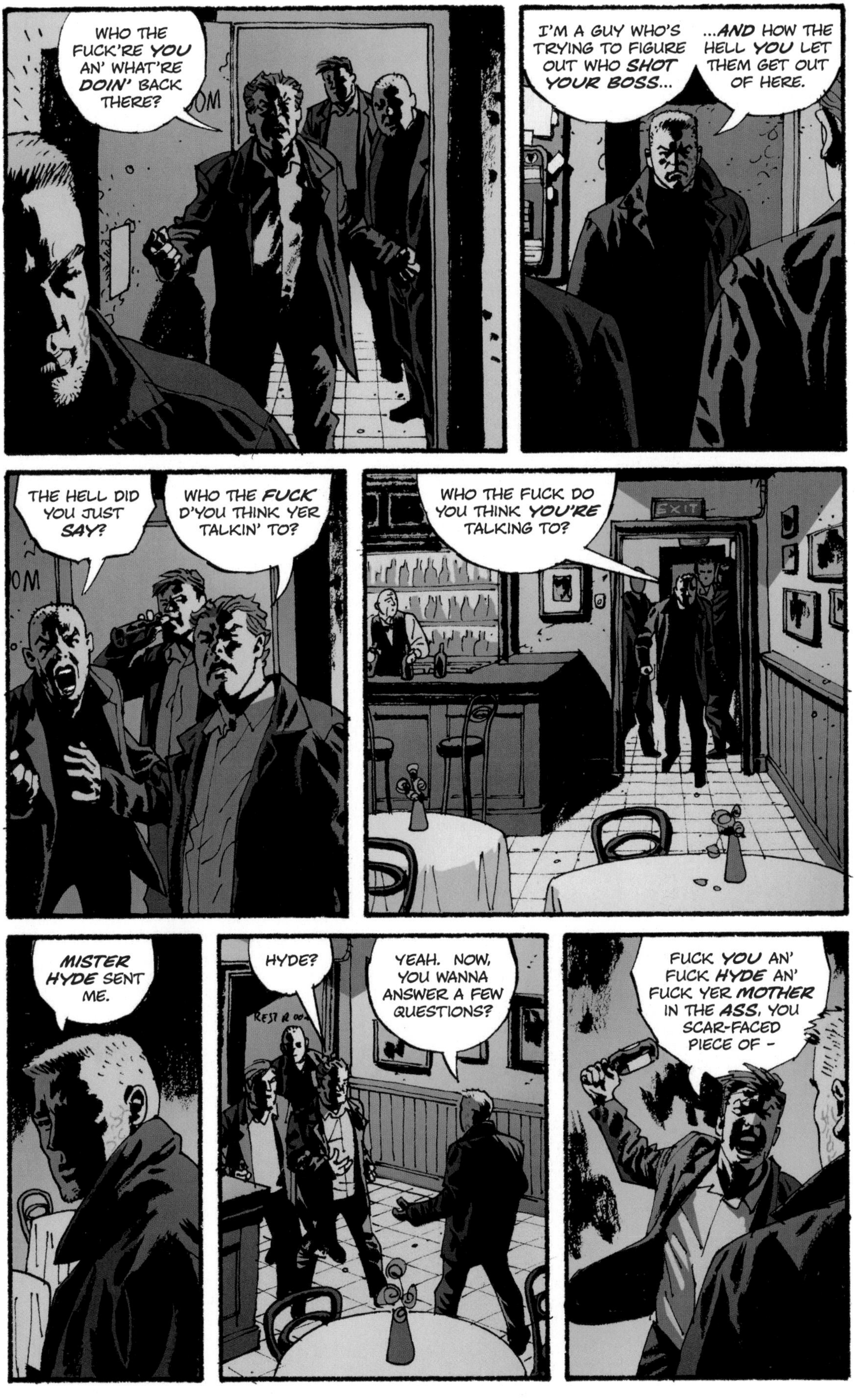
WHO THE FUCK'RE YOU AN' WHAT'RE DOIN' BACK THERE?
I'M A GUY WHO'S TRYING TO FIGURE OUT WHO SHOT YOUR BOSS...
...AND HOW THE HELL YOU LET THEM GET OUT OF HERE.
THE HELL DID YOU JUST SAY?
WHO THE FUCK D'YOU THINK YER TALKIN' TO?
EXIT
WHO THE FUCK DO YOU THINK YOU'RE TALKING TO?
MISTER HYDE SENT ME.
HYDE?
YEAH. NOW, YOU WANNA ANSWER A FEW QUESTIONS?
FUCK YOU AN' FUCK HYDE AN' FUCK YER MOTHER IN THE ASS, YOU SCAR-FACED PIECE OF -

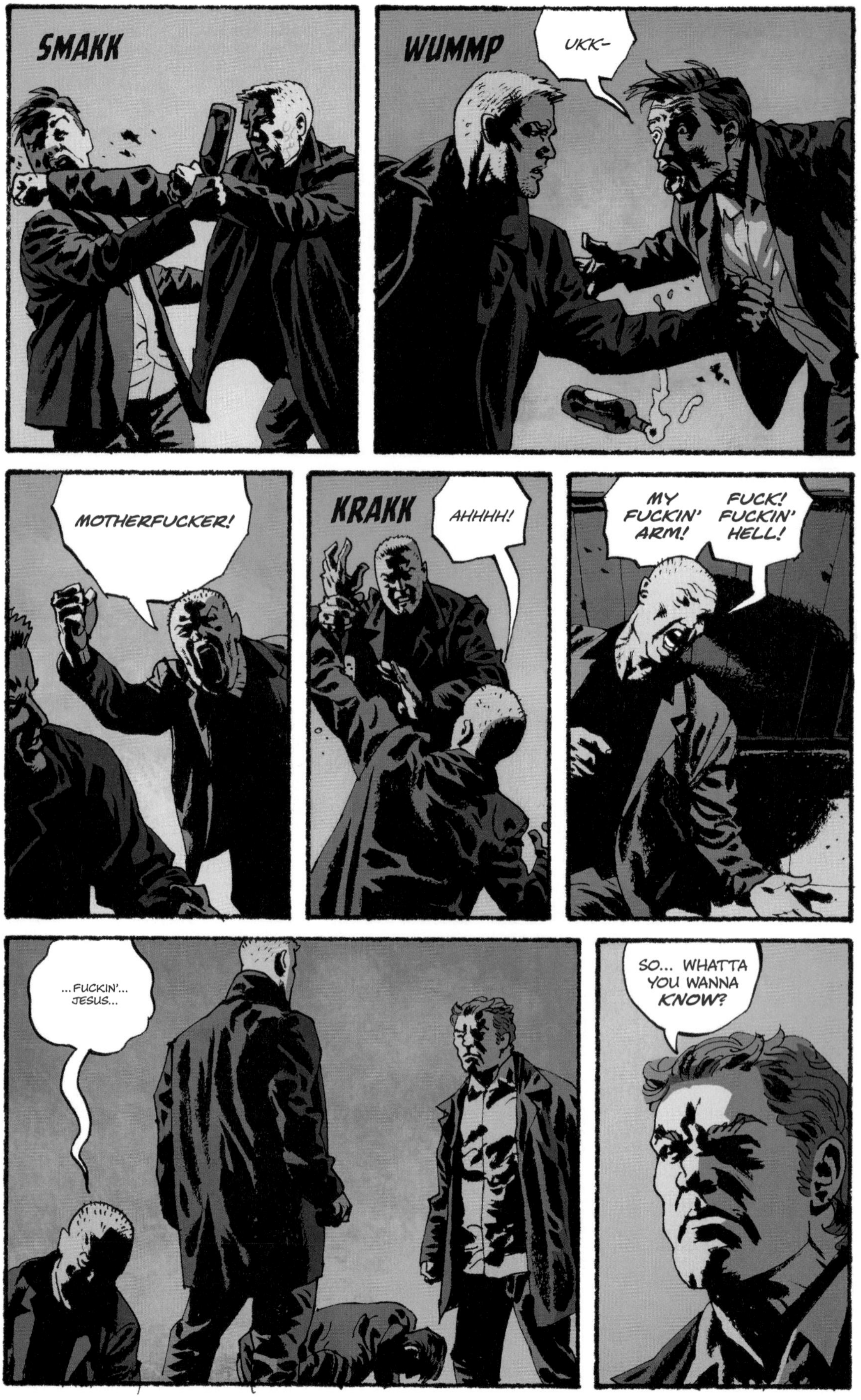
SMAKK
WUMMP
UKK-
MOTHERFUCKER!
KRAKK
AHHHH!
MY FUCKIN' ARM!
FUCK! FUCKIN' HELL!
...FUCKIN'... JESUS...
SO... WHATTA YOU WANNA KNOW?

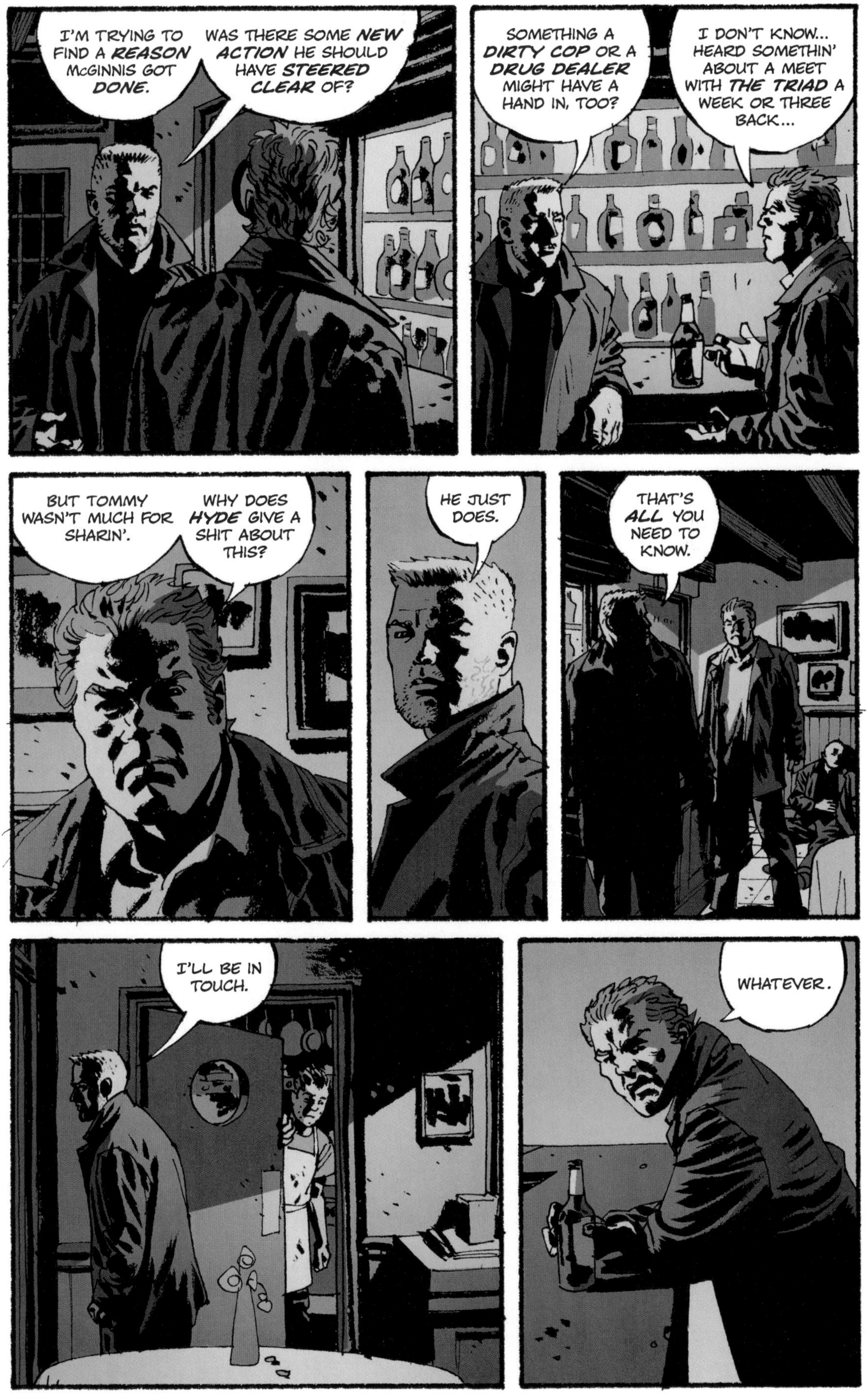
I'M TRYING TO FIND A REASON McGINNIS GOT DONE.
WAS THERE SOME NEW ACTION HE SHOULD HAVE STEERED CLEAR OF?
SOMETHING A DIRTY COP OR A DRUG DEALER MIGHT HAVE A HAND IN, TOO?
I DON'T KNOW... HEARD SOMETHIN' ABOUT A MEET WITH THE TRIAD A WEEK OR THREE BACK...
BUT TOMMY WASN'T MUCH FOR SHARIN'.
WHY DOES HYDE GIVE A SHIT ABOUT THIS?
HE JUST DOES.
THAT'S ALL YOU NEED TO KNOW.
I'LL BE IN TOUCH.
WHATEVER.

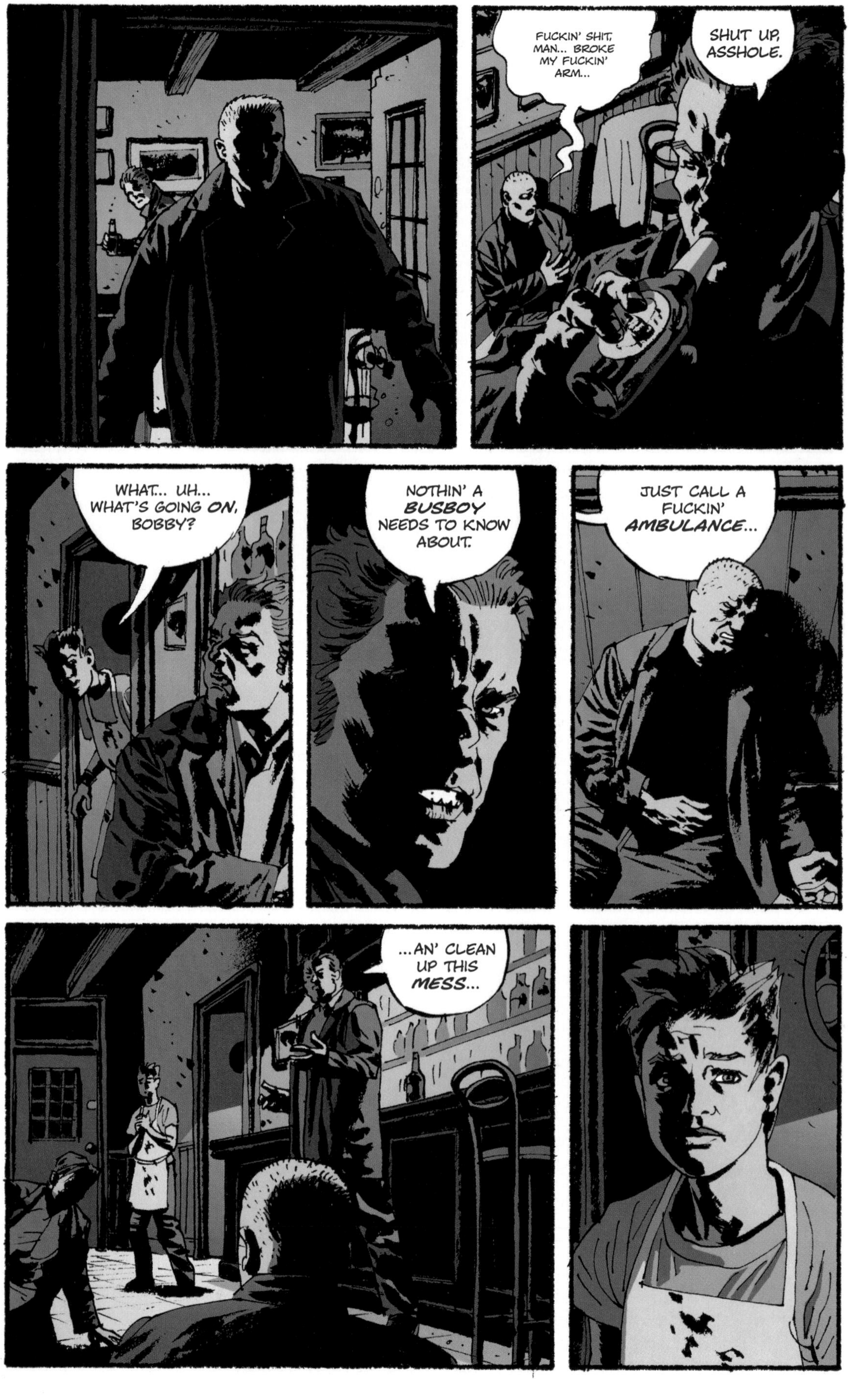
FUCKIN' SHIT, MAN... BROKE MY FUCKIN' ARM...
SHUT UP, ASSHOLE.
WHAT... UH... WHAT'S GOING ON, BOBBY?
NOTHIN' A BUSBOY NEEDS TO KNOW ABOUT.
JUST CALL A FUCKIN' AMBULANCE...
...AN' CLEAN UP THIS MESS...

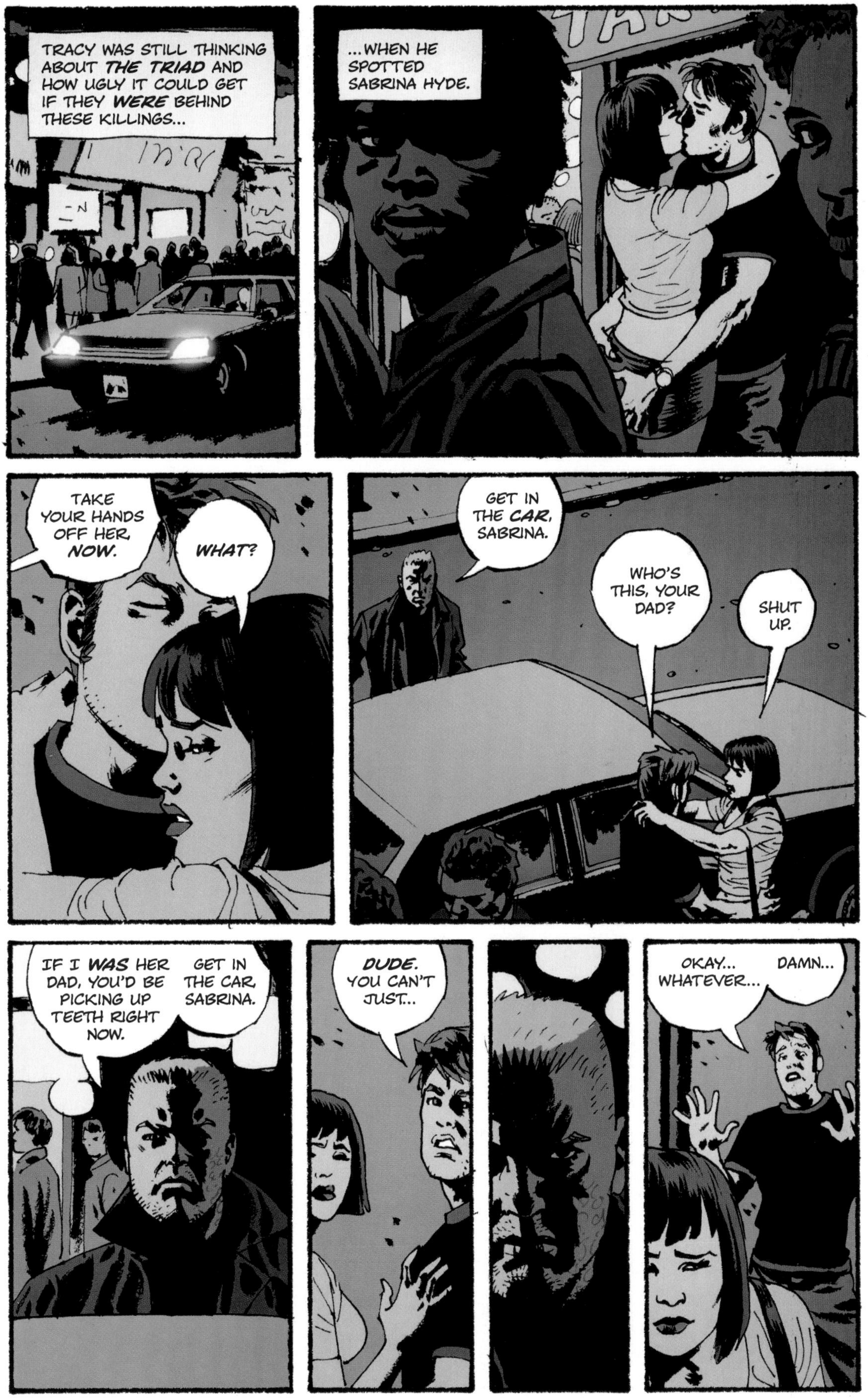
TRACY WAS STILL THINKING ABOUT THE TRIAD AND HOW UGLY IT COULD GET IF THEY WERE BEHIND THESE KILLINGS...
...WHEN HE SPOTTED SABRINA HYDE.
TAKE YOUR HANDS OFF HER, NOW.
WHAT?
GET IN THE CAR, SABRINA.
WHO'S THIS, YOUR DAD?
SHUT UP.
IF I WAS HER DAD, YOU'D BE PICKING UP TEETH RIGHT NOW.
GET IN THE CAR, SABRINA.
DUDE. YOU CAN'T JUST...
OKAY... WHATEVER...
DAMN...

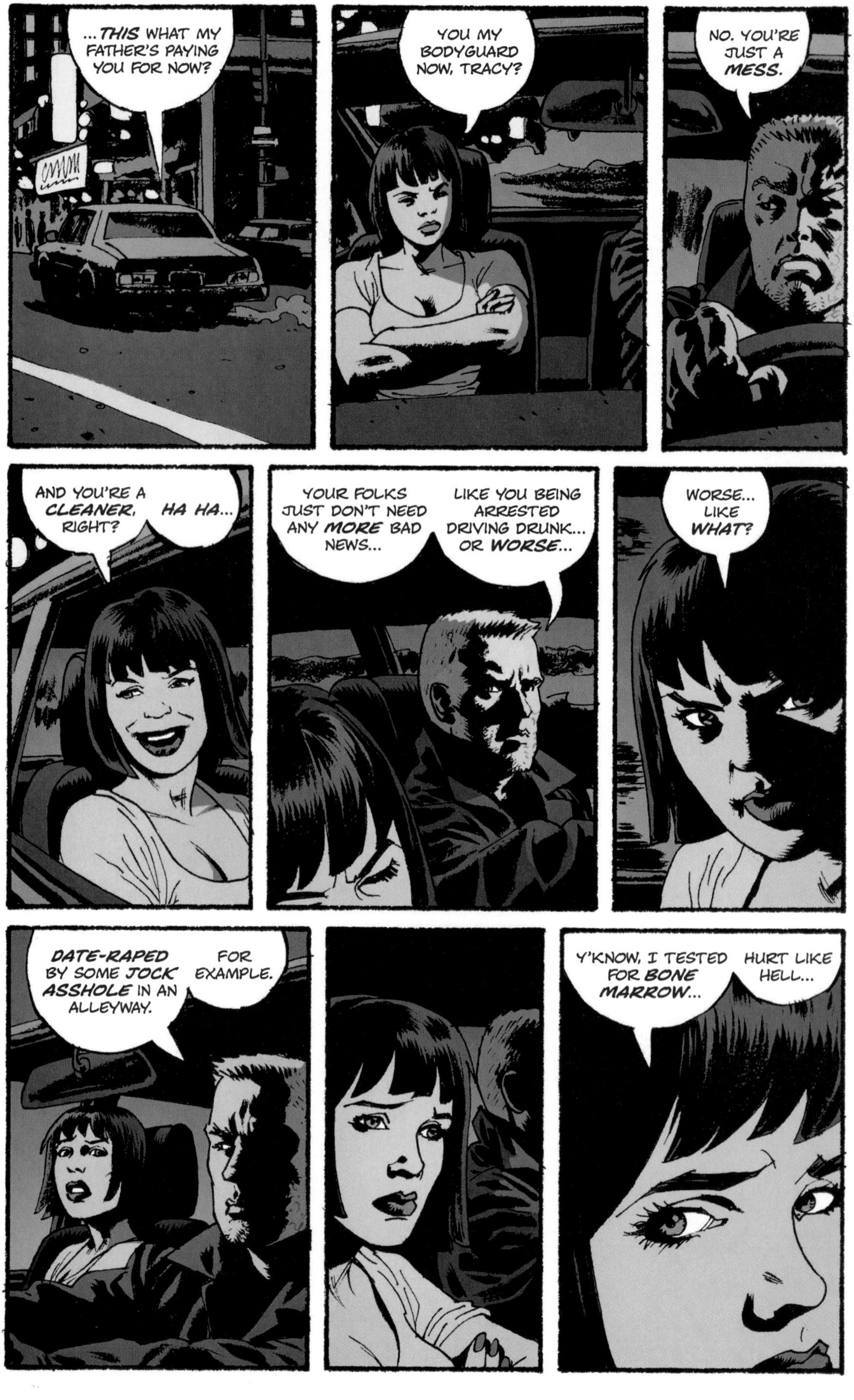
...THIS WHAT MY FATHER'S PAYING YOU FOR NOW?
YOU MY BODYGUARD NOW, TRACY?
NO. YOU'RE JUST A MESS.
AND YOU'RE A CLEANER, RIGHT?
HA HA...
YOUR FOLKS JUST DON'T NEED ANY MORE BAD NEWS...
LIKE YOU BEING ARRESTED DRIVING DRUNK... OR WORSE...
WORSE... LIKE WHAT?
DATE-RAPED BY SOME JOCK ASSHOLE IN AN ALLEYWAY.
FOR EXAMPLE.
Y'KNOW, I TESTED FOR BONE MARROW...
HURT LIKE HELL...

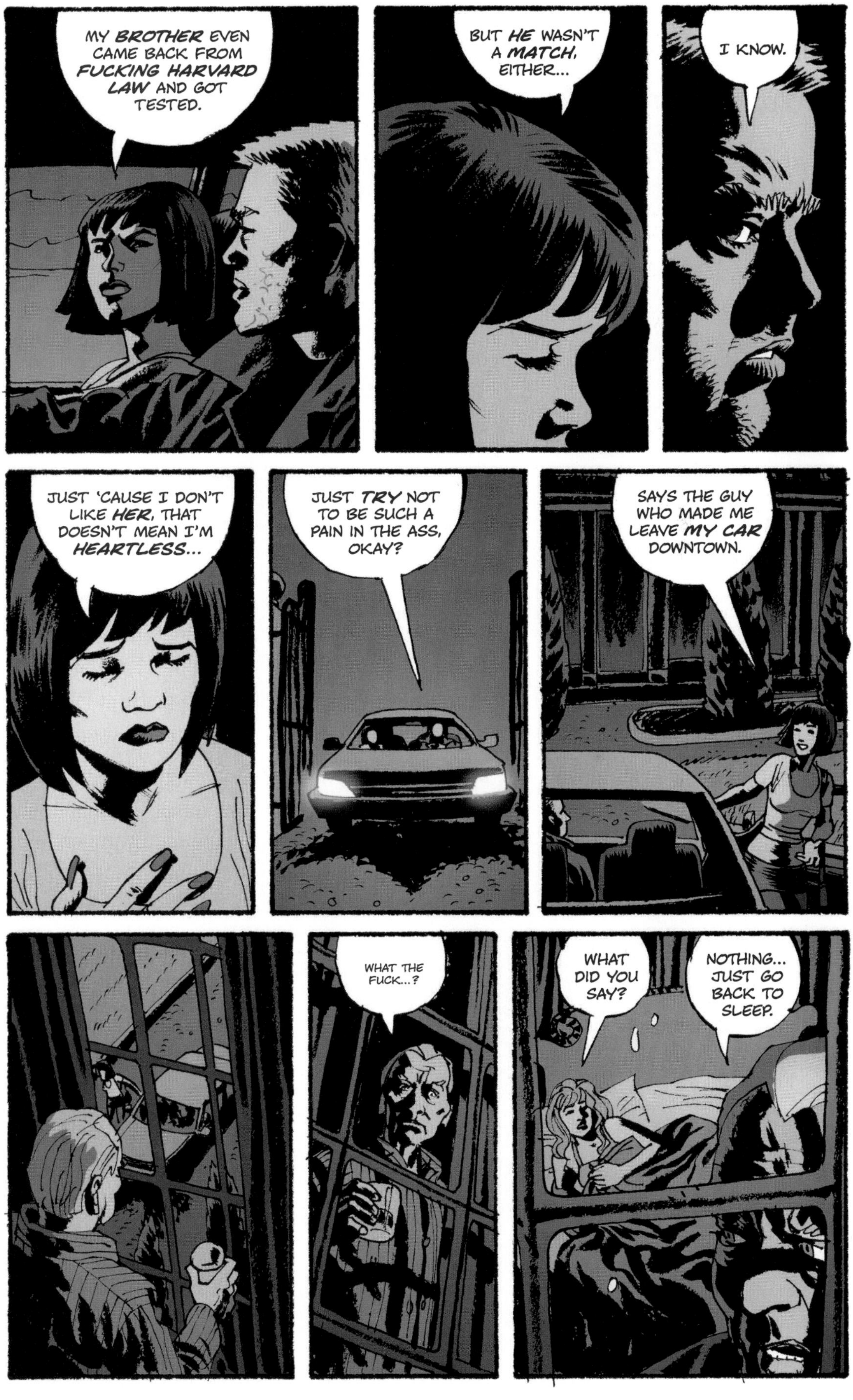
MY BROTHER EVEN CAME BACK FROM FUCKING HARVARD LAW AND GOT TESTED.
BUT HE WASN'T A MATCH, EITHER...
I KNOW.
JUST 'CAUSE I DON'T LIKE HER, THAT DOESN'T MEAN I'M HEARTLESS...
JUST TRY NOT TO BE SUCH A PAIN IN THE ASS, OKAY?
SAYS THE GUY WHO MADE ME LEAVE MY CAR DOWNTOWN.
WHAT THE FUCK...?
WHAT DID YOU SAY?
NOTHING... JUST GO BACK TO SLEEP.

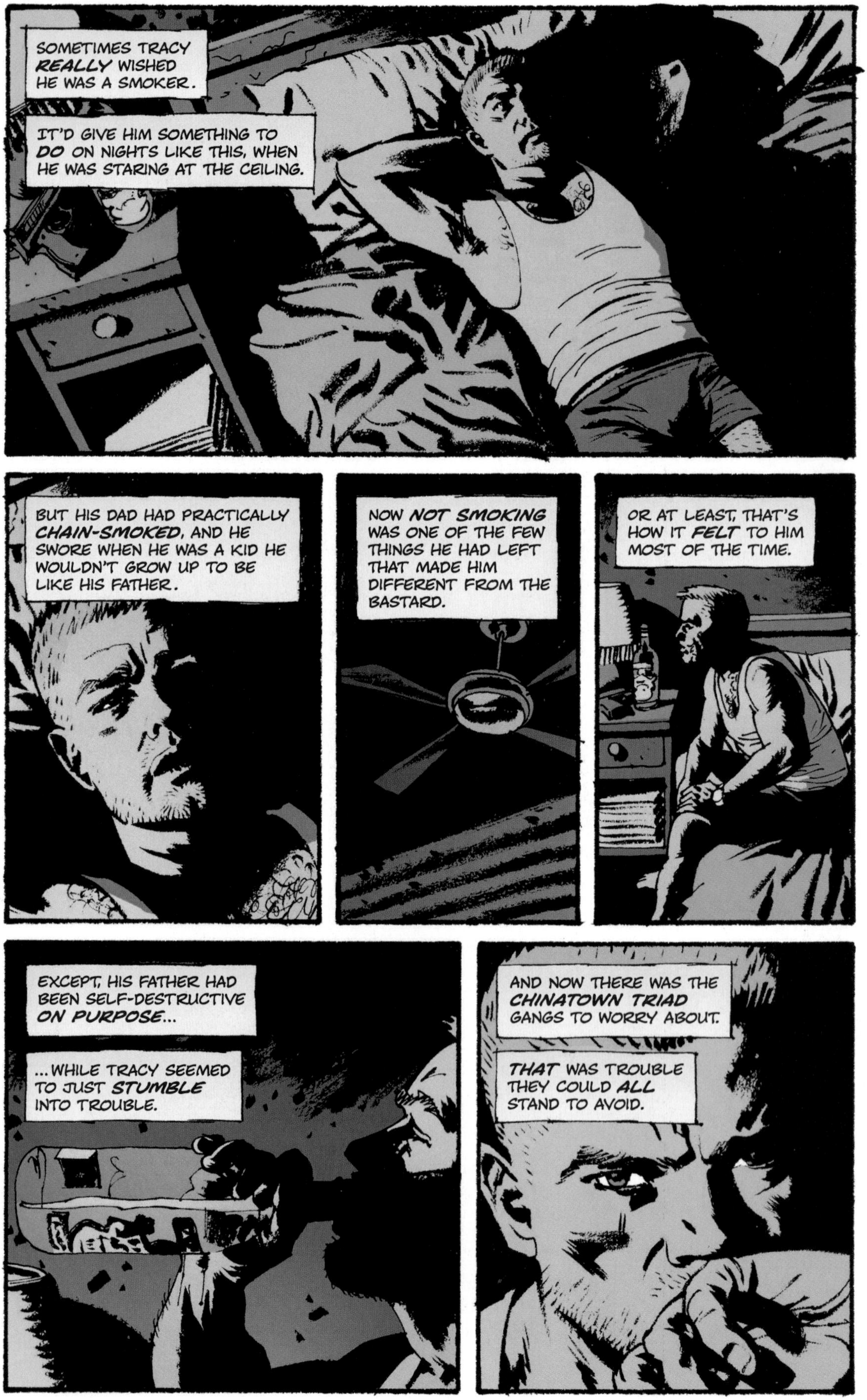
SOMETIMES TRACY REALLY WISHED HE WAS A SMOKER.
IT'D GIVE HIM SOMETHING TO DO ON NIGHTS LIKE THIS, WHEN HE WAS STARING AT THE CEILING.
BUT HIS DAD HAD PRACTICALLY CHAIN-SMOKED, AND HE SWORE WHEN HE WAS A KID HE WOULDN'T GROW UP TO BE LIKE HIS FATHER.
NOW NOT SMOKING WAS ONE OF THE FEW THINGS HE HAD LEFT THAT MADE HIM DIFFERENT FROM THE BASTARD.
OR AT LEAST, THAT'S HOW IT FELT TO HIM MOST OF THE TIME.
EXCEPT, HIS FATHER HAD BEEN SELF-DESTRUCTIVE ON PURPOSE...
...WHILE TRACY SEEMED TO JUST STUMBLE INTO TROUBLE.
AND NOW THERE WAS THE CHINATOWN TRIAD GANGS TO WORRY ABOUT.
THAT WAS TROUBLE THEY COULD ALL STAND TO AVOID.

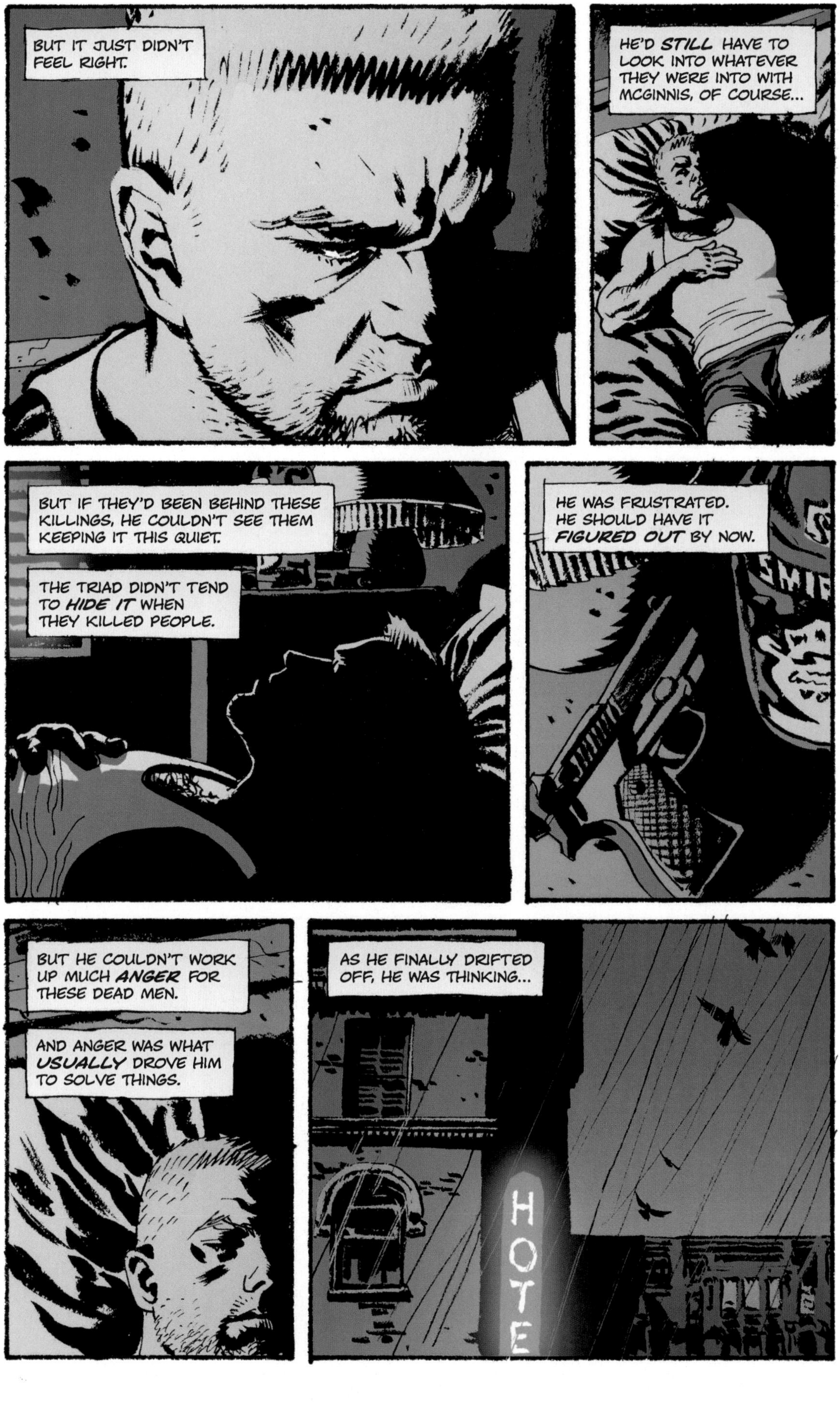
BUT IT JUST DIDN'T FEEL RIGHT.
HE'D *STILL* HAVE TO LOOK INTO WHATEVER THEY WERE INTO WITH MCGINNIS, OF COURSE...
BUT IF THEY'D BEEN BEHIND THESE KILLINGS, HE COULDN'T SEE THEM KEEPING IT THIS QUIET.
THE TRIAD DIDN'T TEND TO *HIDE IT* WHEN THEY KILLED PEOPLE.
HE WAS FRUSTRATED. HE SHOULD HAVE IT *FIGURED OUT* BY NOW.
BUT HE COULDN'T WORK UP MUCH *ANGER* FOR THESE DEAD MEN.
AND ANGER WAS WHAT *USUALLY* DROVE HIM TO SOLVE THINGS.
AS HE FINALLY DRIFTED OFF, HE WAS THINKING...
HOTE

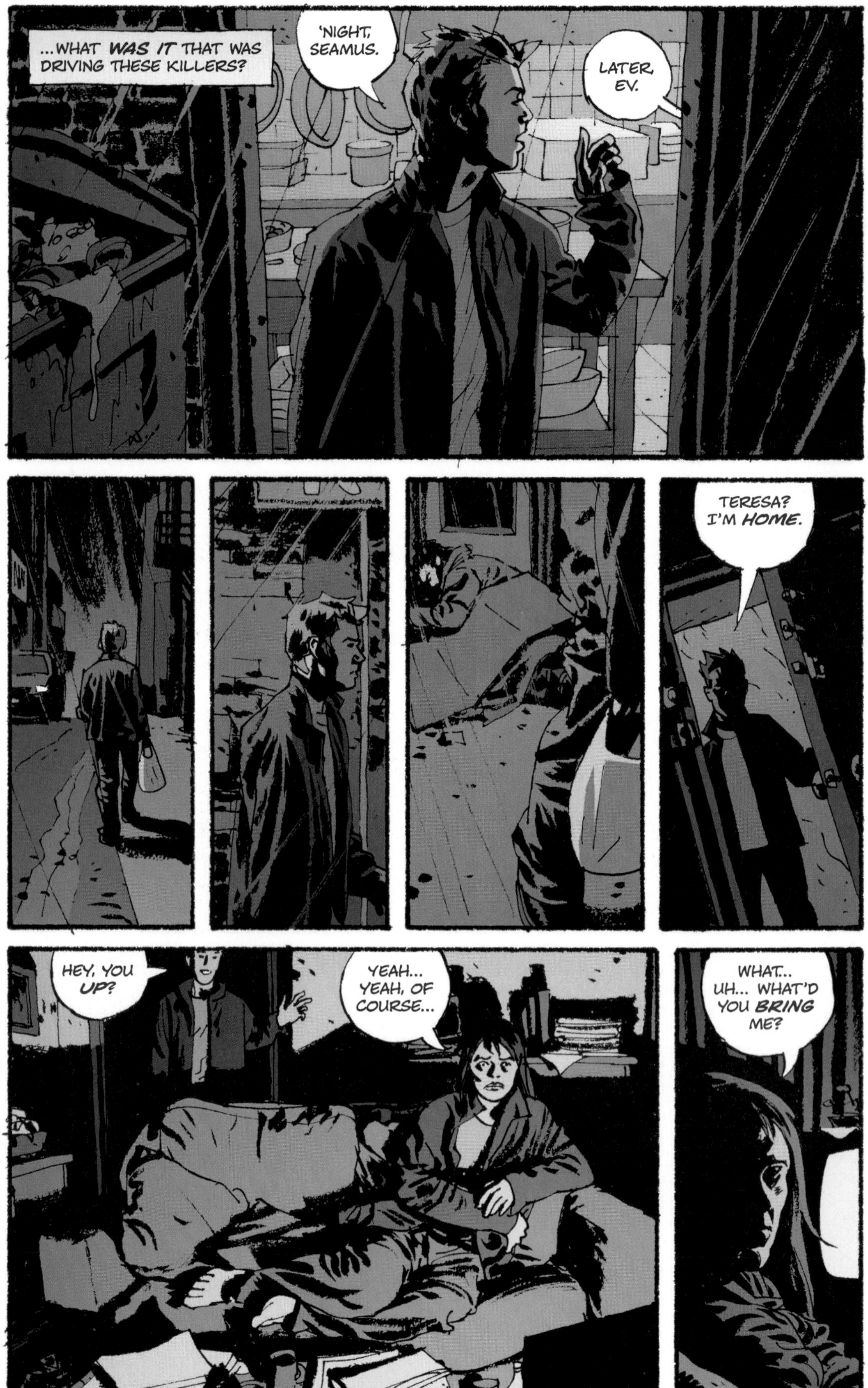
...WHAT WAS IT THAT WAS DRIVING THESE KILLERS?
'NIGHT, SEAMUS.
LATER, EV.
TERESA? I'M HOME.
HEY, YOU UP?
YEAH... YEAH, OF COURSE...
WHAT... UH... WHAT'D YOU BRING ME?

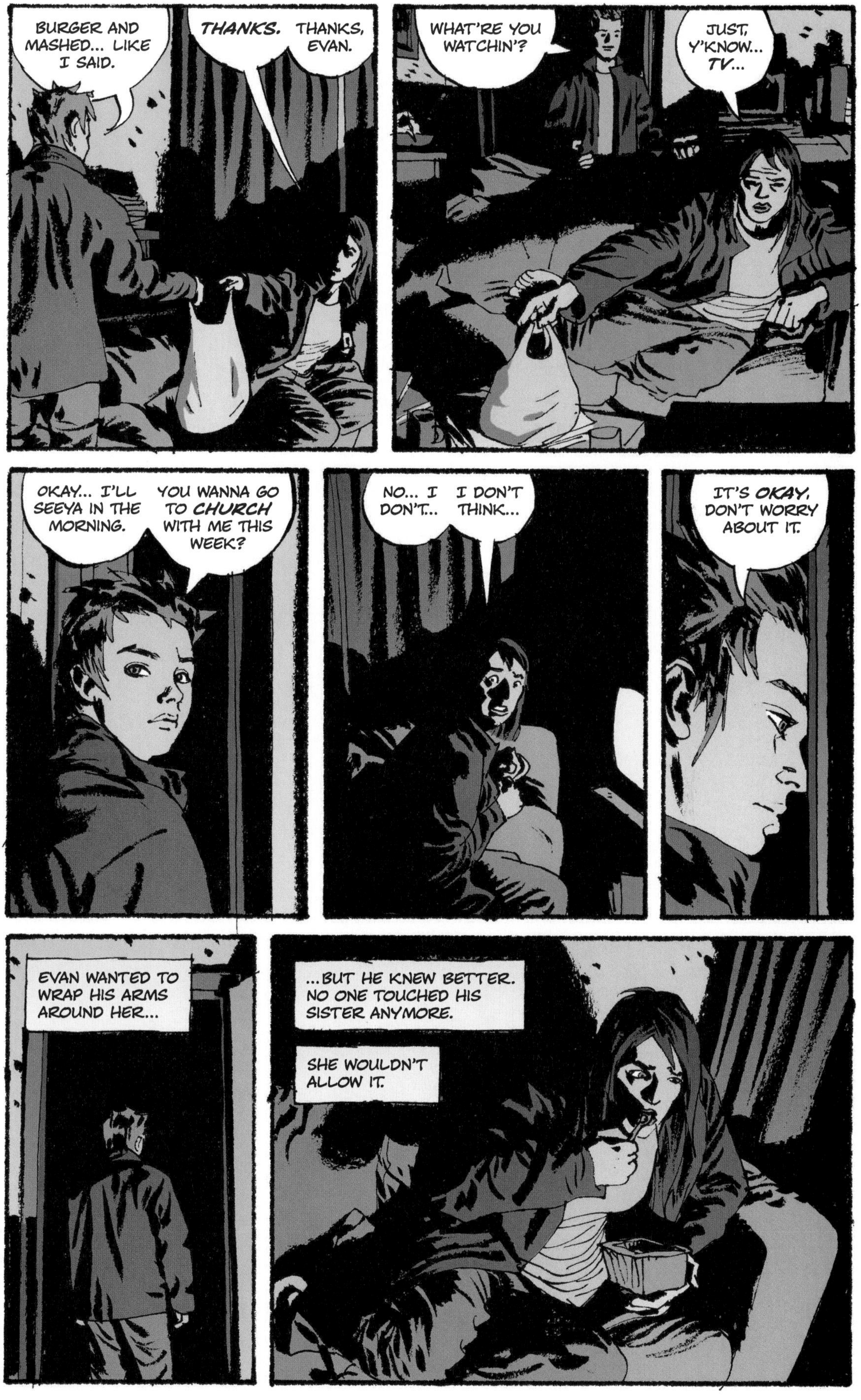

BURGER AND MASHED... LIKE I SAID.
THANKS.
THANKS, EVAN.
WHAT'RE YOU WATCHIN'?
JUST, Y'KNOW... TV...
OKAY... I'LL SEEYA IN THE MORNING.
YOU WANNA GO TO CHURCH WITH ME THIS WEEK?
NO... I DON'T...
I DON'T THINK...
IT'S OKAY, DON'T WORRY ABOUT IT.
EVAN WANTED TO WRAP HIS ARMS AROUND HER...
...BUT HE KNEW BETTER. NO ONE TOUCHED HIS SISTER ANYMORE.
SHE WOULDN'T ALLOW IT.

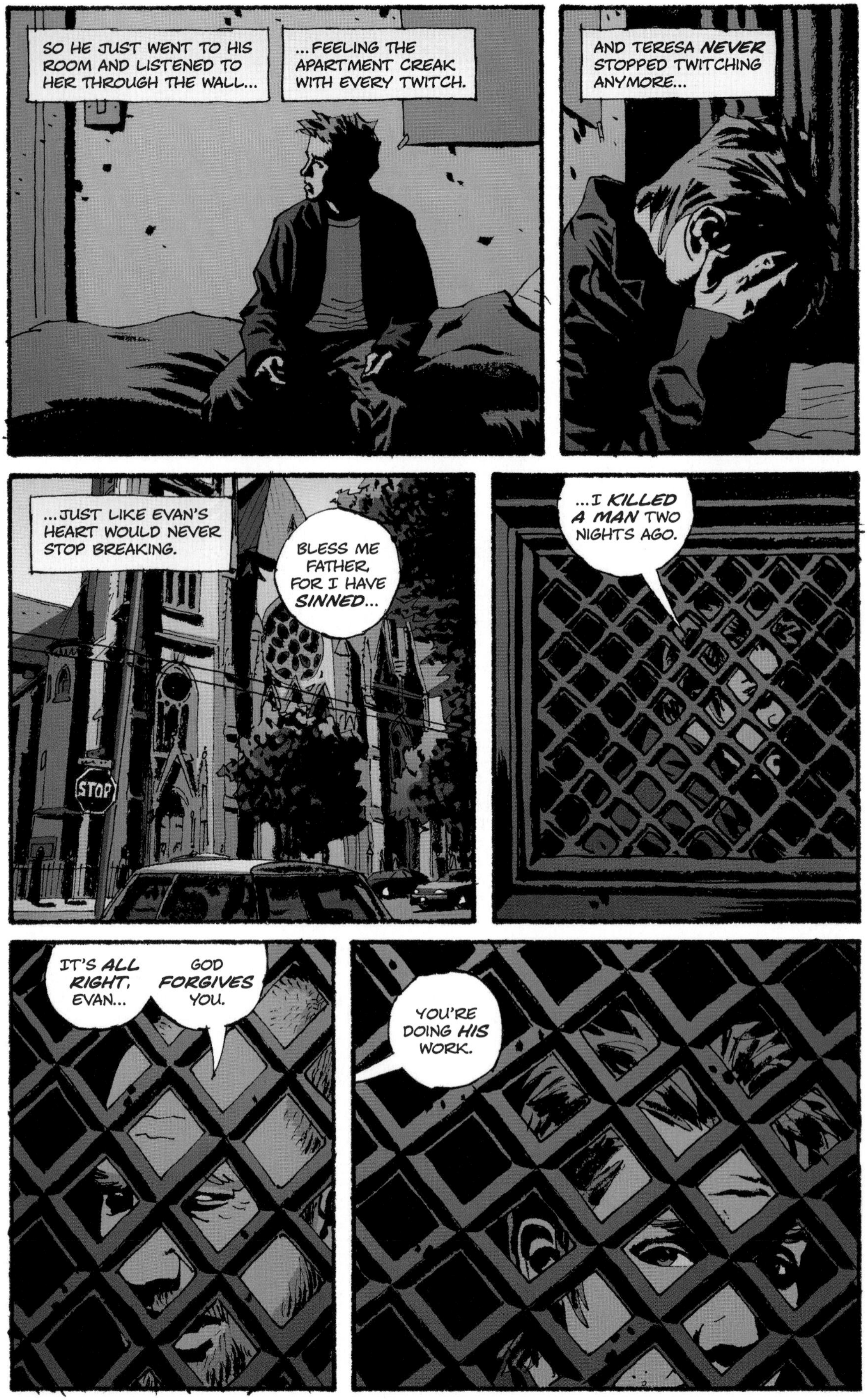
SO HE JUST WENT TO HIS ROOM AND LISTENED TO HER THROUGH THE WALL...
...FEELING THE APARTMENT CREAK WITH EVERY TWITCH.
AND TERESA NEVER STOPPED TWITCHING ANYMORE...
...JUST LIKE EVAN'S HEART WOULD NEVER STOP BREAKING.
BLESS ME FATHER, FOR I HAVE SINNED...
STOP
...I KILLED A MAN TWO NIGHTS AGO.
IT'S ALL RIGHT, EVAN...
GOD FORGIVES YOU.
YOU'RE DOING HIS WORK.

The Sinners Part Three

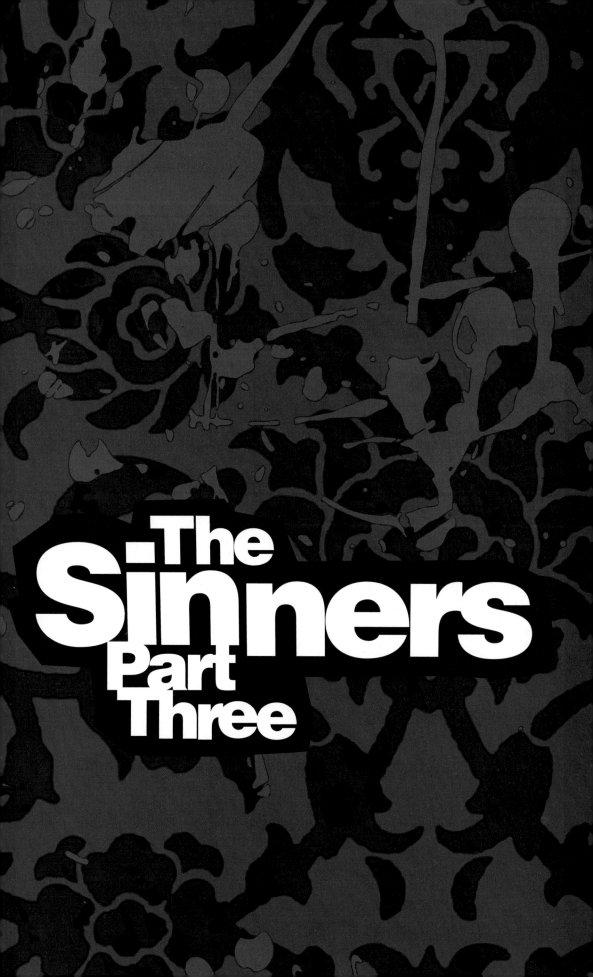

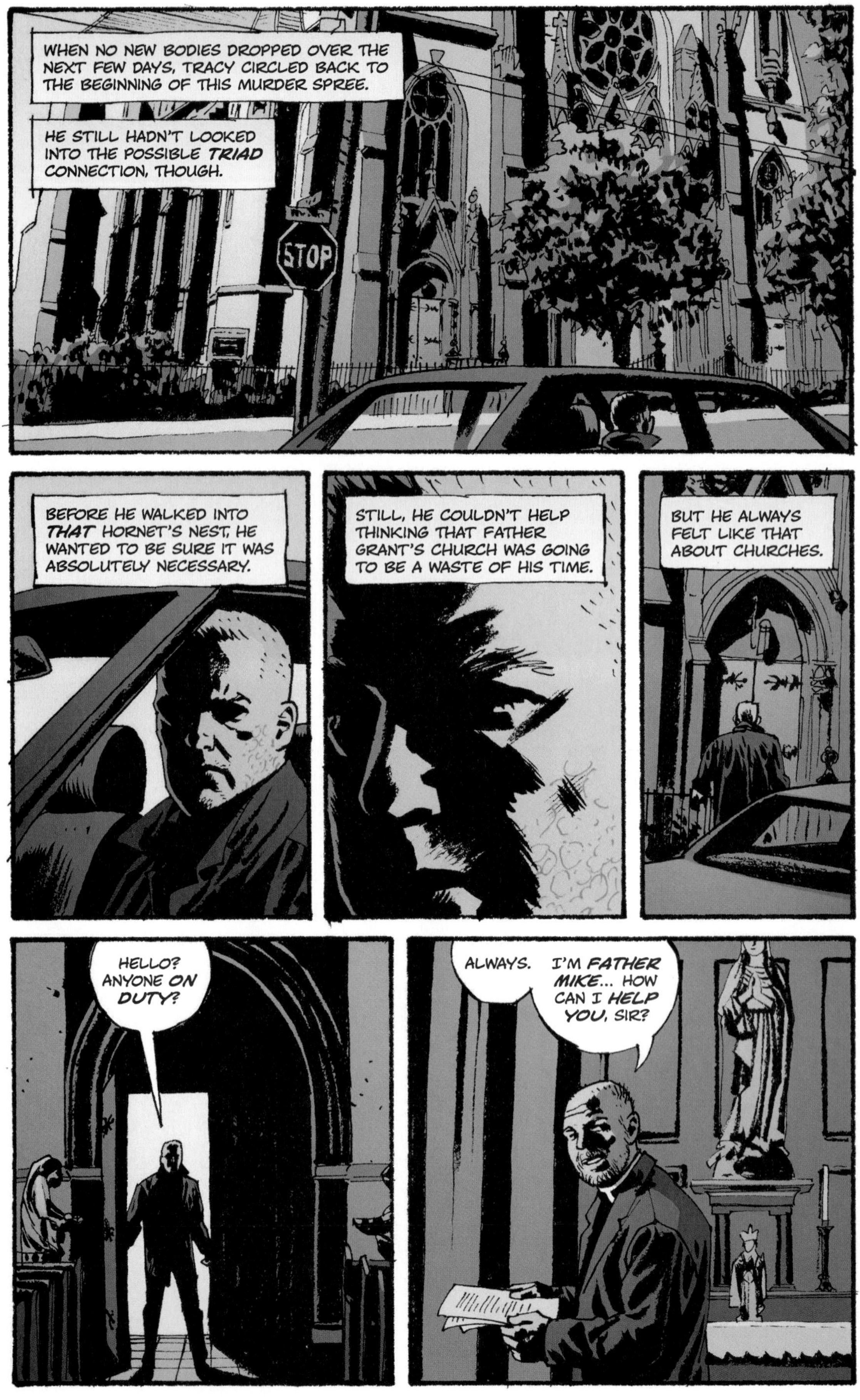
WHEN NO NEW BODIES DROPPED OVER THE NEXT FEW DAYS, TRACY CIRCLED BACK TO THE BEGINNING OF THIS MURDER SPREE.
HE STILL HADN'T LOOKED INTO THE POSSIBLE TRIAD CONNECTION, THOUGH.
STOP
BEFORE HE WALKED INTO THAT HORNET'S NEST, HE WANTED TO BE SURE IT WAS ABSOLUTELY NECESSARY.
STILL, HE COULDN'T HELP THINKING THAT FATHER GRANT'S CHURCH WAS GOING TO BE A WASTE OF HIS TIME.
BUT HE ALWAYS FELT LIKE THAT ABOUT CHURCHES.
HELLO? ANYONE ON DUTY?
ALWAYS.
I'M FATHER MIKE... HOW CAN I HELP YOU, SIR?

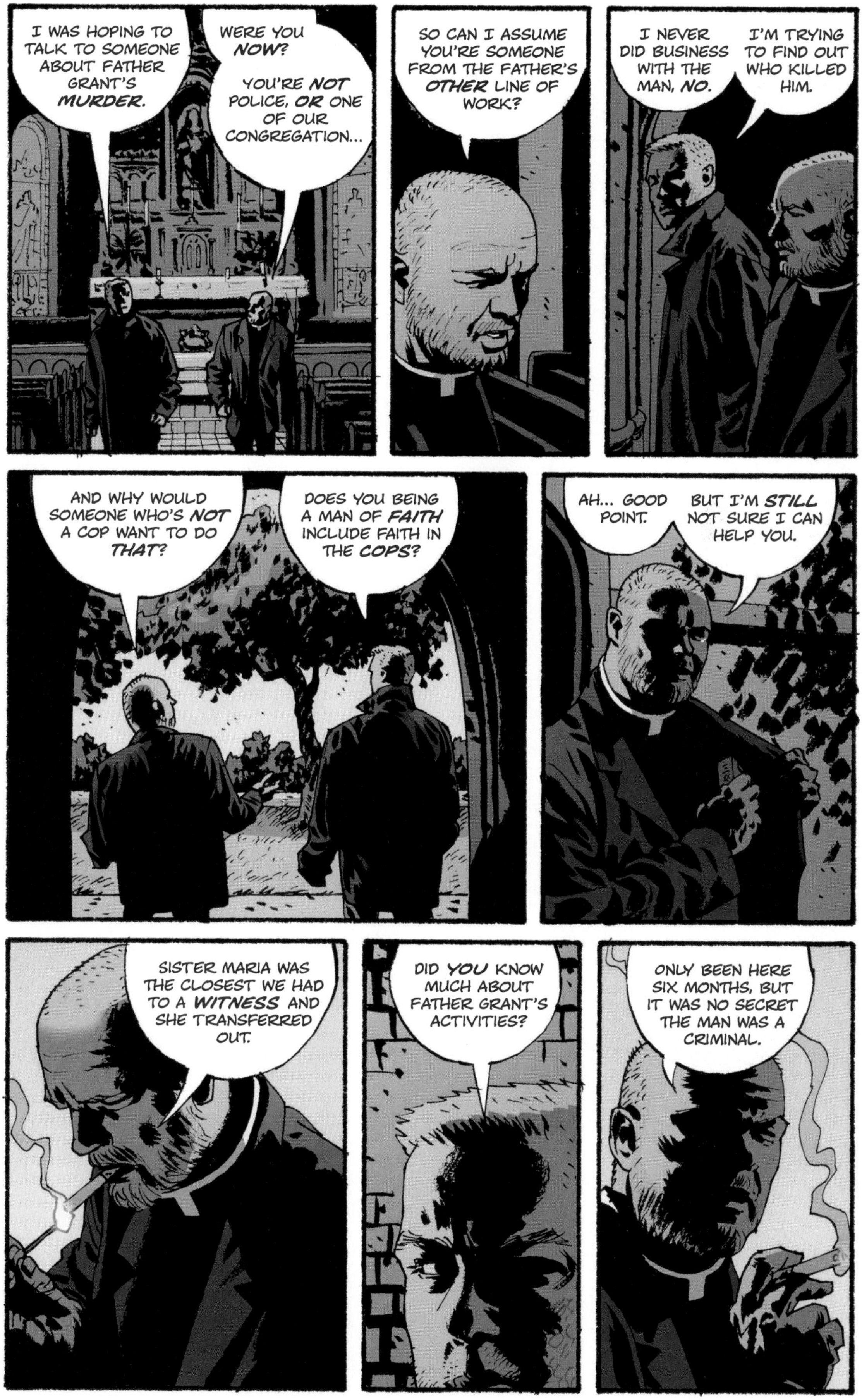
I WAS HOPING TO TALK TO SOMEONE ABOUT FATHER GRANT'S MURDER.
WERE YOU NOW?
YOU'RE NOT POLICE, OR ONE OF OUR CONGREGATION...
SO CAN I ASSUME YOU'RE SOMEONE FROM THE FATHER'S OTHER LINE OF WORK?
I NEVER DID BUSINESS WITH THE MAN, NO.
I'M TRYING TO FIND OUT WHO KILLED HIM.
AND WHY WOULD SOMEONE WHO'S NOT A COP WANT TO DO THAT?
DOES YOU BEING A MAN OF FAITH INCLUDE FAITH IN THE COPS?
AH... GOOD POINT.
BUT I'M STILL NOT SURE I CAN HELP YOU.
SISTER MARIA WAS THE CLOSEST WE HAD TO A WITNESS AND SHE TRANSFERRED OUT.
DID YOU KNOW MUCH ABOUT FATHER GRANT'S ACTIVITIES?
ONLY BEEN HERE SIX MONTHS, BUT IT WAS NO SECRET THE MAN WAS A CRIMINAL.

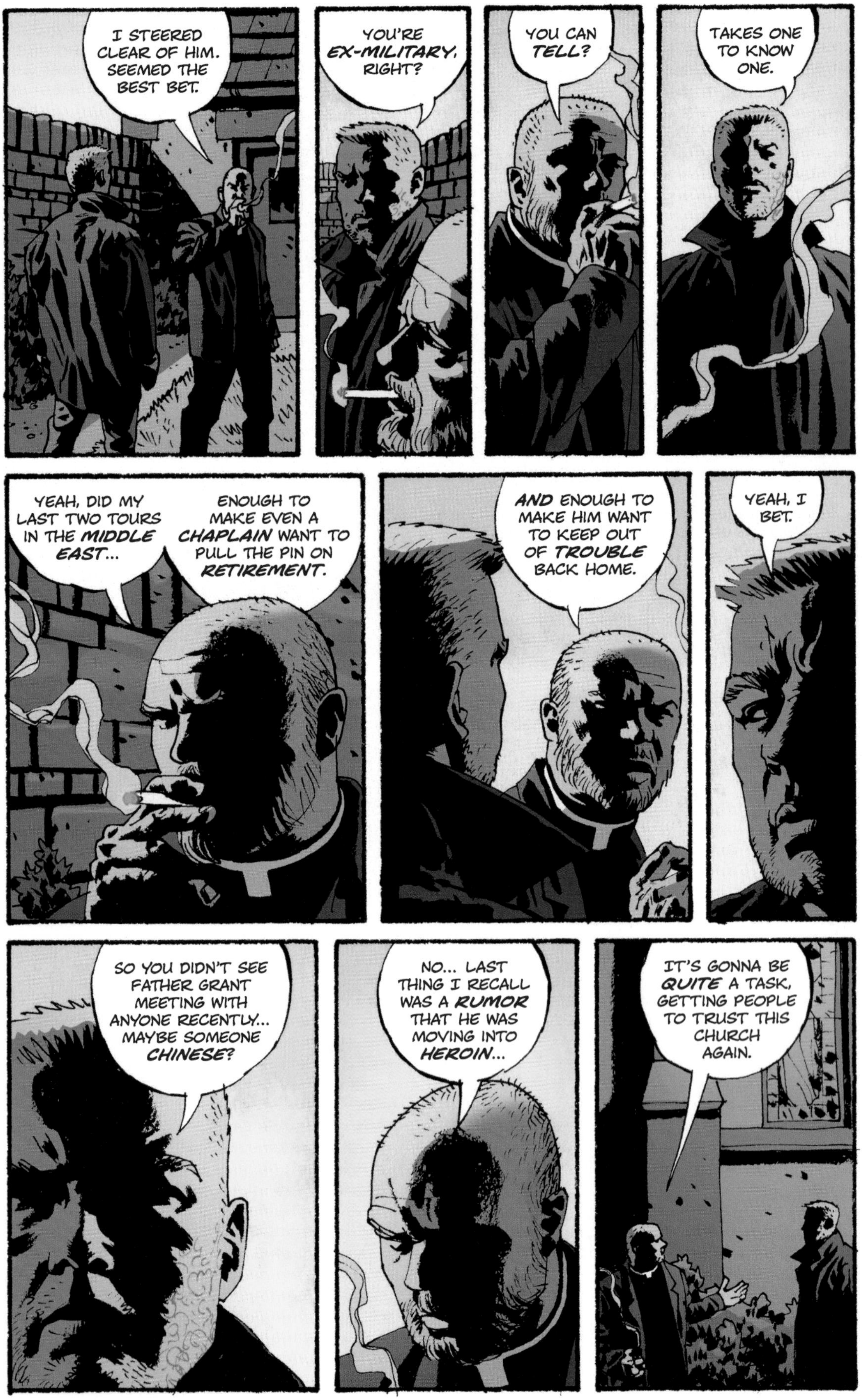
I STEERED CLEAR OF HIM. SEEMED THE BEST BET.
YOU'RE *EX-MILITARY*, RIGHT?
YOU CAN *TELL*?
TAKES ONE TO KNOW ONE.
YEAH, DID MY LAST TWO TOURS IN THE *MIDDLE EAST*...
ENOUGH TO MAKE EVEN A *CHAPLAIN* WANT TO PULL THE PIN ON *RETIREMENT*.
AND ENOUGH TO MAKE HIM WANT TO KEEP OUT OF *TROUBLE* BACK HOME.
YEAH, I BET.
SO YOU DIDN'T SEE FATHER GRANT MEETING WITH ANYONE RECENTLY... MAYBE SOMEONE *CHINESE*?
NO... LAST THING I RECALL WAS A *RUMOR* THAT HE WAS MOVING INTO *HEROIN*...
IT'S GONNA BE *QUITE* A TASK, GETTING PEOPLE TO TRUST THIS CHURCH AGAIN.

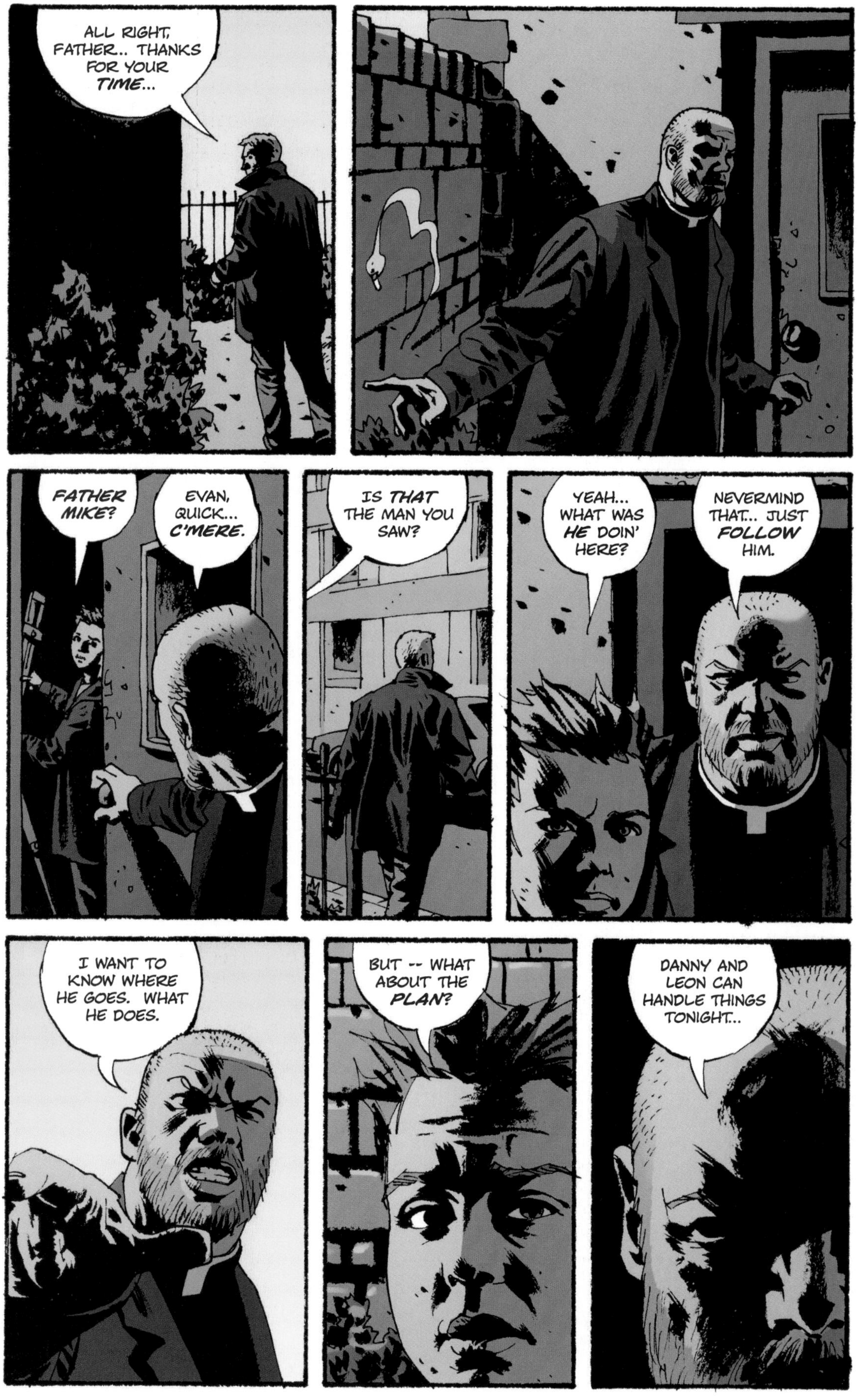
ALL RIGHT, FATHER... THANKS FOR YOUR *TIME*...
FATHER MIKE?
EVAN, QUICK... *C'MERE*.
IS *THAT* THE MAN YOU SAW?
YEAH... WHAT WAS *HE* DOIN' HERE?
NEVERMIND THAT... JUST *FOLLOW* HIM.
I WANT TO KNOW WHERE HE GOES. WHAT HE DOES.
BUT -- WHAT ABOUT THE *PLAN?*
DANNY AND LEON CAN HANDLE THINGS TONIGHT...

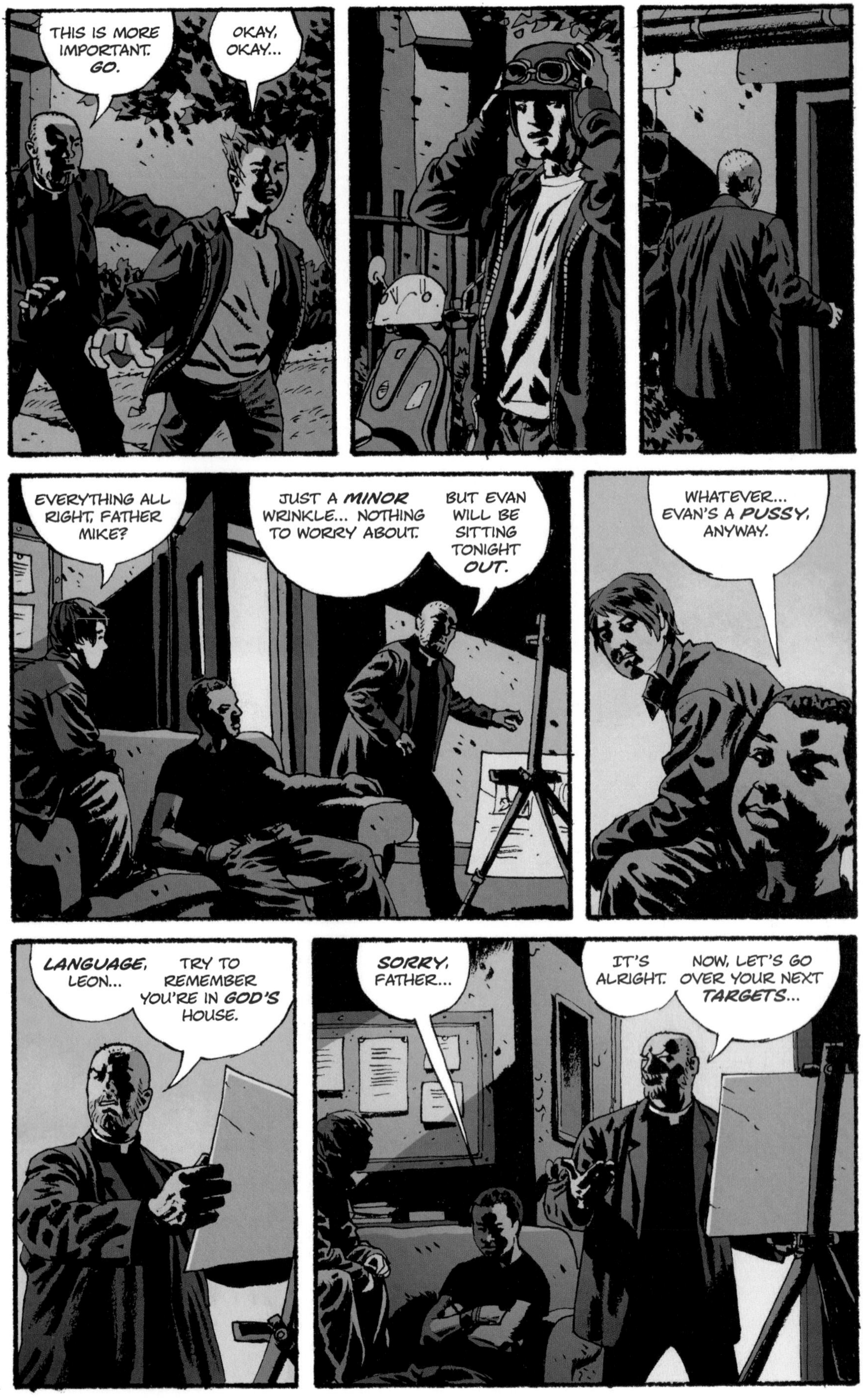
THIS IS MORE IMPORTANT. *GO.*
OKAY, OKAY...
EVERYTHING ALL RIGHT, FATHER MIKE?
JUST A *MINOR* WRINKLE... NOTHING TO WORRY ABOUT.
BUT EVAN WILL BE SITTING TONIGHT *OUT.*
WHATEVER... EVAN'S A *PUSSY,* ANYWAY.
LANGUAGE, LEON...
TRY TO REMEMBER YOU'RE IN *GOD'S* HOUSE.
SORRY, FATHER...
IT'S ALRIGHT.
NOW, LET'S GO OVER YOUR NEXT *TARGETS...*

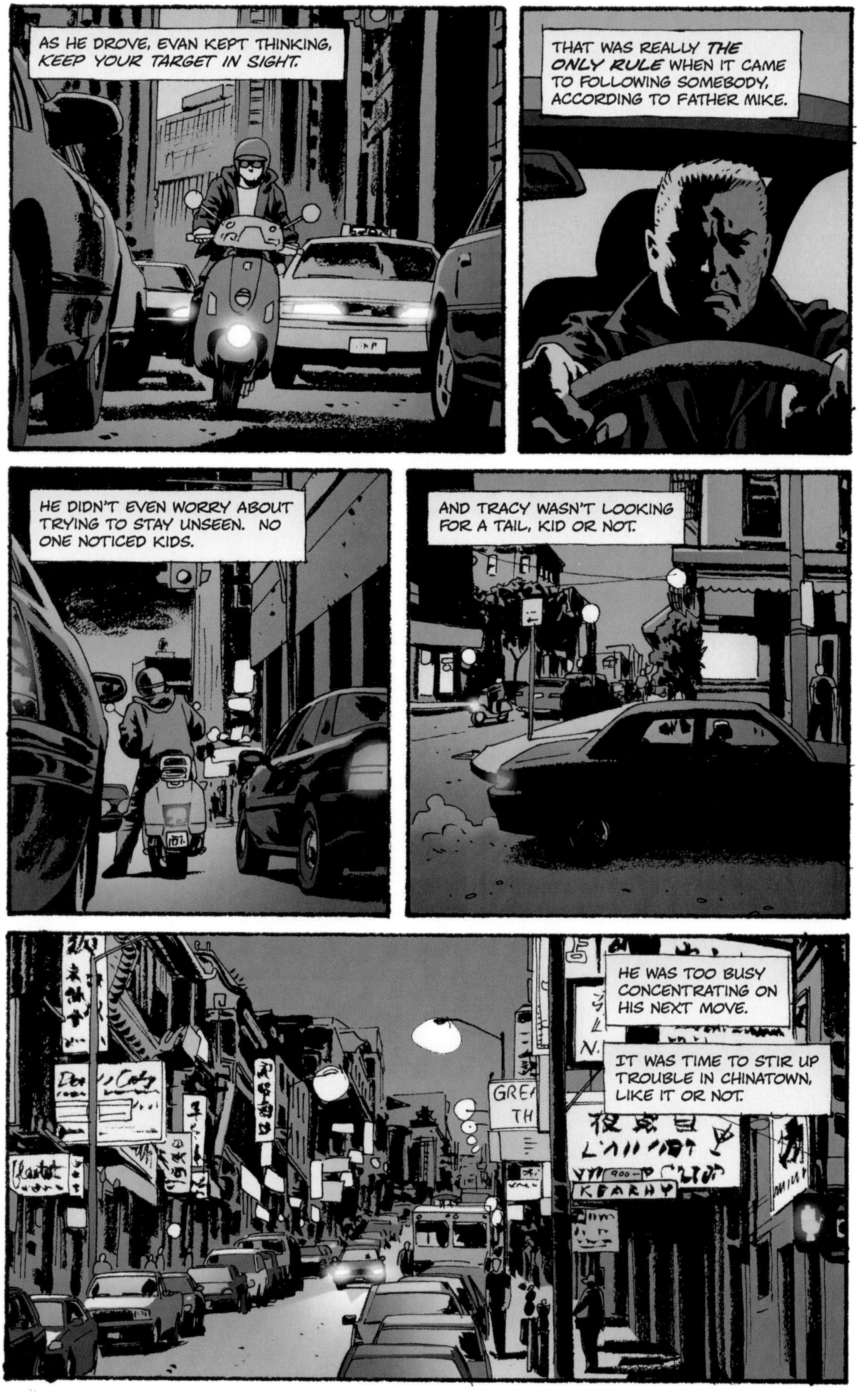
AS HE DROVE, EVAN KEPT THINKING, KEEP YOUR TARGET IN SIGHT.
THAT WAS REALLY THE ONLY RULE WHEN IT CAME TO FOLLOWING SOMEBODY, ACCORDING TO FATHER MIKE.
HE DIDN'T EVEN WORRY ABOUT TRYING TO STAY UNSEEN. NO ONE NOTICED KIDS.
AND TRACY WASN'T LOOKING FOR A TAIL, KID OR NOT.
HE WAS TOO BUSY CONCENTRATING ON HIS NEXT MOVE.
IT WAS TIME TO STIR UP TROUBLE IN CHINATOWN, LIKE IT OR NOT.
KEARNY

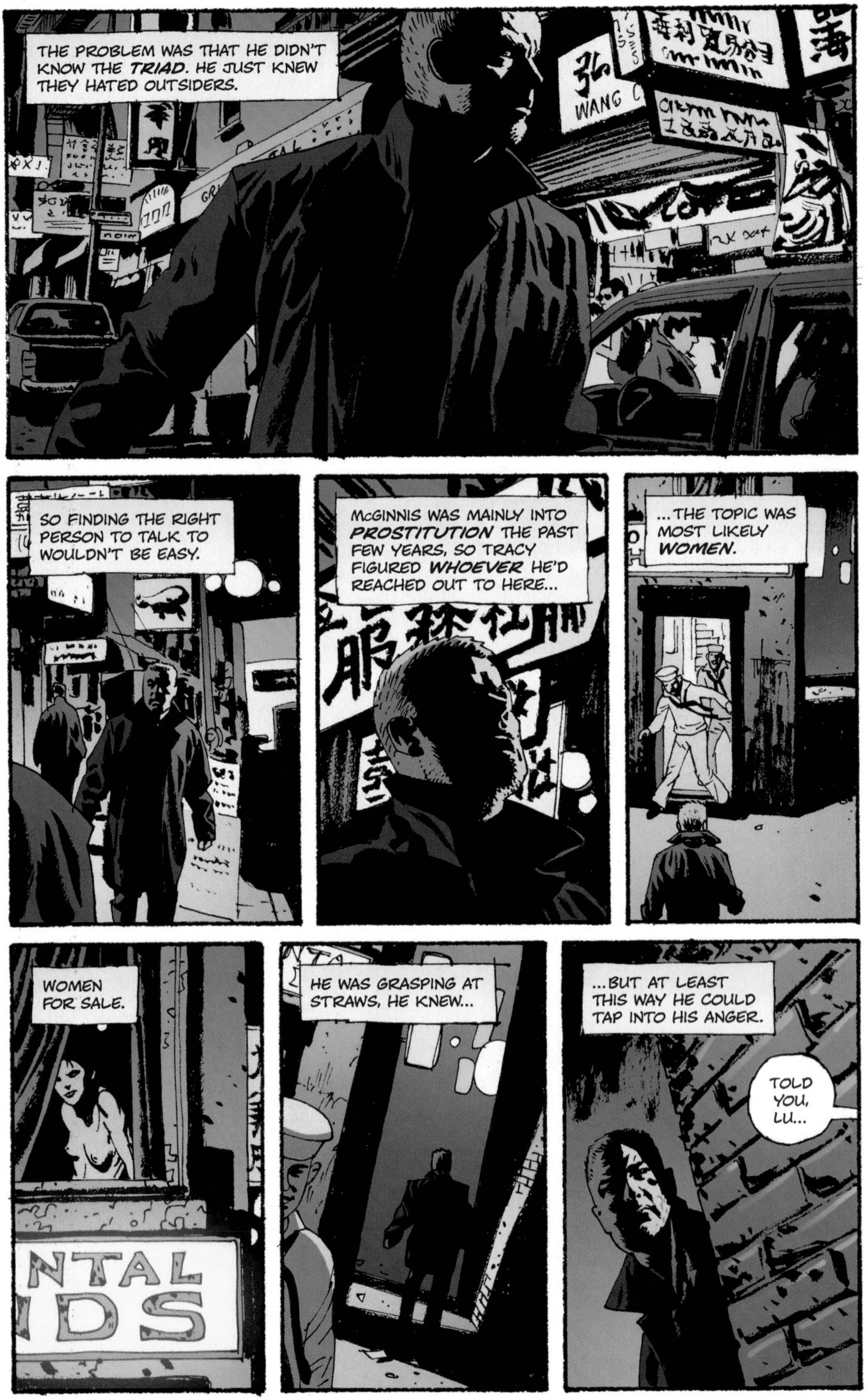
THE PROBLEM WAS THAT HE DIDN'T KNOW THE *TRIAD*. HE JUST KNEW THEY HATED OUTSIDERS.
WANG C
SO FINDING THE RIGHT PERSON TO TALK TO WOULDN'T BE EASY.
McGINNIS WAS MAINLY INTO *PROSTITUTION* THE PAST FEW YEARS, SO TRACY FIGURED *WHOEVER* HE'D REACHED OUT TO HERE...
...THE TOPIC WAS MOST LIKELY *WOMEN*.
WOMEN FOR SALE.
NTAL
DS
HE WAS GRASPING AT STRAWS, HE KNEW...
...BUT AT LEAST THIS WAY HE COULD TAP INTO HIS ANGER.
TOLD YOU, LU...

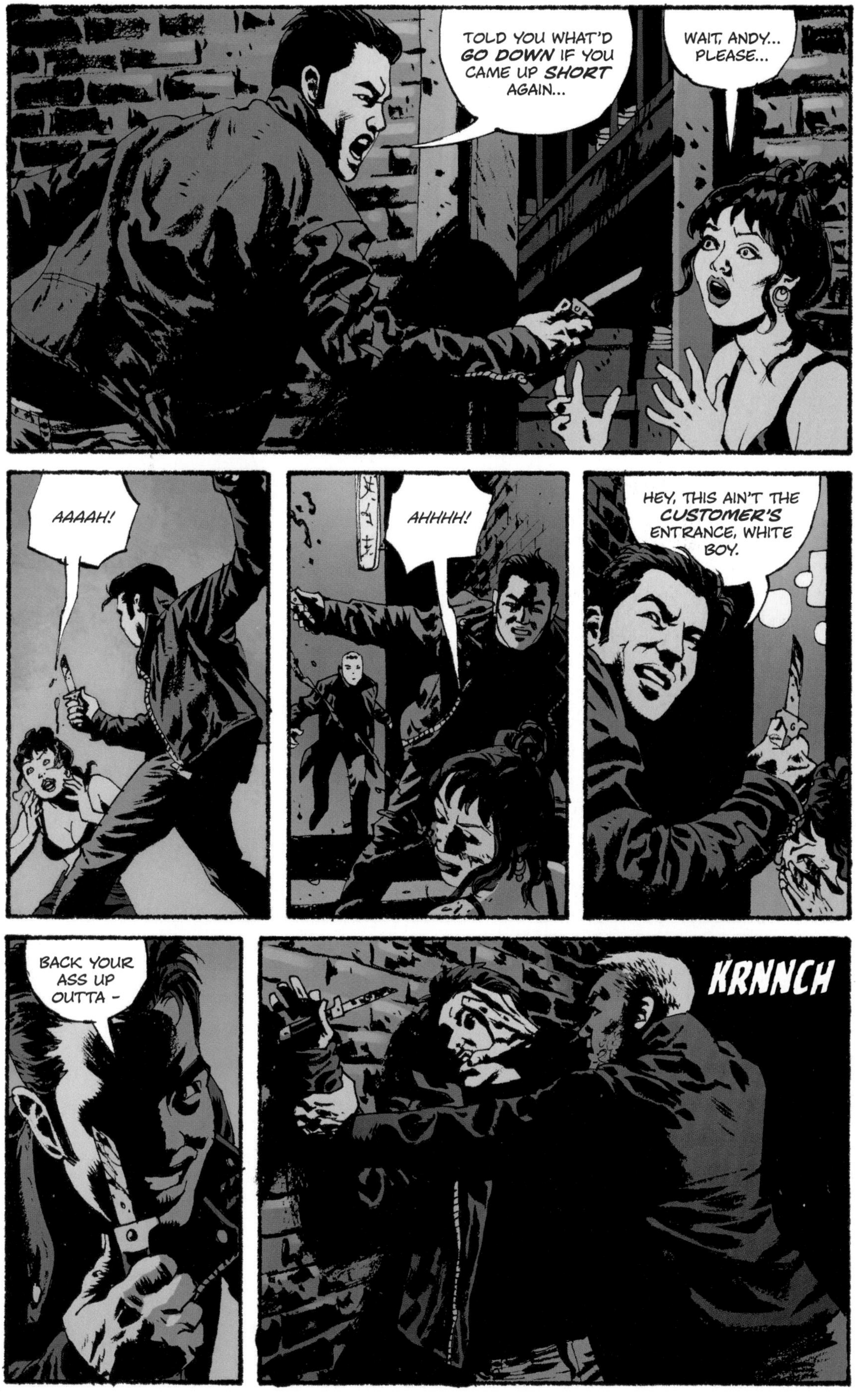
TOLD YOU WHAT'D *GO DOWN* IF YOU CAME UP *SHORT* AGAIN...
WAIT, ANDY... PLEASE...
AAAAH!
AHHHH!
HEY, THIS AIN'T THE *CUSTOMER'S* ENTRANCE, WHITE BOY.
BACK YOUR ASS UP OUTTA -
KRNNCH

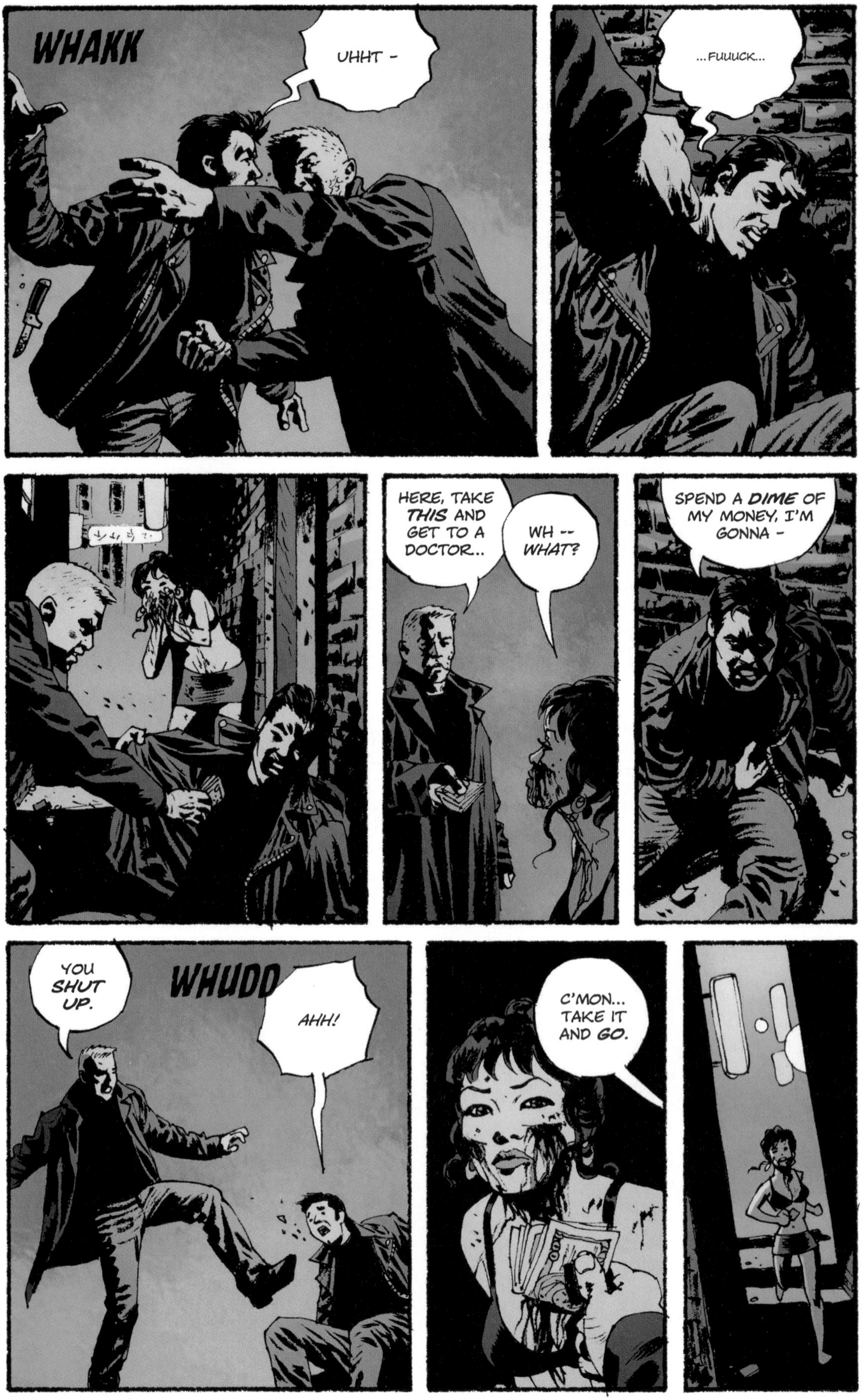
WHAKK
UHHT -
...FUUUCK...
HERE, TAKE THIS AND GET TO A DOCTOR..
WH -- WHAT?
SPEND A DIME OF MY MONEY, I'M GONNA -
YOU SHUT UP.
WHUDD
AHH!
C'MON... TAKE IT AND GO.

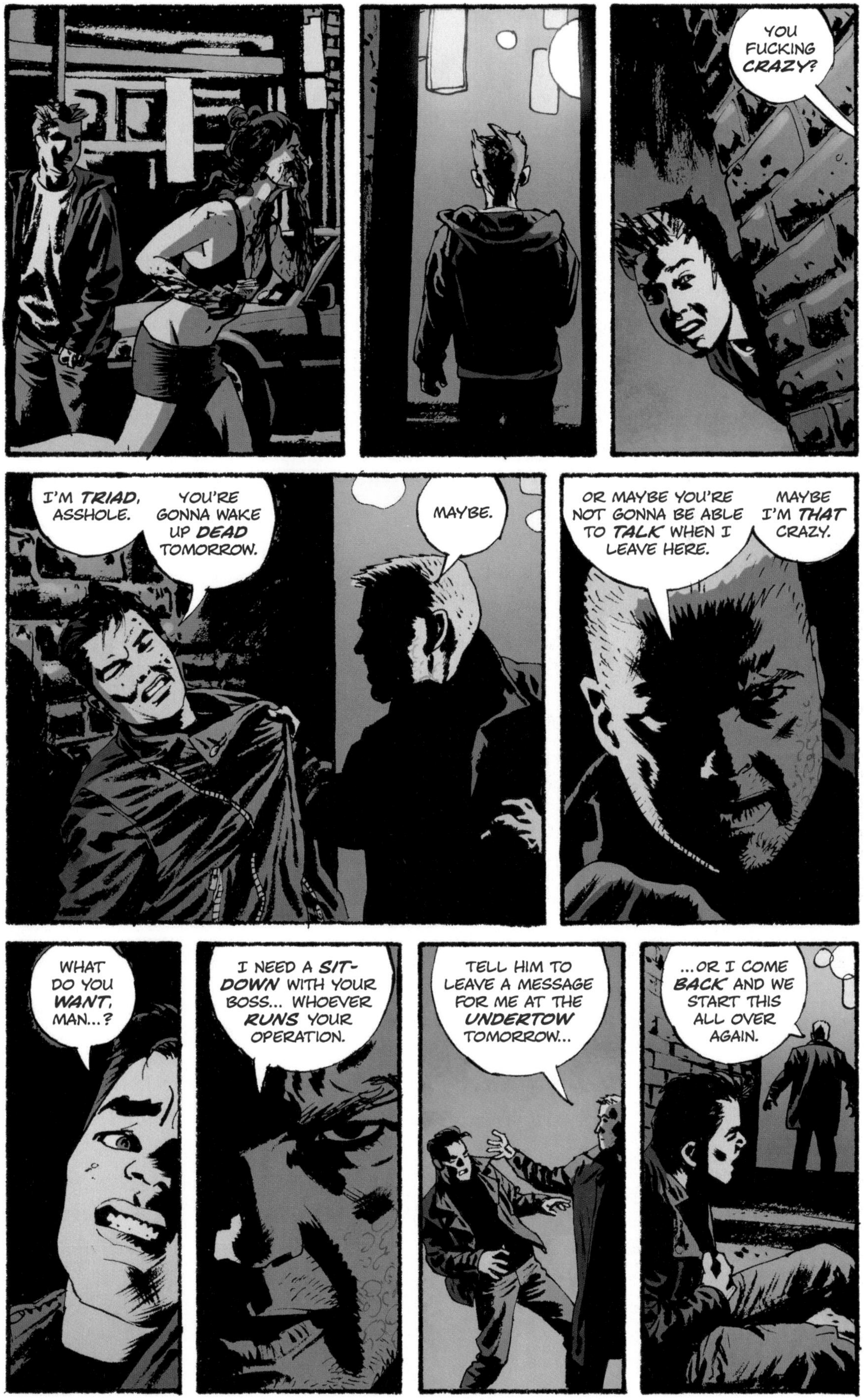
YOU FUCKING CRAZY?
I'M TRIAD, ASSHOLE.
YOU'RE GONNA WAKE UP DEAD TOMORROW.
MAYBE.
OR MAYBE YOU'RE NOT GONNA BE ABLE TO TALK WHEN I LEAVE HERE.
MAYBE I'M THAT CRAZY.
WHAT DO YOU WANT, MAN...?
I NEED A SIT-DOWN WITH YOUR BOSS... WHOEVER RUNS YOUR OPERATION.
TELL HIM TO LEAVE A MESSAGE FOR ME AT THE UNDERTOW TOMORROW...
...OR I COME BACK AND WE START THIS ALL OVER AGAIN.

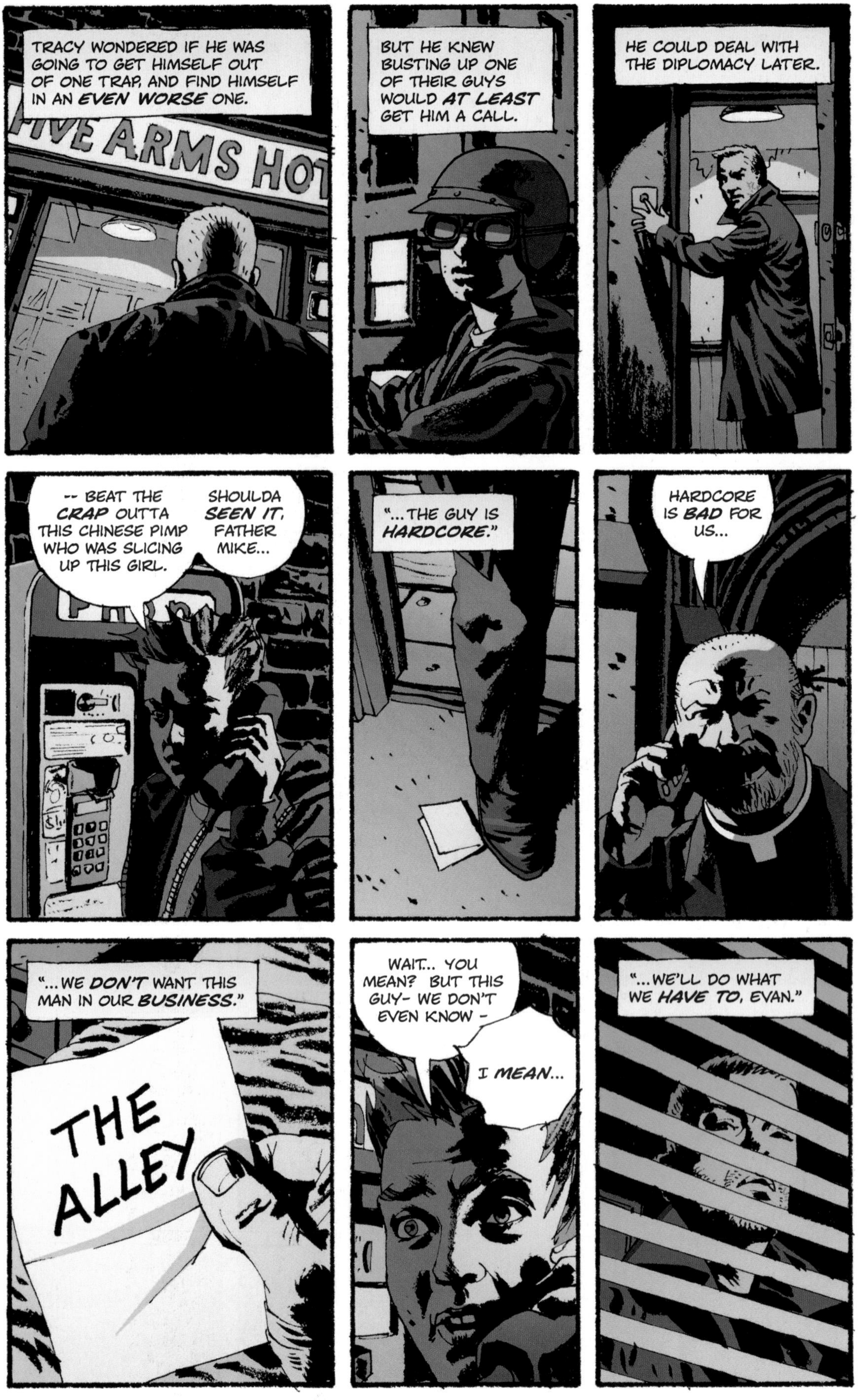
TRACY WONDERED IF HE WAS GOING TO GET HIMSELF OUT OF ONE TRAP, AND FIND HIMSELF IN AN EVEN WORSE ONE.
FIVE ARMS HOT
BUT HE KNEW BUSTING UP ONE OF THEIR GUYS WOULD AT LEAST GET HIM A CALL.
HE COULD DEAL WITH THE DIPLOMACY LATER.
-- BEAT THE CRAP OUTTA THIS CHINESE PIMP WHO WAS SLICING UP THIS GIRL.
SHOULDA SEEN IT, FATHER MIKE...
"...THE GUY IS HARDCORE."
HARDCORE IS BAD FOR US...
"...WE DON'T WANT THIS MAN IN OUR BUSINESS."
THE ALLEY
WAIT... YOU MEAN? BUT THIS GUY- WE DON'T EVEN KNOW -
I MEAN...
"...WE'LL DO WHAT WE HAVE TO, EVAN."

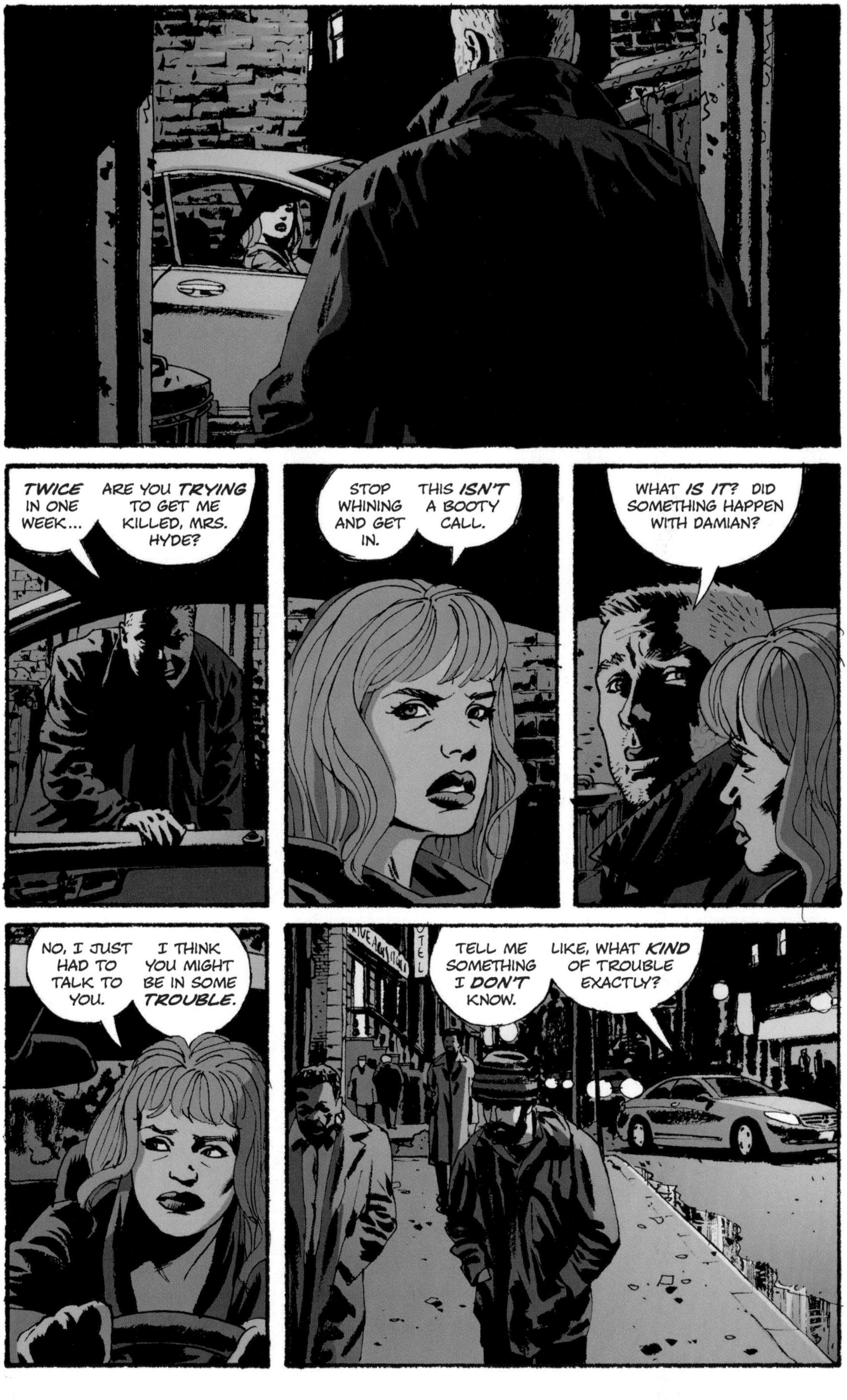
TWICE IN ONE WEEK...
ARE YOU TRYING TO GET ME KILLED, MRS. HYDE?
STOP WHINING AND GET IN.
THIS ISN'T A BOOTY CALL.
WHAT IS IT? DID SOMETHING HAPPEN WITH DAMIAN?
NO, I JUST HAD TO TALK TO YOU.
I THINK YOU MIGHT BE IN SOME TROUBLE.
TELL ME SOMETHING I DON'T KNOW.
LIKE, WHAT KIND OF TROUBLE EXACTLY?

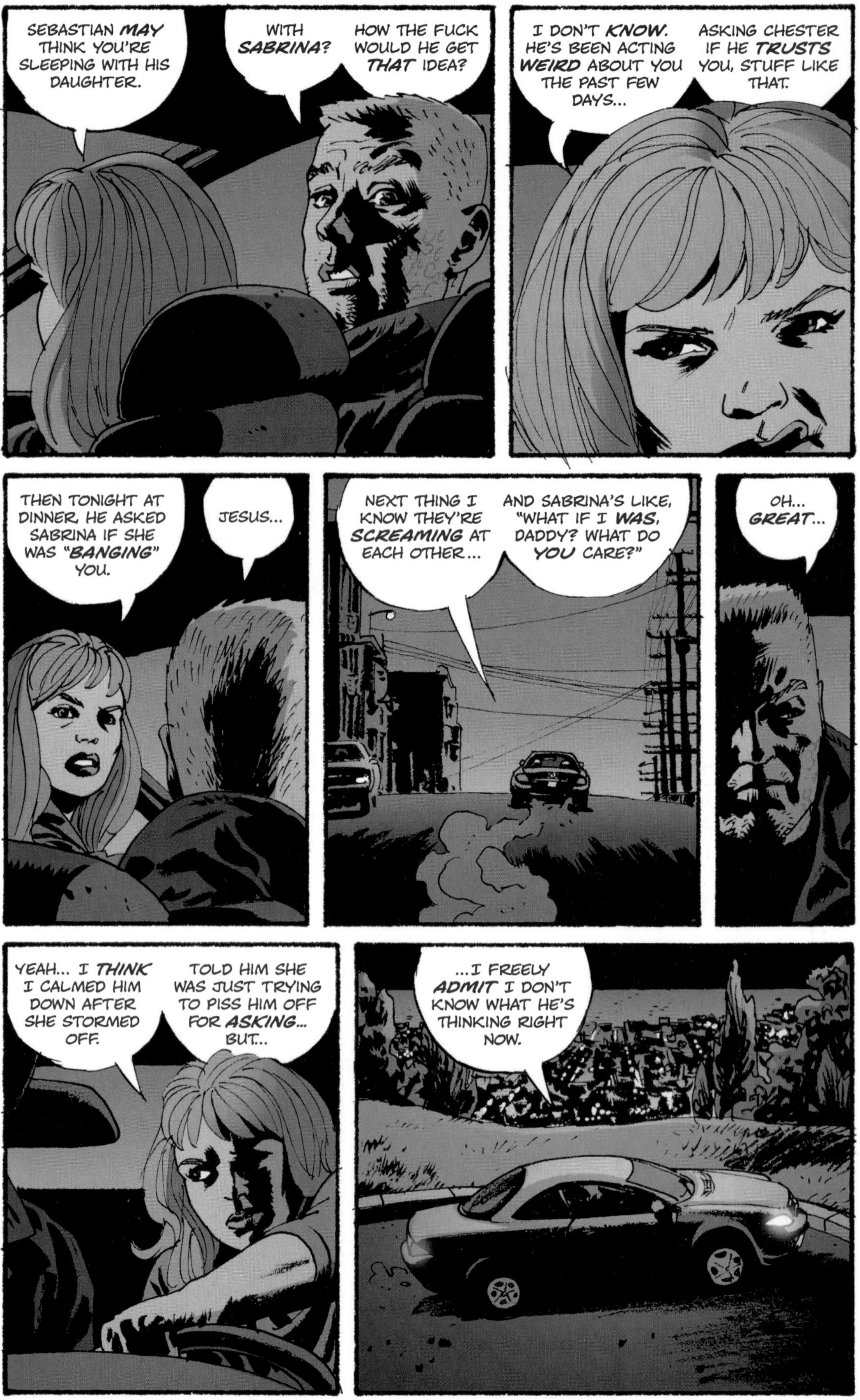
SEBASTIAN MAY THINK YOU'RE SLEEPING WITH HIS DAUGHTER.
WITH SABRINA?
HOW THE FUCK WOULD HE GET THAT IDEA?
I DON'T KNOW. HE'S BEEN ACTING WEIRD ABOUT YOU THE PAST FEW DAYS...
ASKING CHESTER IF HE TRUSTS YOU, STUFF LIKE THAT.
THEN TONIGHT AT DINNER, HE ASKED SABRINA IF SHE WAS "BANGING" YOU.
JESUS...
NEXT THING I KNOW THEY'RE SCREAMING AT EACH OTHER...
AND SABRINA'S LIKE, "WHAT IF I WAS, DADDY? WHAT DO YOU CARE?"
OH... GREAT...
YEAH... I THINK I CALMED HIM DOWN AFTER SHE STORMED OFF.
TOLD HIM SHE WAS JUST TRYING TO PISS HIM OFF FOR ASKING... BUT...
...I FREELY ADMIT I DON'T KNOW WHAT HE'S THINKING RIGHT NOW.

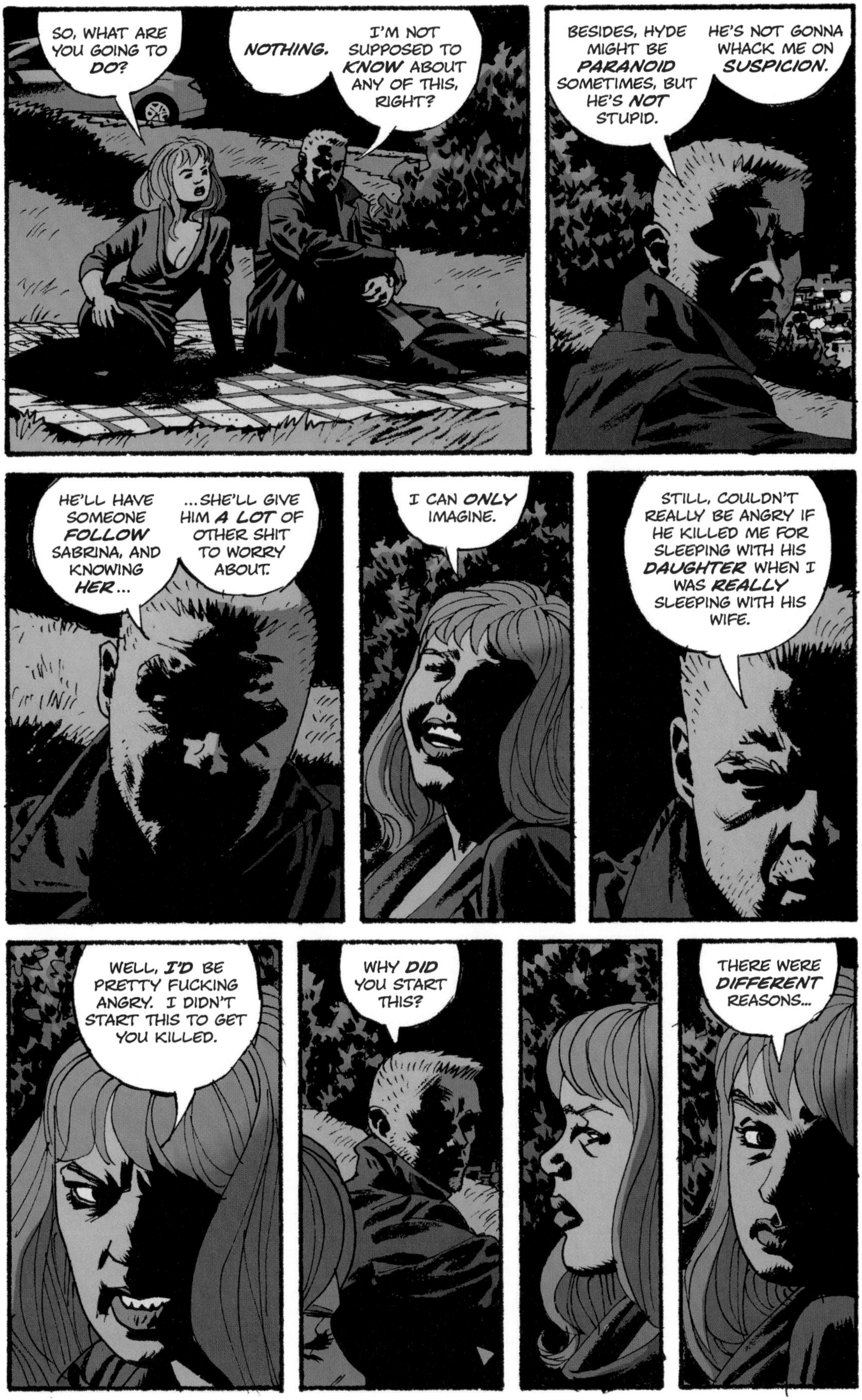
SO, WHAT ARE YOU GOING TO DO?
NOTHING.
I'M NOT SUPPOSED TO KNOW ABOUT ANY OF THIS, RIGHT?
BESIDES, HYDE MIGHT BE PARANOID SOMETIMES, BUT HE'S NOT STUPID.
HE'S NOT GONNA WHACK ME ON SUSPICION.
HE'LL HAVE SOMEONE FOLLOW SABRINA, AND KNOWING HER...
...SHE'LL GIVE HIM A LOT OF OTHER SHIT TO WORRY ABOUT.
I CAN ONLY IMAGINE.
STILL, COULDN'T REALLY BE ANGRY IF HE KILLED ME FOR SLEEPING WITH HIS DAUGHTER WHEN I WAS REALLY SLEEPING WITH HIS WIFE.
WELL, I'D BE PRETTY FUCKING ANGRY. I DIDN'T START THIS TO GET YOU KILLED.
WHY DID YOU START THIS?
THERE WERE DIFFERENT REASONS...

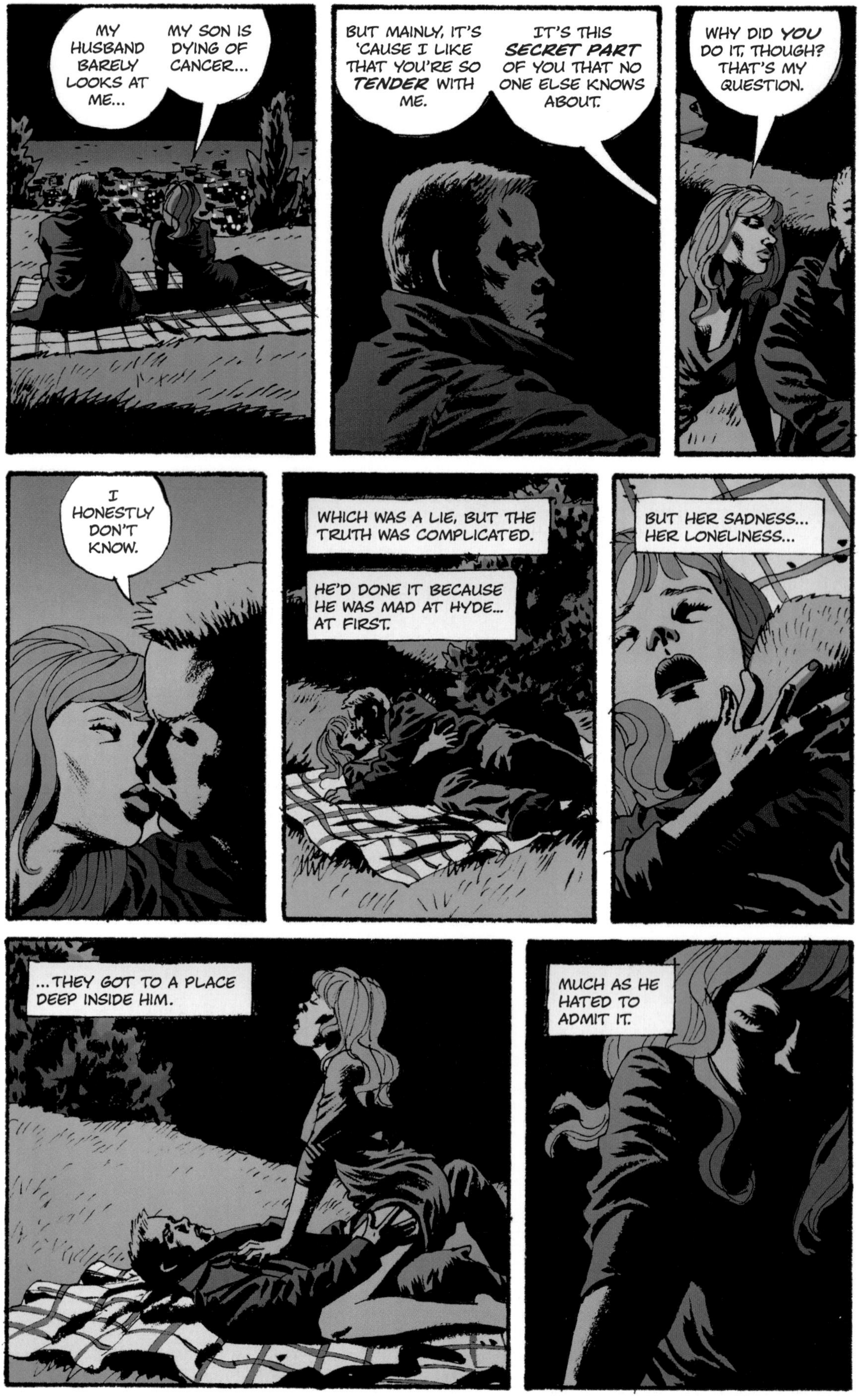
MY HUSBAND BARELY LOOKS AT ME...
MY SON IS DYING OF CANCER...
BUT MAINLY, IT'S 'CAUSE I LIKE THAT YOU'RE SO TENDER WITH ME.
IT'S THIS SECRET PART OF YOU THAT NO ONE ELSE KNOWS ABOUT.
WHY DID YOU DO IT, THOUGH? THAT'S MY QUESTION.
I HONESTLY DON'T KNOW.
WHICH WAS A LIE, BUT THE TRUTH WAS COMPLICATED.
HE'D DONE IT BECAUSE HE WAS MAD AT HYDE... AT FIRST.
BUT HER SADNESS... HER LONELINESS...
...THEY GOT TO A PLACE DEEP INSIDE HIM.
MUCH AS HE HATED TO ADMIT IT.

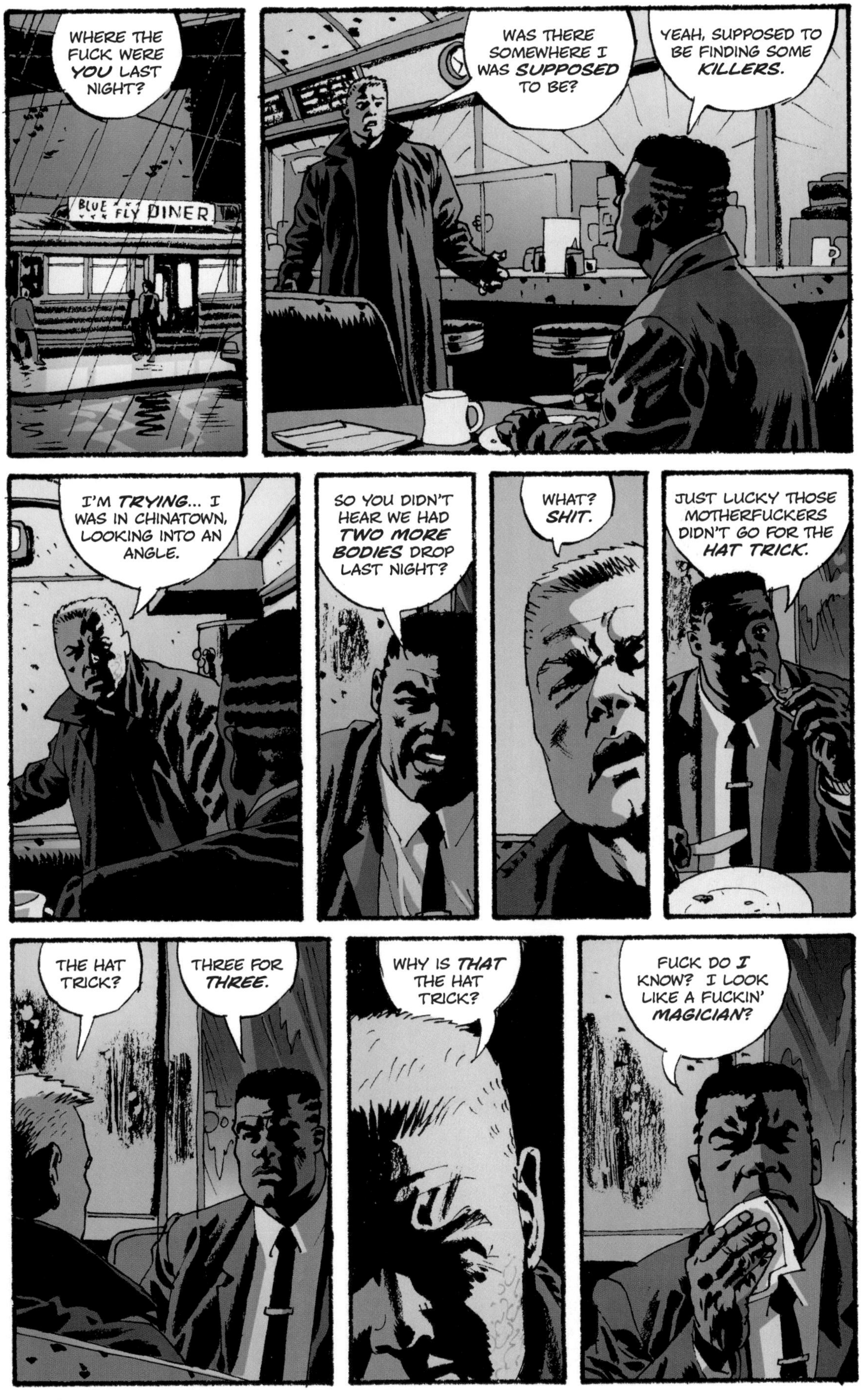
WHERE THE FUCK WERE YOU LAST NIGHT?
BLUE FLY DINER
WAS THERE SOMEWHERE I WAS SUPPOSED TO BE?
YEAH, SUPPOSED TO BE FINDING SOME KILLERS.
I'M TRYING... I WAS IN CHINATOWN, LOOKING INTO AN ANGLE.
SO YOU DIDN'T HEAR WE HAD TWO MORE BODIES DROP LAST NIGHT?
WHAT? SHIT.
JUST LUCKY THOSE MOTHERFUCKERS DIDN'T GO FOR THE HAT TRICK.
THE HAT TRICK?
THREE FOR THREE.
WHY IS THAT THE HAT TRICK?
FUCK DO I KNOW? I LOOK LIKE A FUCKIN' MAGICIAN?

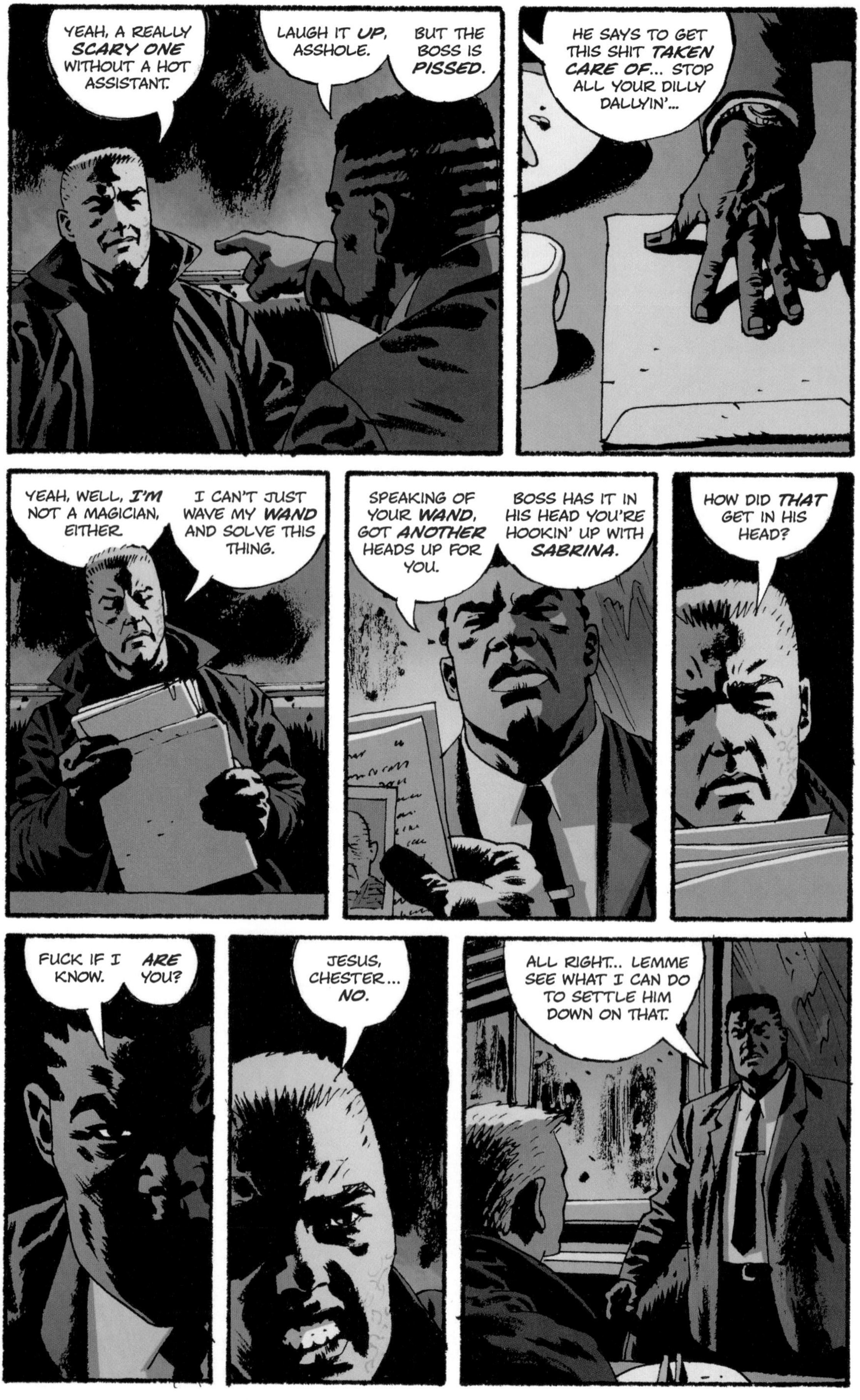
YEAH, A REALLY SCARY ONE WITHOUT A HOT ASSISTANT.
LAUGH IT UP, ASSHOLE.
BUT THE BOSS IS PISSED.
HE SAYS TO GET THIS SHIT TAKEN CARE OF... STOP ALL YOUR DILLY DALLYIN'...
YEAH, WELL, I'M NOT A MAGICIAN, EITHER.
I CAN'T JUST WAVE MY WAND AND SOLVE THIS THING.
SPEAKING OF YOUR WAND, GOT ANOTHER HEADS UP FOR YOU.
BOSS HAS IT IN HIS HEAD YOU'RE HOOKIN' UP WITH SABRINA.
HOW DID THAT GET IN HIS HEAD?
FUCK IF I KNOW.
ARE YOU?
JESUS, CHESTER... NO.
ALL RIGHT... LEMME SEE WHAT I CAN DO TO SETTLE HIM DOWN ON THAT.

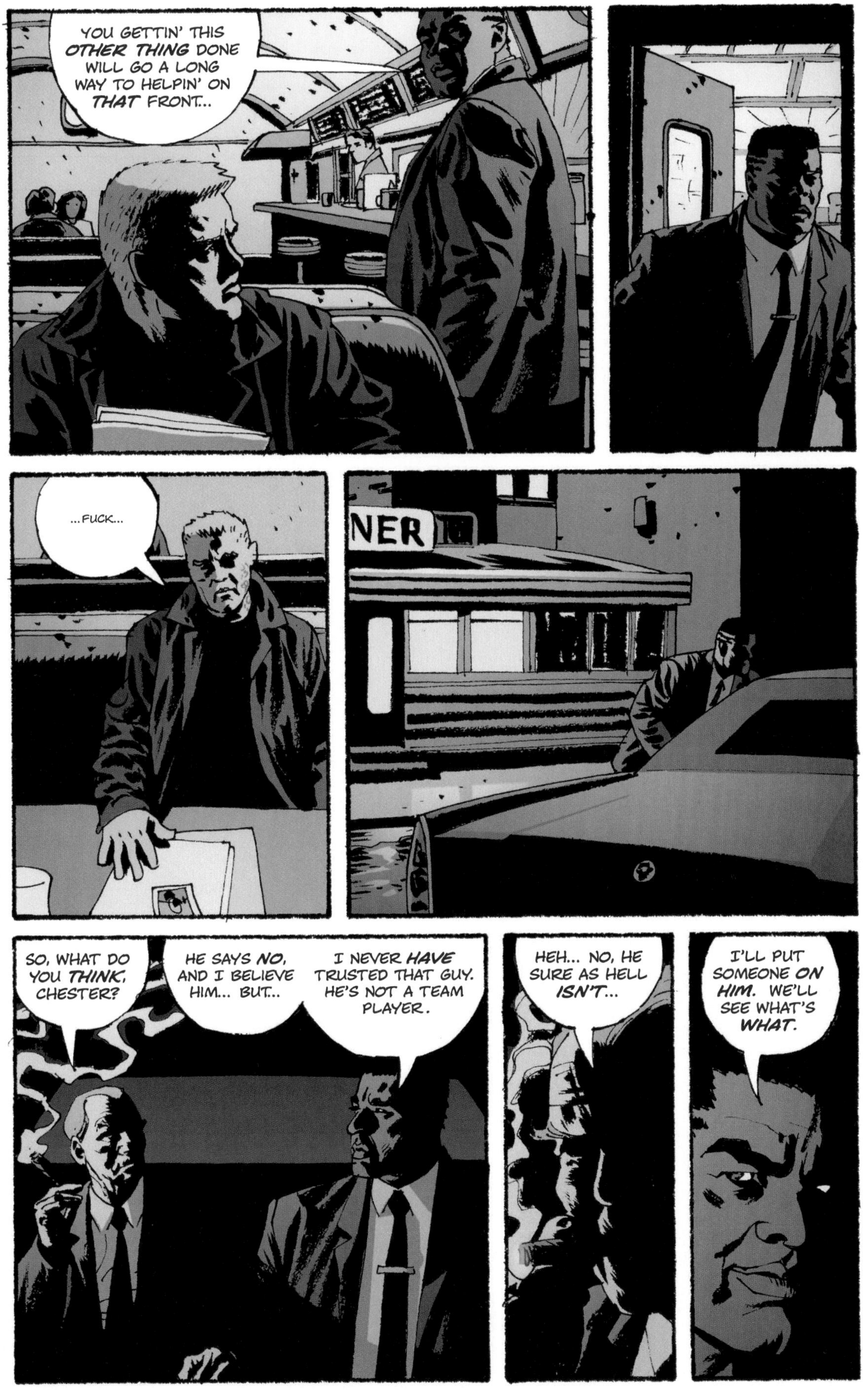
YOU GETTIN' THIS OTHER THING DONE WILL GO A LONG WAY TO HELPIN' ON THAT FRONT...
...FUCK...
NER
SO, WHAT DO YOU THINK, CHESTER?
HE SAYS NO, AND I BELIEVE HIM... BUT...
I NEVER HAVE TRUSTED THAT GUY. HE'S NOT A TEAM PLAYER.
HEH... NO, HE SURE AS HELL ISN'T...
I'LL PUT SOMEONE ON HIM. WE'LL SEE WHAT'S WHAT.

EVAN HAD *HEARD* OF THE *UNDERTOW* BEFORE LAST NIGHT, BUT HE'D NEVER BEEN THERE.

IT LOOKED JUST LIKE ANY OTHER BAR, AS FAR AS HE COULD TELL.

NOTHING SCREAMED OUT *UNDERWORLD LEGEND,* WHICH WAS DISAPPOINTING, EVEN TO A KID LIKE HIM, WHO *HATED* MOST CRIMINALS.

HE WASN'T EVEN SURE *WHY* HE WAS THERE, REALLY.

IT JUST DIDN'T SIT *RIGHT* WITH HIM, WHAT FATHER MIKE WAS TALKING ABOUT DOING.

HE DIDN'T THINK THIS TRACY LAWLESS *DESERVED* TO BE ON THEIR LIST.

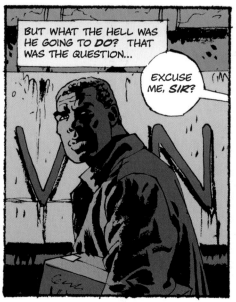

BUT WHAT THE HELL WAS HE GOING TO *DO?* THAT WAS THE QUESTION...

EXCUSE ME, *SIR?*

ARE YOU JACOB BROWN, THE *PROPRIETOR* HERE?

THAT'S AN AWFUL *BIG* WORD FOR A COP IN *THIS* CITY.

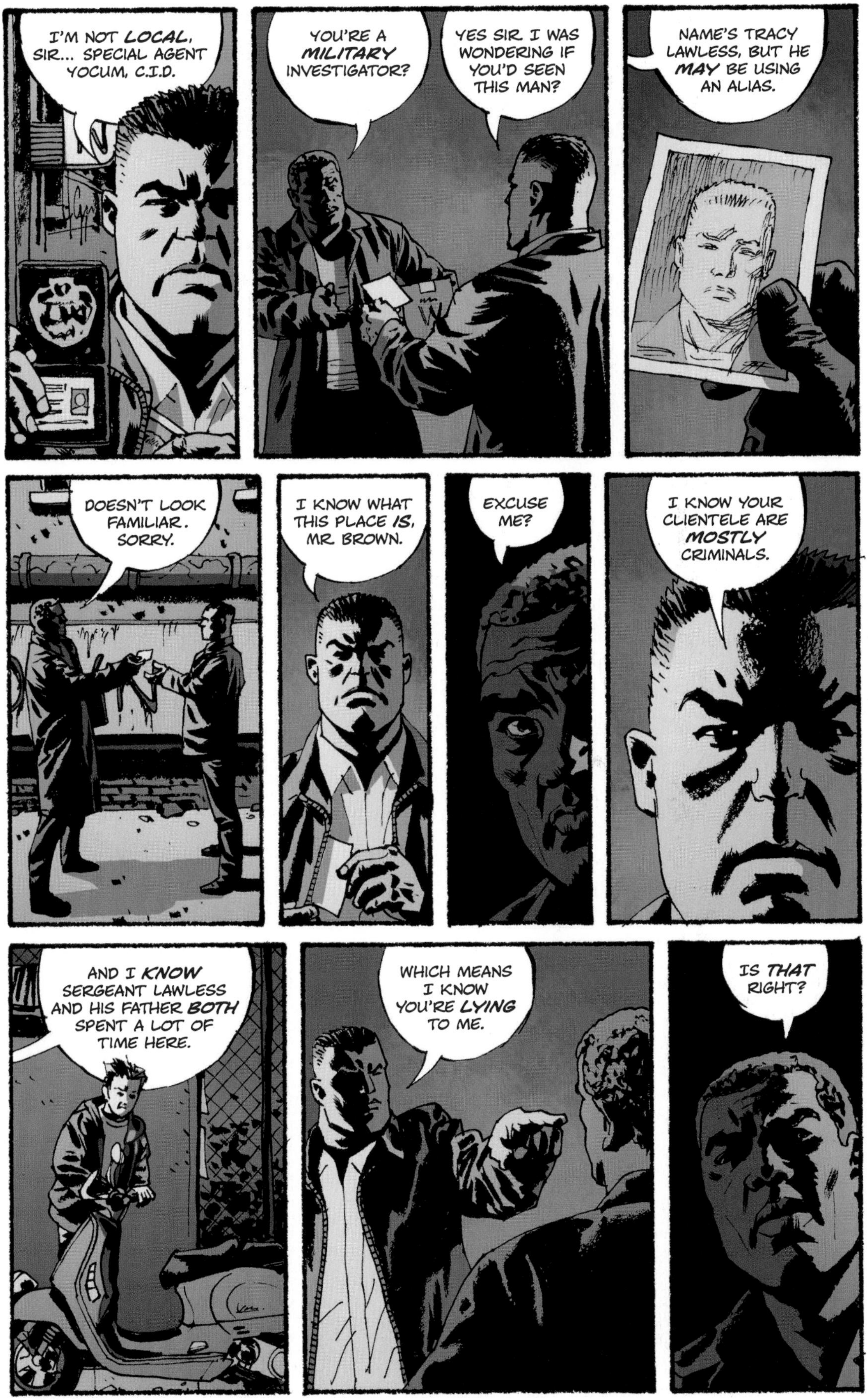
I'M NOT LOCAL, SIR... SPECIAL AGENT YOCUM, C.I.D.
YOU'RE A MILITARY INVESTIGATOR?
YES SIR. I WAS WONDERING IF YOU'D SEEN THIS MAN?
NAME'S TRACY LAWLESS, BUT HE MAY BE USING AN ALIAS.
DOESN'T LOOK FAMILIAR. SORRY.
I KNOW WHAT THIS PLACE IS, MR BROWN.
EXCUSE ME?
I KNOW YOUR CLIENTELE ARE MOSTLY CRIMINALS.
AND I KNOW SERGEANT LAWLESS AND HIS FATHER BOTH SPENT A LOT OF TIME HERE.
WHICH MEANS I KNOW YOU'RE LYING TO ME.
IS THAT RIGHT?

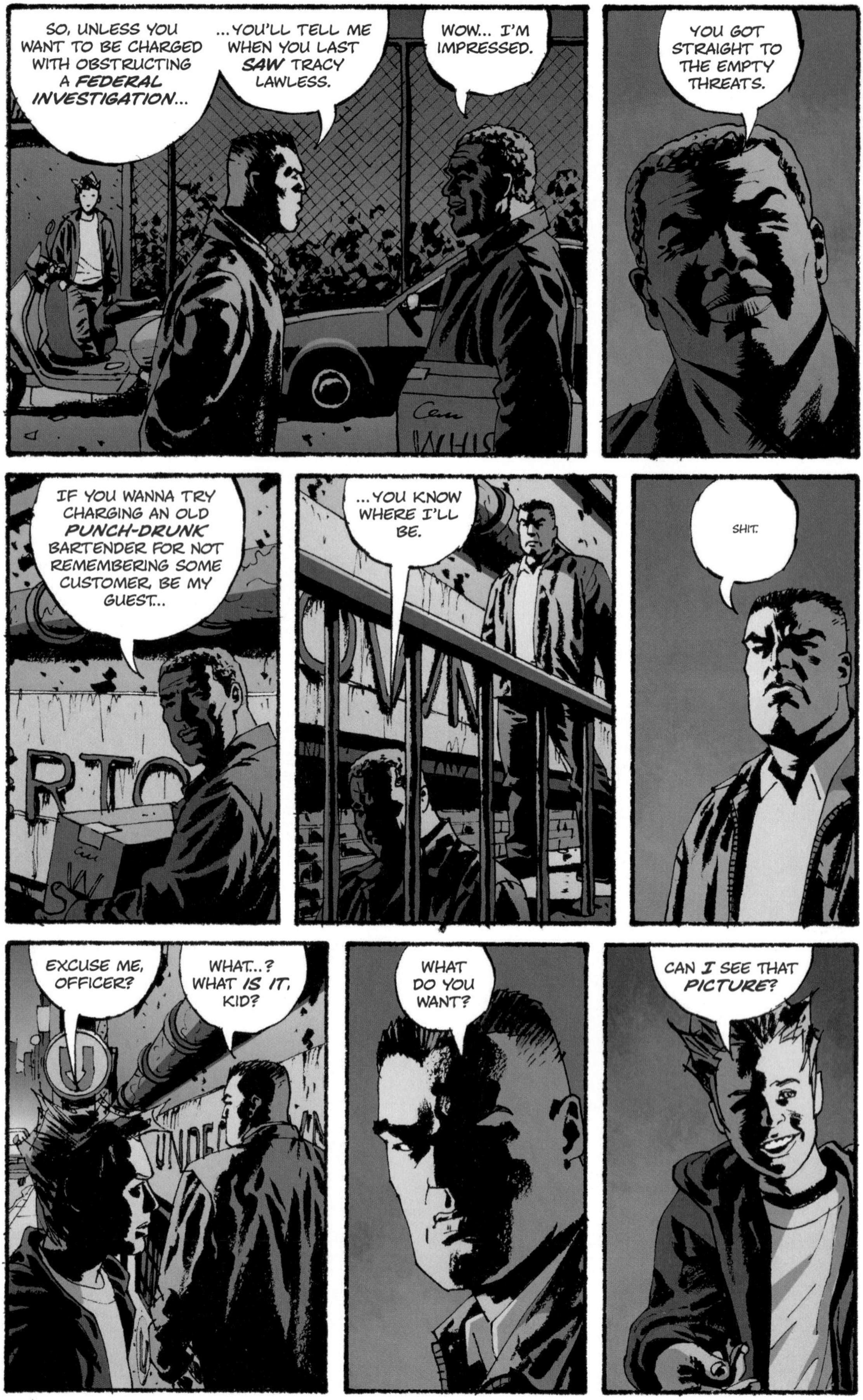
SO, UNLESS YOU WANT TO BE CHARGED WITH OBSTRUCTING A FEDERAL INVESTIGATION...
...YOU'LL TELL ME WHEN YOU LAST SAW TRACY LAWLESS.
WOW... I'M IMPRESSED.
YOU GOT STRAIGHT TO THE EMPTY THREATS.
IF YOU WANNA TRY CHARGING AN OLD PUNCH-DRUNK BARTENDER FOR NOT REMEMBERING SOME CUSTOMER, BE MY GUEST...
...YOU KNOW WHERE I'LL BE.
SHIT.
EXCUSE ME, OFFICER?
WHAT...? WHAT IS IT, KID?
WHAT DO YOU WANT?
CAN I SEE THAT PICTURE?

THE PICTURES CHESTER HAD GIVEN TRACY TOLD THE SAME STORY THE PREVIOUS CRIME SCENES HAD.

MADE MEN KILLED WITH NO WITNESSES.

LAST NIGHT AT TEN MINUTES AFTER MIDNIGHT, GIACOMO SANTANGELO WAS POPPED IN THE PARKING LOT BEHIND A LIQUOR STORE.

TWO SHOTS IN THE BACK OF THE HEAD.

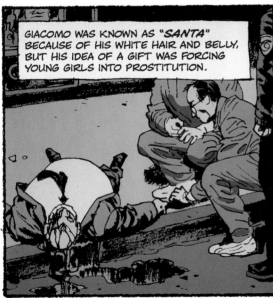

GIACOMO WAS KNOWN AS "*SANTA*" BECAUSE OF HIS WHITE HAIR AND BELLY, BUT HIS IDEA OF A GIFT WAS FORCING YOUNG GIRLS INTO PROSTITUTION.

THE MAFIA WASN'T A LARGE PRESENCE IN THE CITY, BUT LIKE THE IRISH MOB, THEY STILL COMMANDED A CERTAIN AMOUNT OF RESPECT.

DINER

BUT TO CATCH *SANTA* UNAWARE LIKE THAT, TRACY ALMOST WONDERED IF MAYBE THESE KILLERS WEREN'T WOMEN.

THAT MIGHT FIT, ACTUALLY, SINCE THREE HOURS LATER, ARTHUR TEBBEL HAD FOUR BULLETS PUT INTO HIM IN THE BACK OF HIS OWN JOINT.

AFTER ALL HIS GUYS HAD GONE HOME FOR THE NIGHT.

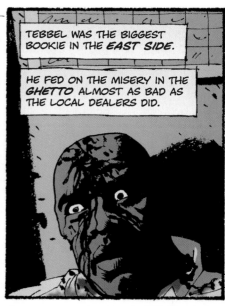

TEBBEL WAS THE BIGGEST BOOKIE IN THE *EAST SIDE*.

HE FED ON THE MISERY IN THE *GHETTO* ALMOST AS BAD AS THE LOCAL DEALERS DID.

WORSE, MAYBE, BECAUSE WITH A GAMBLING ADDICT, YOU COULD HAVE YOUR HOOKS IN THEM FOR DECADES.

JUNKIES NEVER LIVED THAT LONG.

SO WHO WOULD ARTIE LET STAY AFTER HOURS, OTHER THAN SOME WOMAN WHO NEEDED TO PAY OFF A DEBT WITH FLESH?

BUT STILL, HE REMEMBERED DETECTIVE WATERS ADVICE. WHERE WAS THE LINK?

BETWEEN A MAFIA LIEUTENANT, A BLACK BOOKIE, A DRUG DEALER, A LOAN SHARK PRIEST, AN IRISH HOOD, AND A CROOKED COP...

OTHER THAN THAT THEY WERE ALL LOCAL SCUMBAGS WHO WERE NOW DEAD, TRACY COULDN'T SEE ONE.

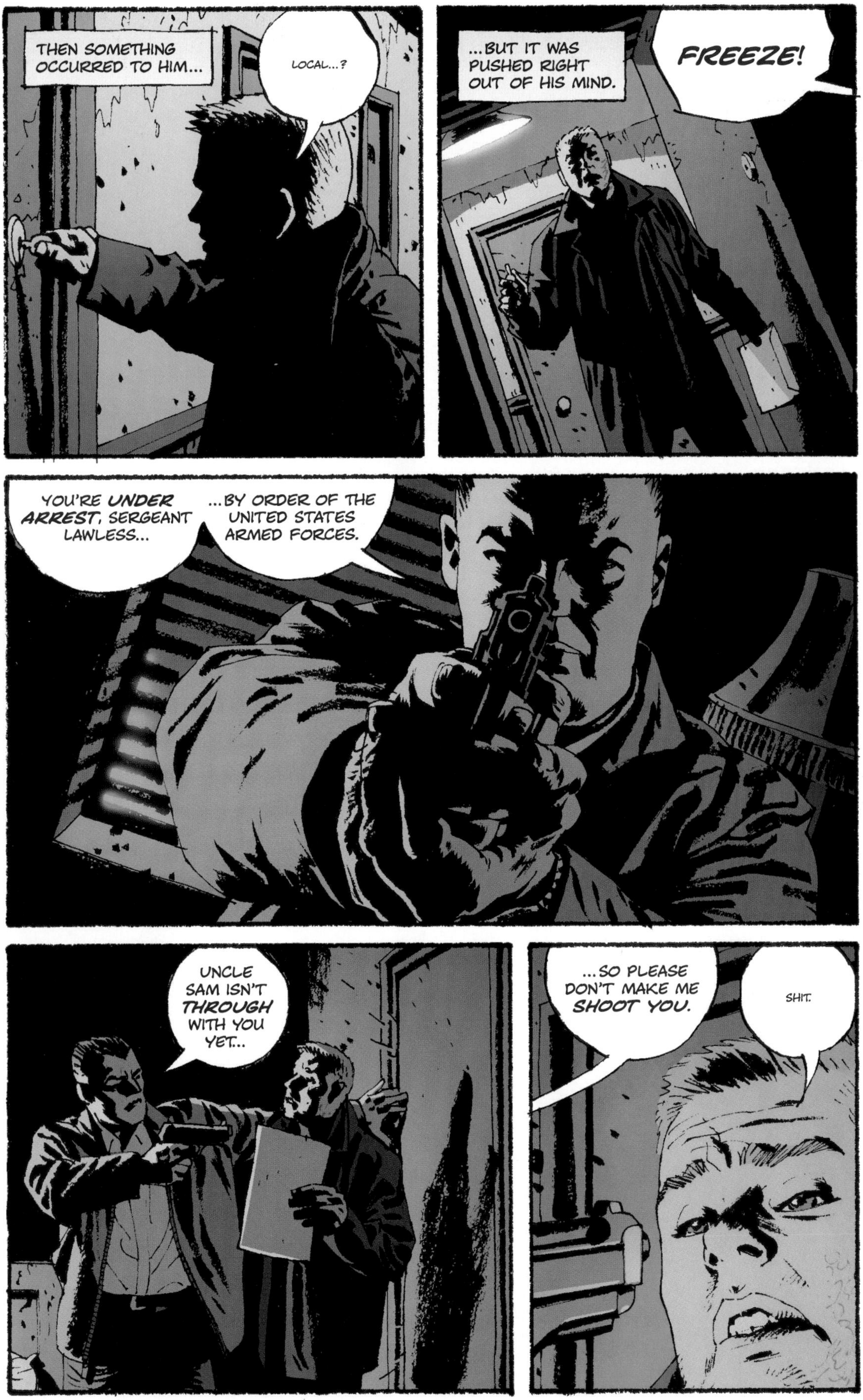
THEN SOMETHING OCCURRED TO HIM...
LOCAL...?
...BUT IT WAS PUSHED RIGHT OUT OF HIS MIND.
FREEZE!
YOU'RE UNDER ARREST, SERGEANT LAWLESS...
...BY ORDER OF THE UNITED STATES ARMED FORCES.
UNCLE SAM ISN'T THROUGH WITH YOU YET...
...SO PLEASE DON'T MAKE ME SHOOT YOU.
SHIT.

The Sinners
Part Four

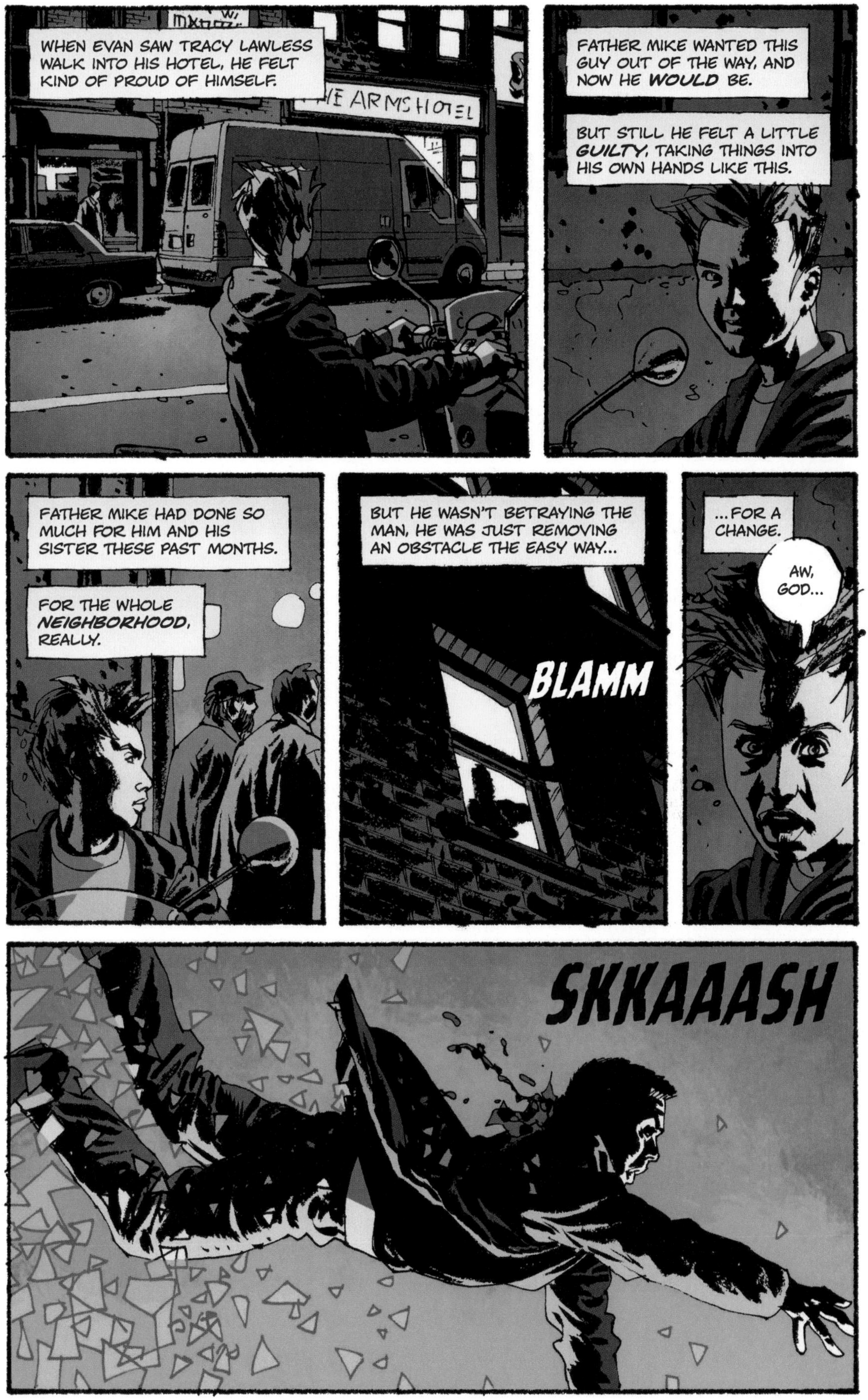
WHEN EVAN SAW TRACY LAWLESS WALK INTO HIS HOTEL, HE FELT KIND OF PROUD OF HIMSELF.
THE ARMS HOTEL
FATHER MIKE WANTED THIS GUY OUT OF THE WAY, AND NOW HE WOULD BE.
BUT STILL HE FELT A LITTLE GUILTY, TAKING THINGS INTO HIS OWN HANDS LIKE THIS.
FATHER MIKE HAD DONE SO MUCH FOR HIM AND HIS SISTER THESE PAST MONTHS.
FOR THE WHOLE NEIGHBORHOOD, REALLY.
BUT HE WASN'T BETRAYING THE MAN, HE WAS JUST REMOVING AN OBSTACLE THE EASY WAY...
BLAMM
...FOR A CHANGE.
AW, GOD...
SKKAAASH

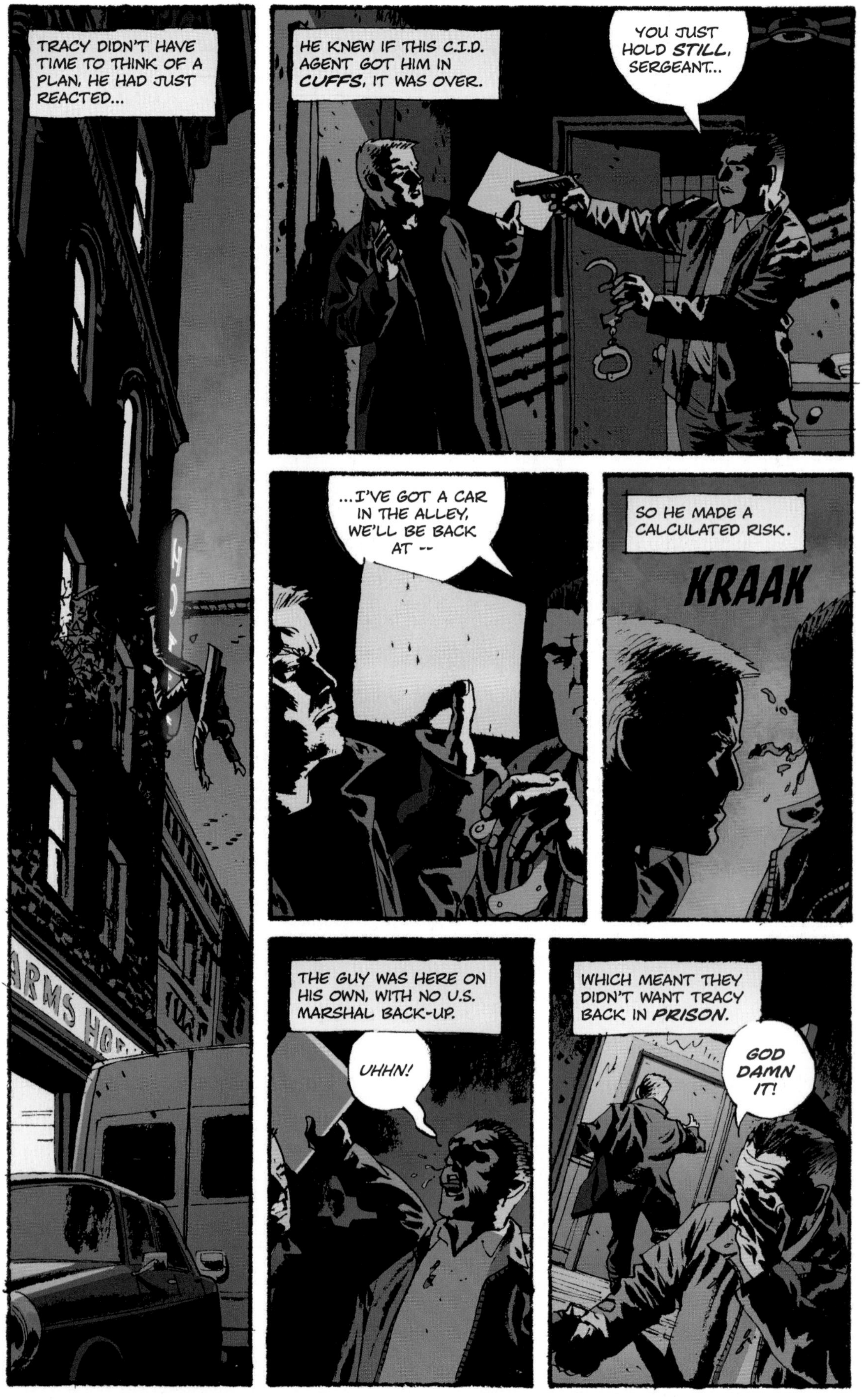
TRACY DIDN'T HAVE TIME TO THINK OF A PLAN, HE HAD JUST REACTED...
HE KNEW IF THIS C.I.D. AGENT GOT HIM IN CUFFS, IT WAS OVER.
YOU JUST HOLD STILL, SERGEANT...
...I'VE GOT A CAR IN THE ALLEY, WE'LL BE BACK AT --
SO HE MADE A CALCULATED RISK.
KRAAK
THE GUY WAS HERE ON HIS OWN, WITH NO U.S. MARSHAL BACK-UP.
UHHN!
WHICH MEANT THEY DIDN'T WANT TRACY BACK IN PRISON.
GOD DAMN IT!

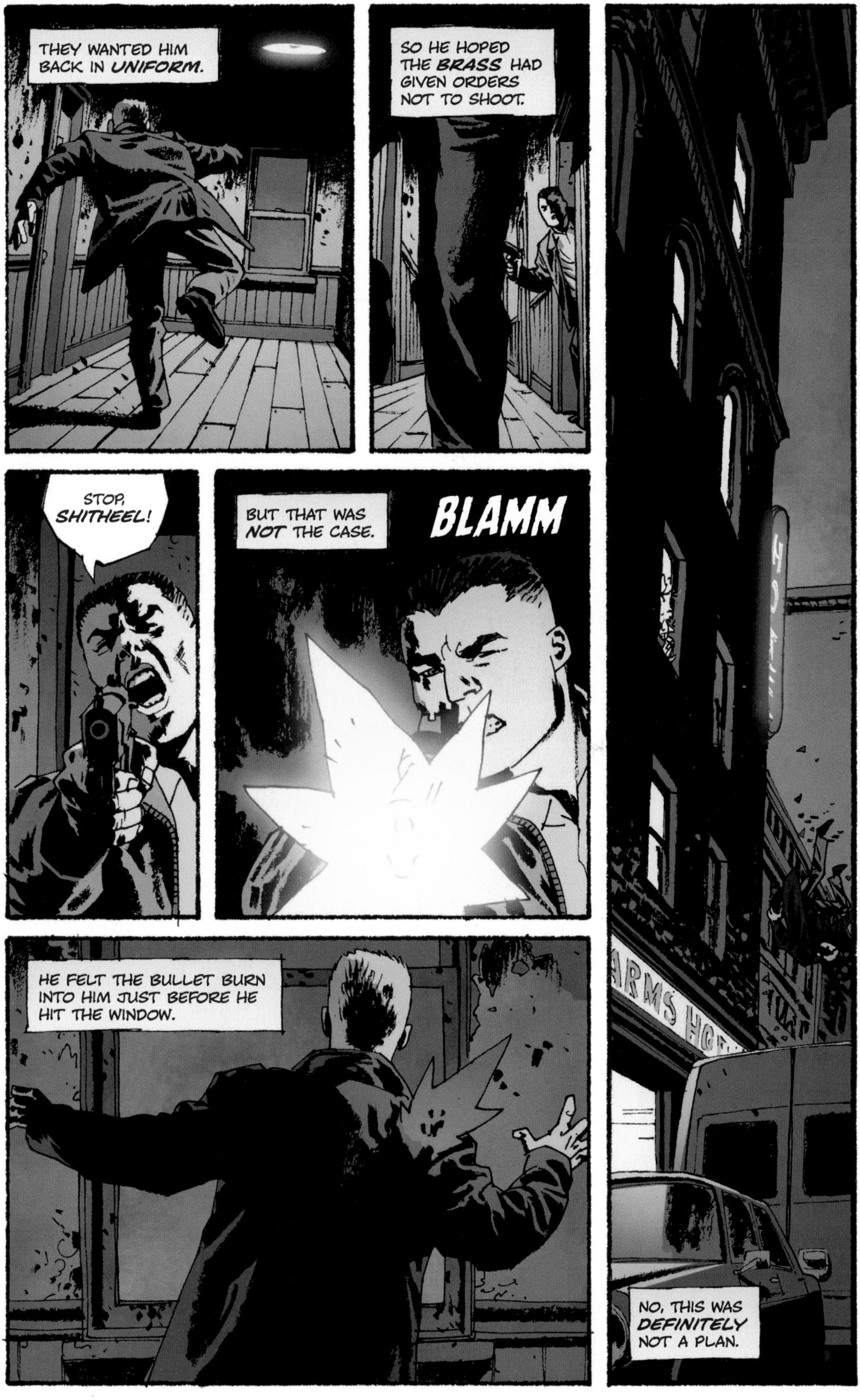
THEY WANTED HIM BACK IN *UNIFORM*.
SO HE HOPED THE **BRASS** HAD GIVEN ORDERS NOT TO SHOOT.
STOP, *SHITHEEL!*
BUT THAT WAS *NOT* THE CASE.
BLAMM
HE FELT THE BULLET BURN INTO HIM JUST BEFORE HE HIT THE WINDOW.
NO, THIS WAS *DEFINITELY* NOT A PLAN.

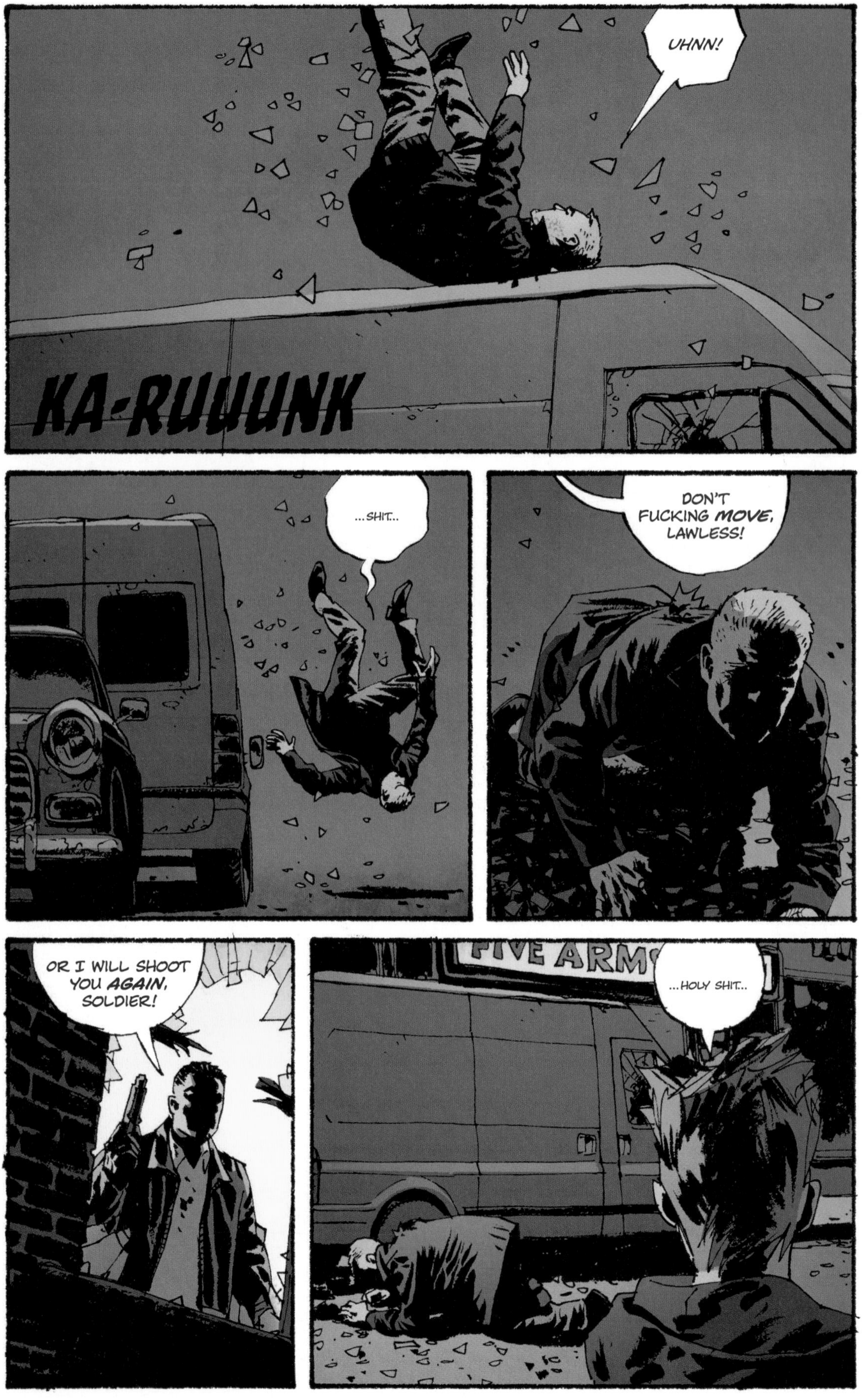
UHNN!
KA-RUUUNK
...SHIT...
DON'T FUCKING MOVE, LAWLESS!
OR I WILL SHOOT YOU AGAIN, SOLDIER!
FIVE ARM
...HOLY SHIT...

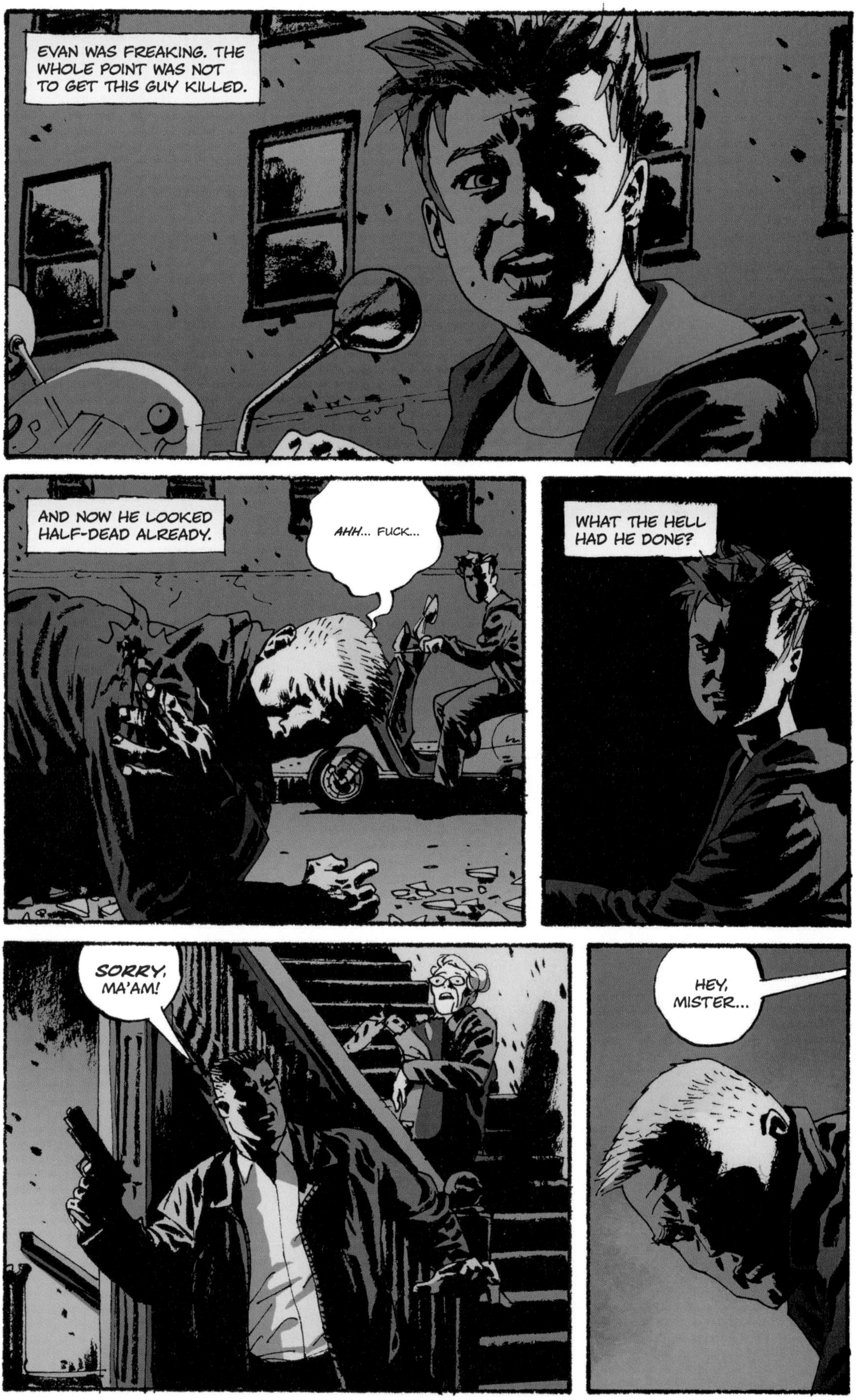
EVAN WAS FREAKING. THE WHOLE POINT WAS NOT TO GET THIS GUY KILLED.
AND NOW HE LOOKED HALF-DEAD ALREADY.
AHH... FUCK...
WHAT THE HELL HAD HE DONE?
SORRY, MA'AM!
HEY, MISTER...

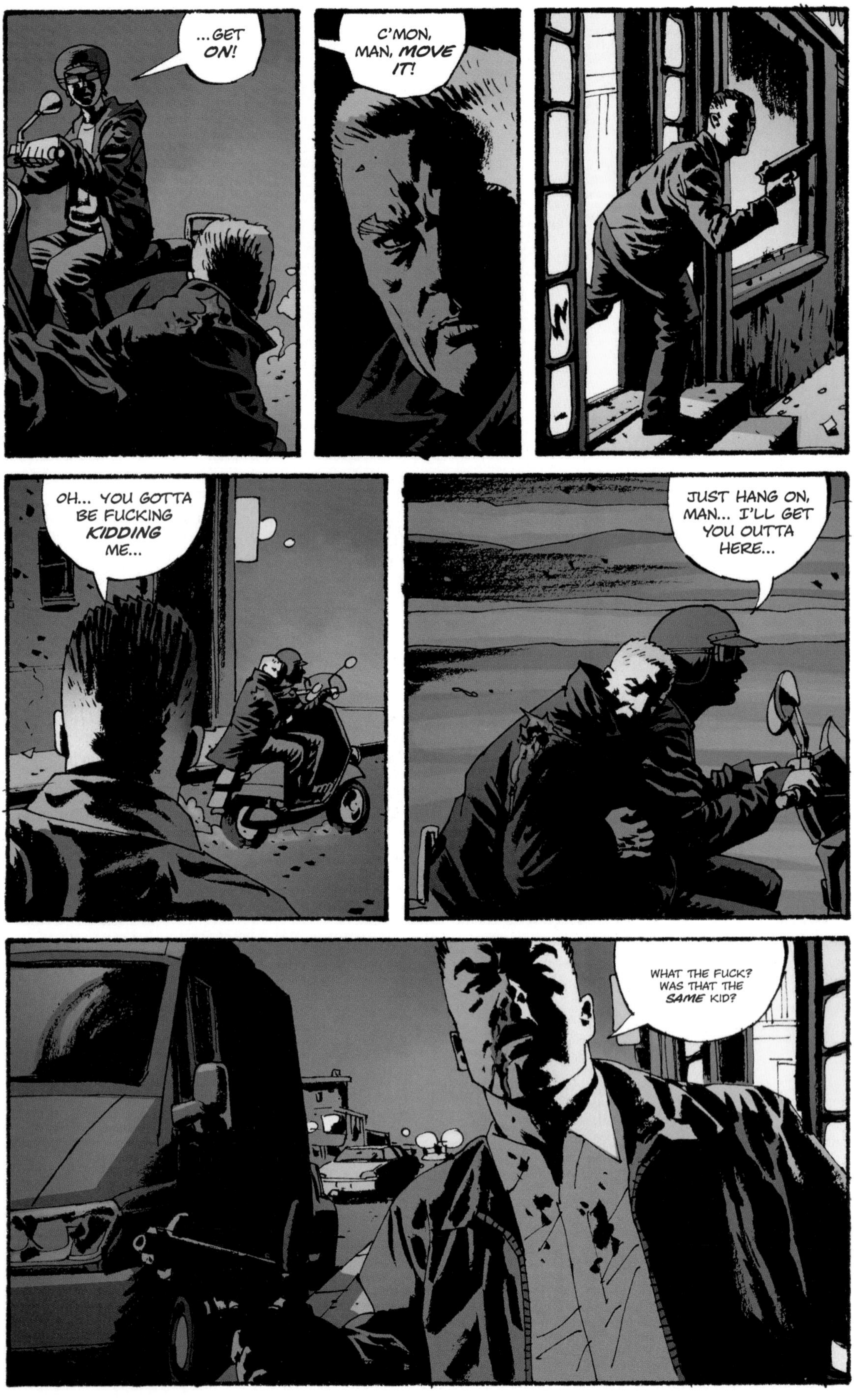
...GET ON!
C'MON, MAN, MOVE IT!
OH... YOU GOTTA BE FUCKING KIDDING ME...
JUST HANG ON, MAN... I'LL GET YOU OUTTA HERE...
WHAT THE FUCK? WAS THAT THE SAME KID?

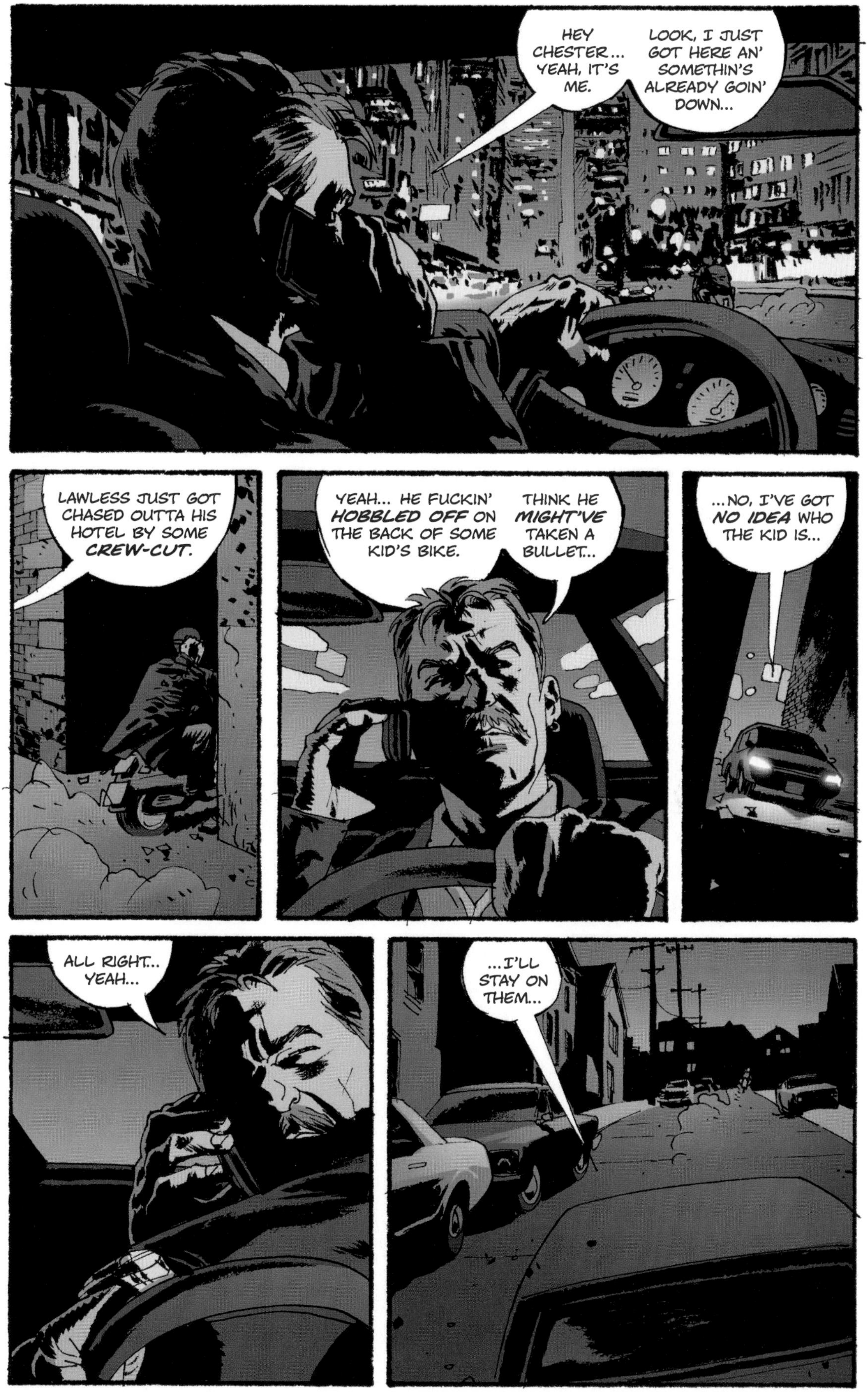
HEY CHESTER... YEAH, IT'S ME.
LOOK, I JUST GOT HERE AN' SOMETHIN'S ALREADY GOIN' DOWN...
LAWLESS JUST GOT CHASED OUTTA HIS HOTEL BY SOME CREW-CUT.
YEAH... HE FUCKIN' HOBBLED OFF ON THE BACK OF SOME KID'S BIKE.
THINK HE MIGHT'VE TAKEN A BULLET...
...NO, I'VE GOT NO IDEA WHO THE KID IS...
ALL RIGHT... YEAH...
...I'LL STAY ON THEM...

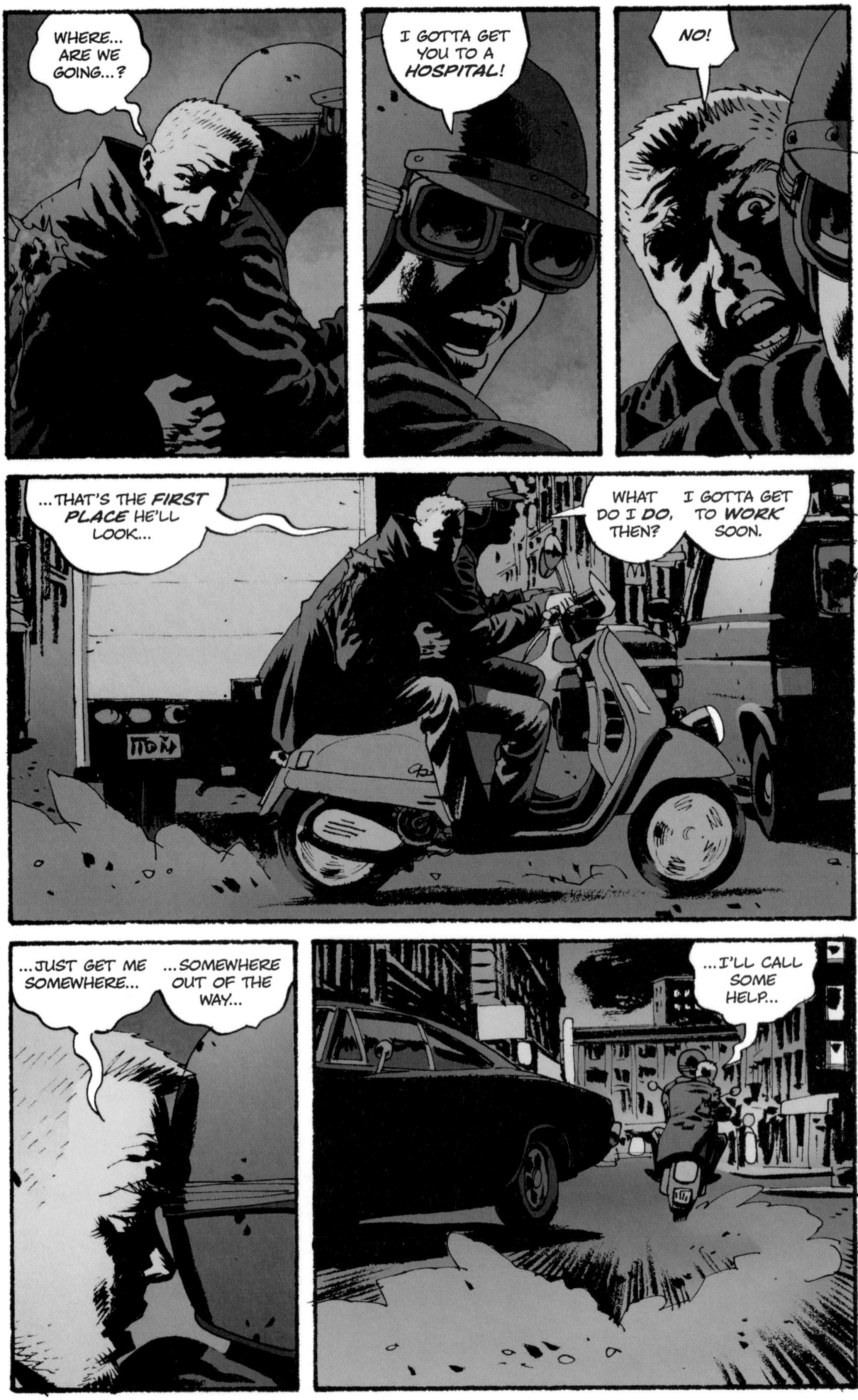
WHERE... ARE WE GOING...?
I GOTTA GET YOU TO A HOSPITAL!
NO!
...THAT'S THE FIRST PLACE HE'LL LOOK...
WHAT DO I DO, THEN?
I GOTTA GET TO WORK SOON.
...JUST GET ME SOMEWHERE...
...SOMEWHERE OUT OF THE WAY...
...I'LL CALL SOME HELP...

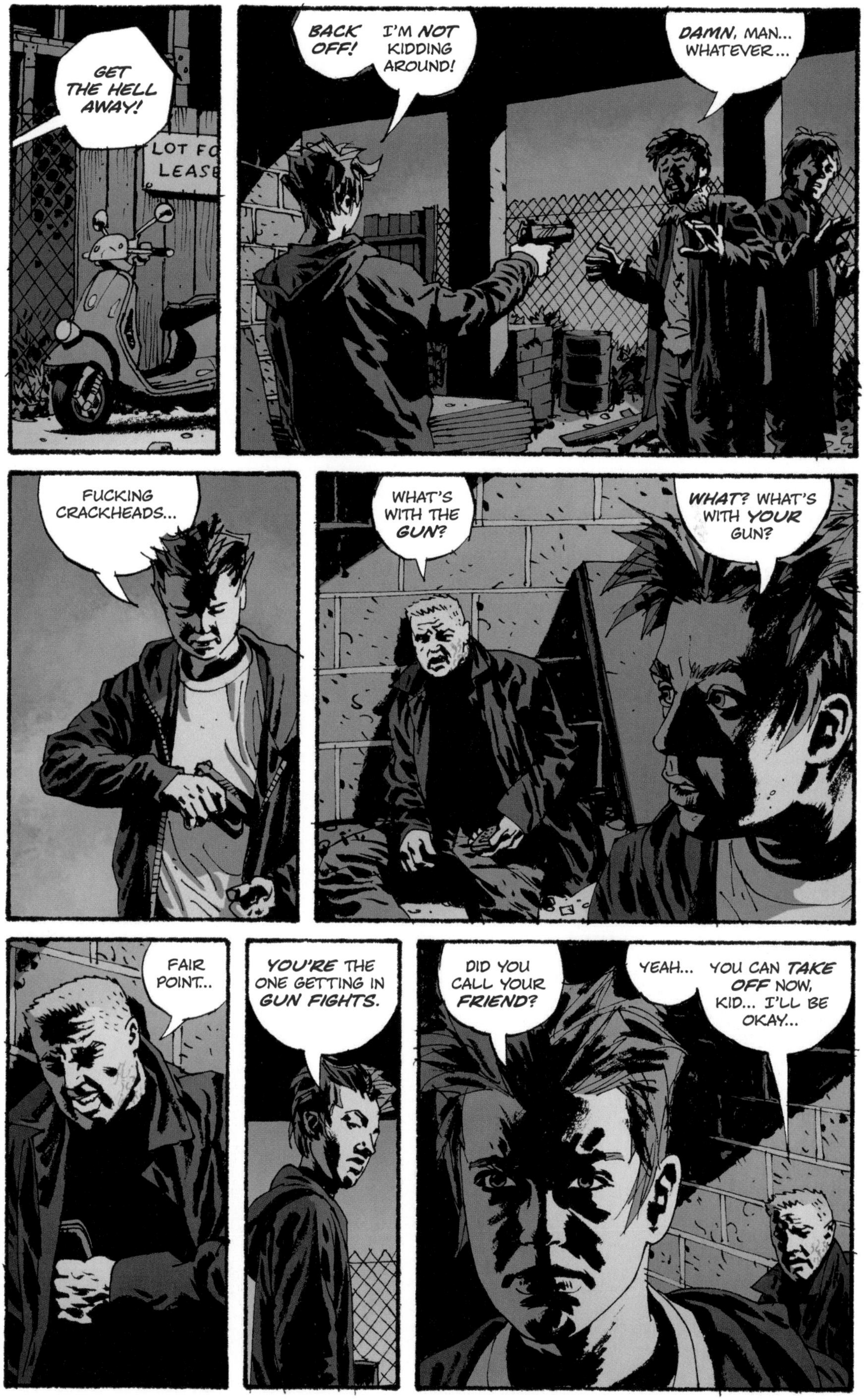
GET THE HELL AWAY!
LOT FO LEASE
BACK OFF!
I'M NOT KIDDING AROUND!
DAMN, MAN... WHATEVER...
FUCKING CRACKHEADS...
WHAT'S WITH THE GUN?
WHAT? WHAT'S WITH YOUR GUN?
FAIR POINT...
YOU'RE THE ONE GETTING IN GUN FIGHTS.
DID YOU CALL YOUR FRIEND?
YEAH...
YOU CAN TAKE OFF NOW, KID... I'LL BE OKAY...

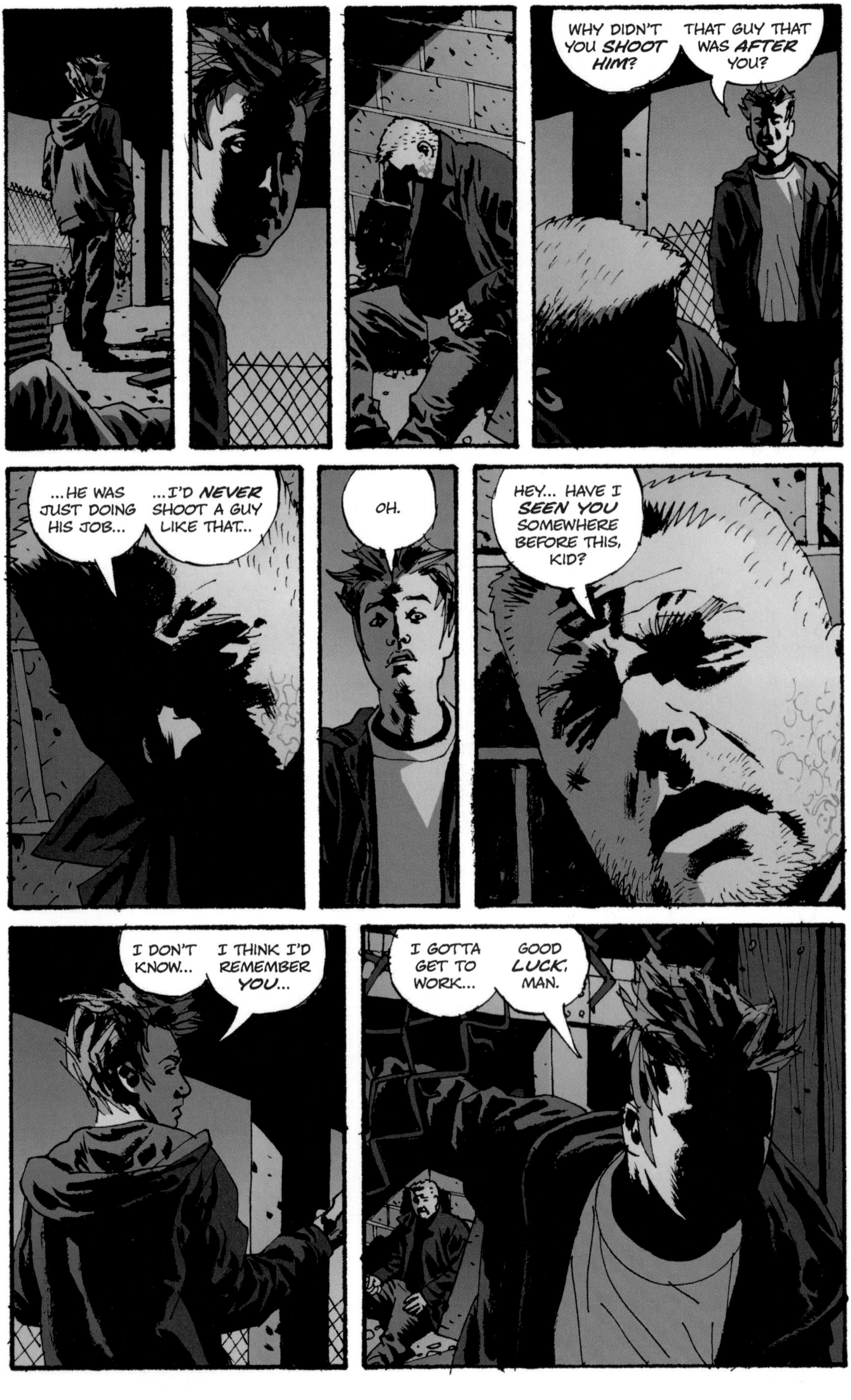
WHY DIDN'T YOU *SHOOT HIM*?
THAT GUY THAT WAS *AFTER* YOU?
...HE WAS JUST DOING HIS JOB...
...I'D *NEVER* SHOOT A GUY LIKE THAT...
OH.
HEY... HAVE I *SEEN YOU* SOMEWHERE BEFORE THIS, KID?
I DON'T KNOW...
I THINK I'D REMEMBER *YOU*...
I GOTTA GET TO WORK...
GOOD *LUCK*, MAN.

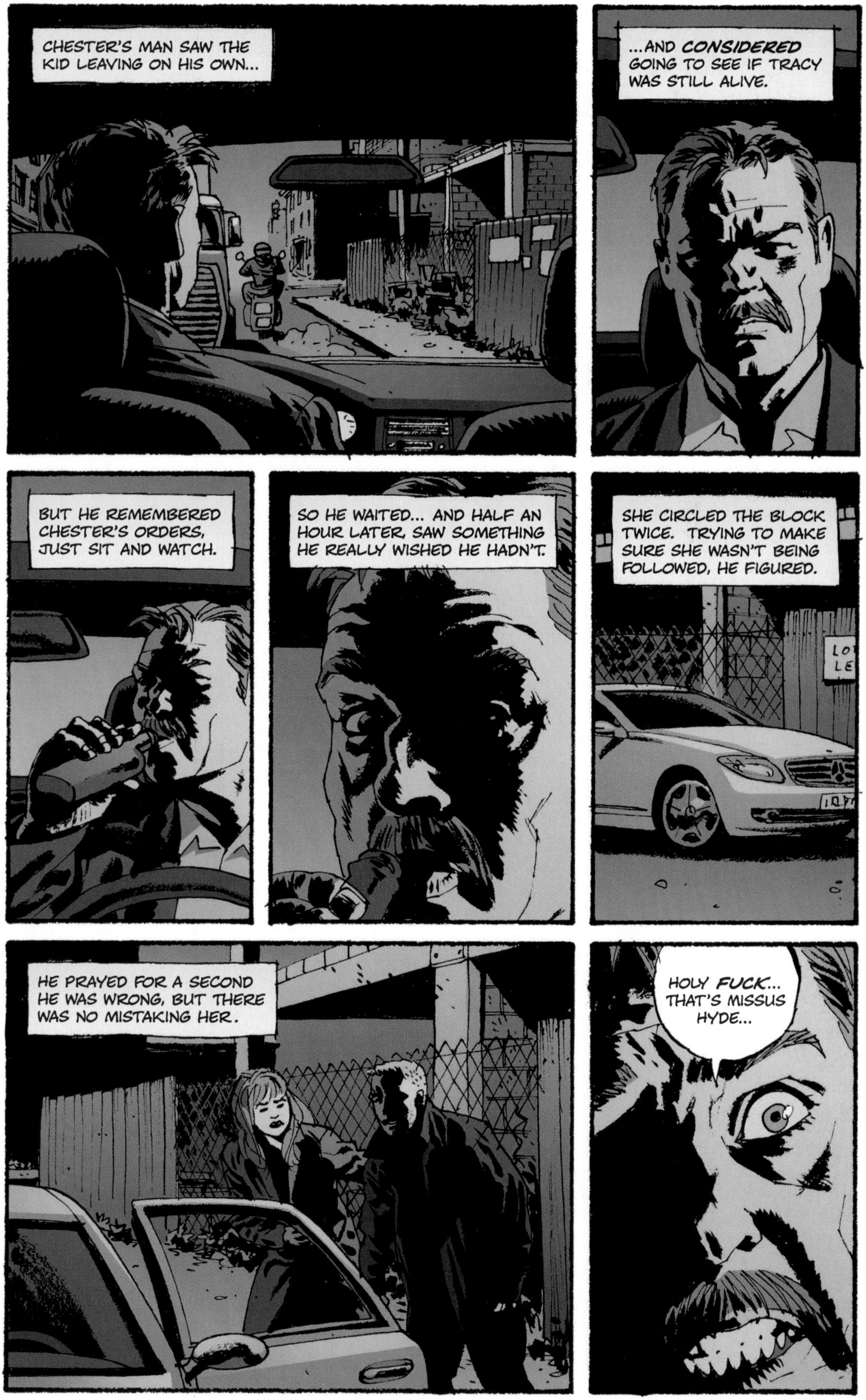
CHESTER'S MAN SAW THE KID LEAVING ON HIS OWN...
...AND CONSIDERED GOING TO SEE IF TRACY WAS STILL ALIVE.
BUT HE REMEMBERED CHESTER'S ORDERS, JUST SIT AND WATCH.
SO HE WAITED... AND HALF AN HOUR LATER, SAW SOMETHING HE REALLY WISHED HE HADN'T.
SHE CIRCLED THE BLOCK TWICE. TRYING TO MAKE SURE SHE WASN'T BEING FOLLOWED, HE FIGURED.
HE PRAYED FOR A SECOND HE WAS WRONG, BUT THERE WAS NO MISTAKING HER.
HOLY FUCK... THAT'S MISSUS HYDE...

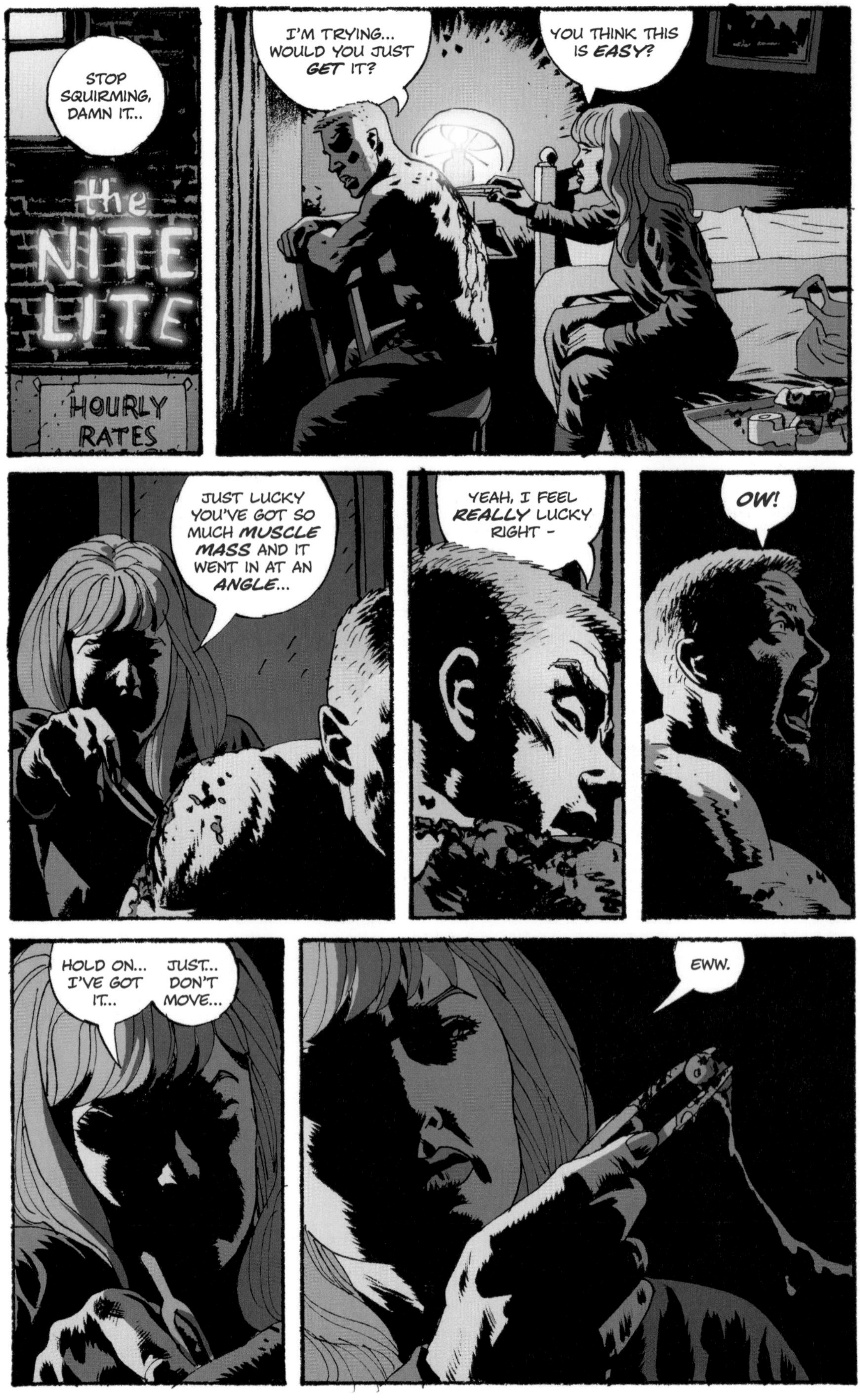
STOP SQUIRMING, DAMN IT...
the NITE LITE
HOURLY RATES
I'M TRYING... WOULD YOU JUST GET IT?
YOU THINK THIS IS EASY?
JUST LUCKY YOU'VE GOT SO MUCH MUSCLE MASS AND IT WENT IN AT AN ANGLE...
YEAH, I FEEL REALLY LUCKY RIGHT -
OW!
HOLD ON... I'VE GOT IT...
JUST... DON'T MOVE...
EWW.

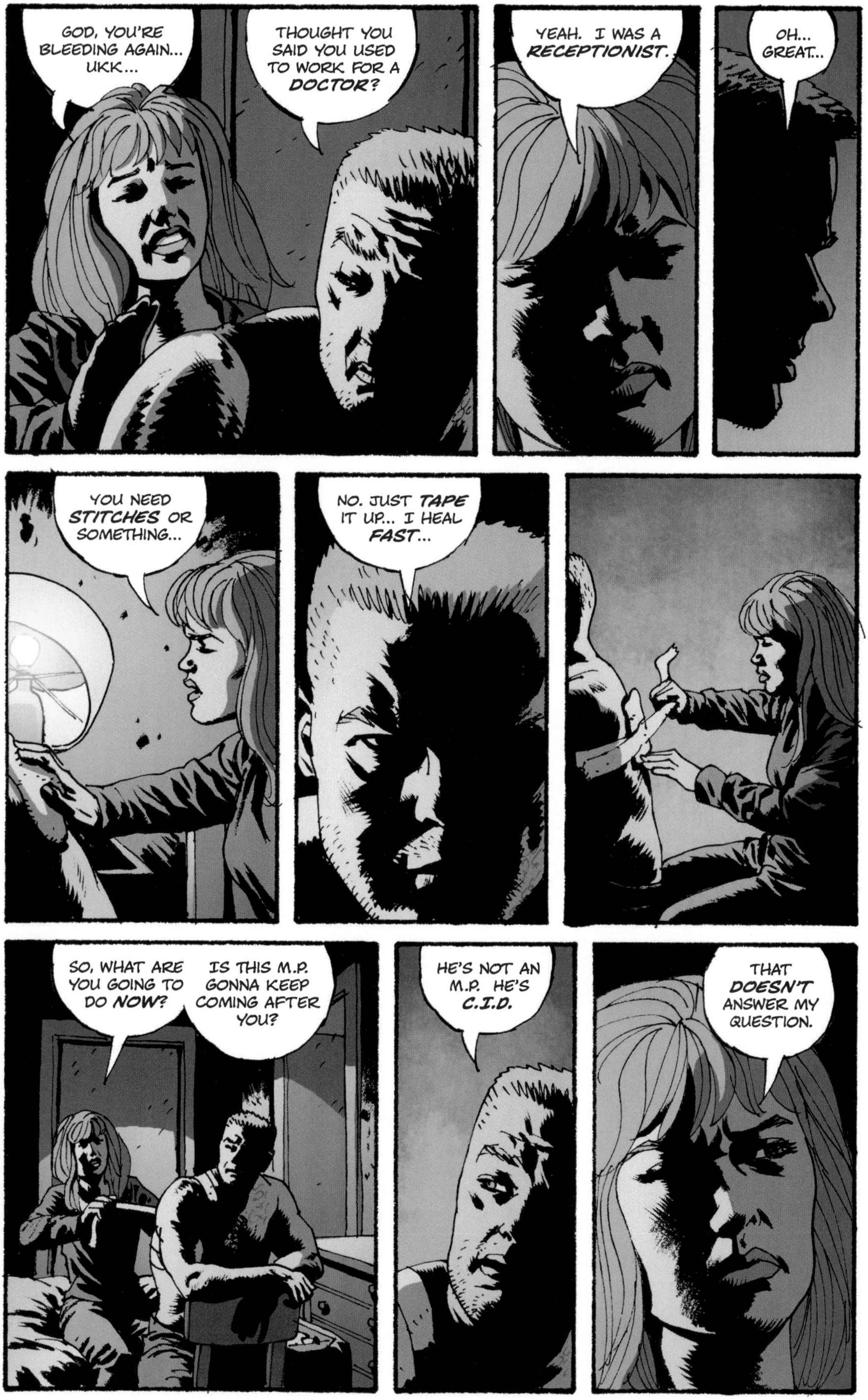
GOD, YOU'RE BLEEDING AGAIN... UKK...
THOUGHT YOU SAID YOU USED TO WORK FOR A DOCTOR?
YEAH. I WAS A RECEPTIONIST.
OH... GREAT...
YOU NEED STITCHES OR SOMETHING...
NO. JUST TAPE IT UP... I HEAL FAST...
SO, WHAT ARE YOU GOING TO DO NOW?
IS THIS M.P. GONNA KEEP COMING AFTER YOU?
HE'S NOT AN M.P. HE'S C.I.D.
THAT DOESN'T ANSWER MY QUESTION.

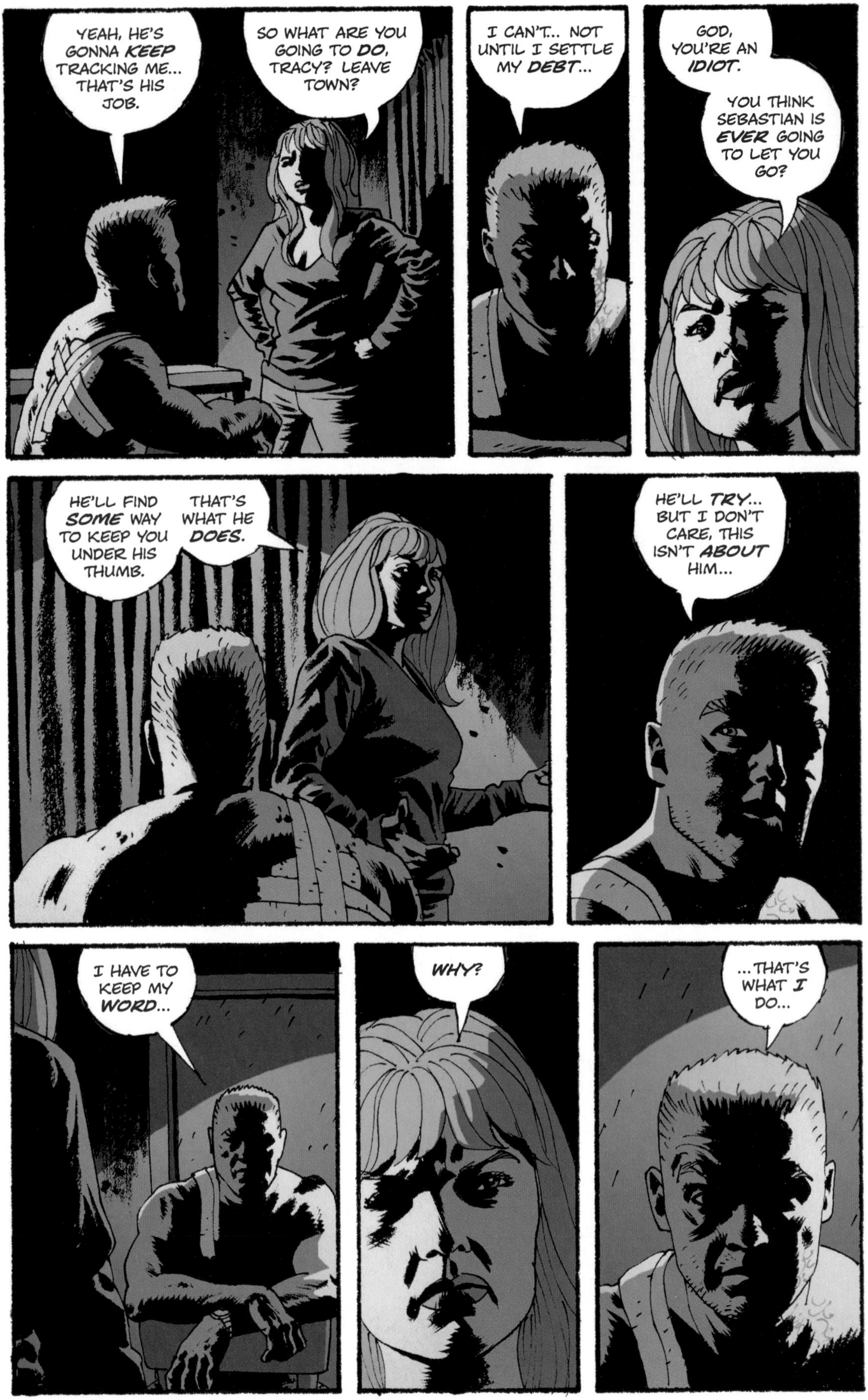
YEAH, HE'S GONNA KEEP TRACKING ME... THAT'S HIS JOB.
SO WHAT ARE YOU GOING TO DO, TRACY? LEAVE TOWN?
I CAN'T... NOT UNTIL I SETTLE MY DEBT...
GOD, YOU'RE AN IDIOT.
YOU THINK SEBASTIAN IS EVER GOING TO LET YOU GO?
HE'LL FIND SOME WAY TO KEEP YOU UNDER HIS THUMB.
THAT'S WHAT HE DOES.
HE'LL TRY... BUT I DON'T CARE, THIS ISN'T ABOUT HIM...
I HAVE TO KEEP MY WORD...
WHY?
...THAT'S WHAT I DO...

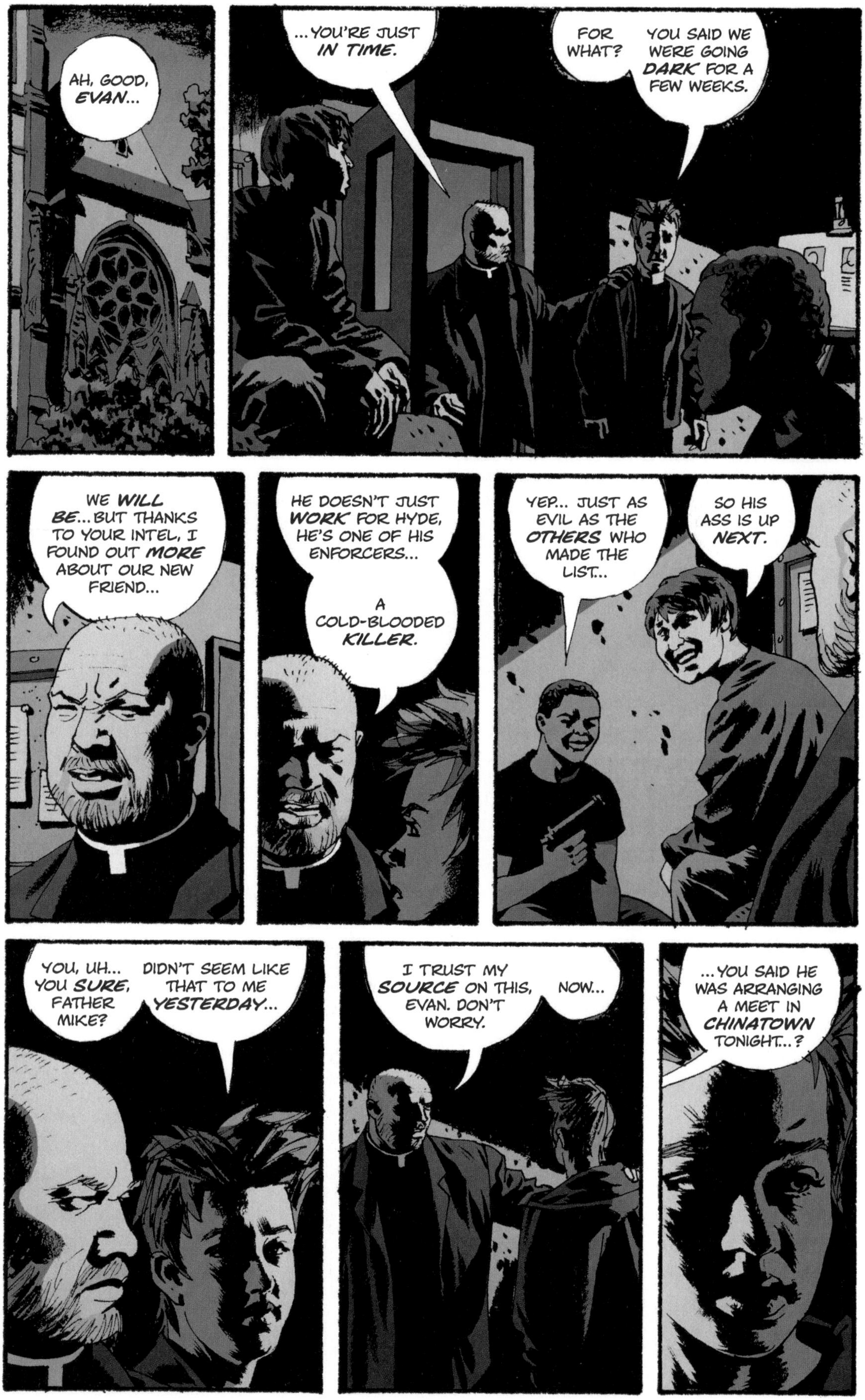
AH, GOOD, EVAN...
...YOU'RE JUST IN TIME.
FOR WHAT?
YOU SAID WE WERE GOING DARK FOR A FEW WEEKS.
WE WILL BE...BUT THANKS TO YOUR INTEL, I FOUND OUT MORE ABOUT OUR NEW FRIEND...
HE DOESN'T JUST WORK FOR HYDE, HE'S ONE OF HIS ENFORCERS...
A COLD-BLOODED KILLER.
YEP... JUST AS EVIL AS THE OTHERS WHO MADE THE LIST...
SO HIS ASS IS UP NEXT.
YOU, UH... YOU SURE, FATHER MIKE?
DIDN'T SEEM LIKE THAT TO ME YESTERDAY...
I TRUST MY SOURCE ON THIS, EVAN. DON'T WORRY.
NOW...
...YOU SAID HE WAS ARRANGING A MEET IN CHINATOWN TONIGHT...?

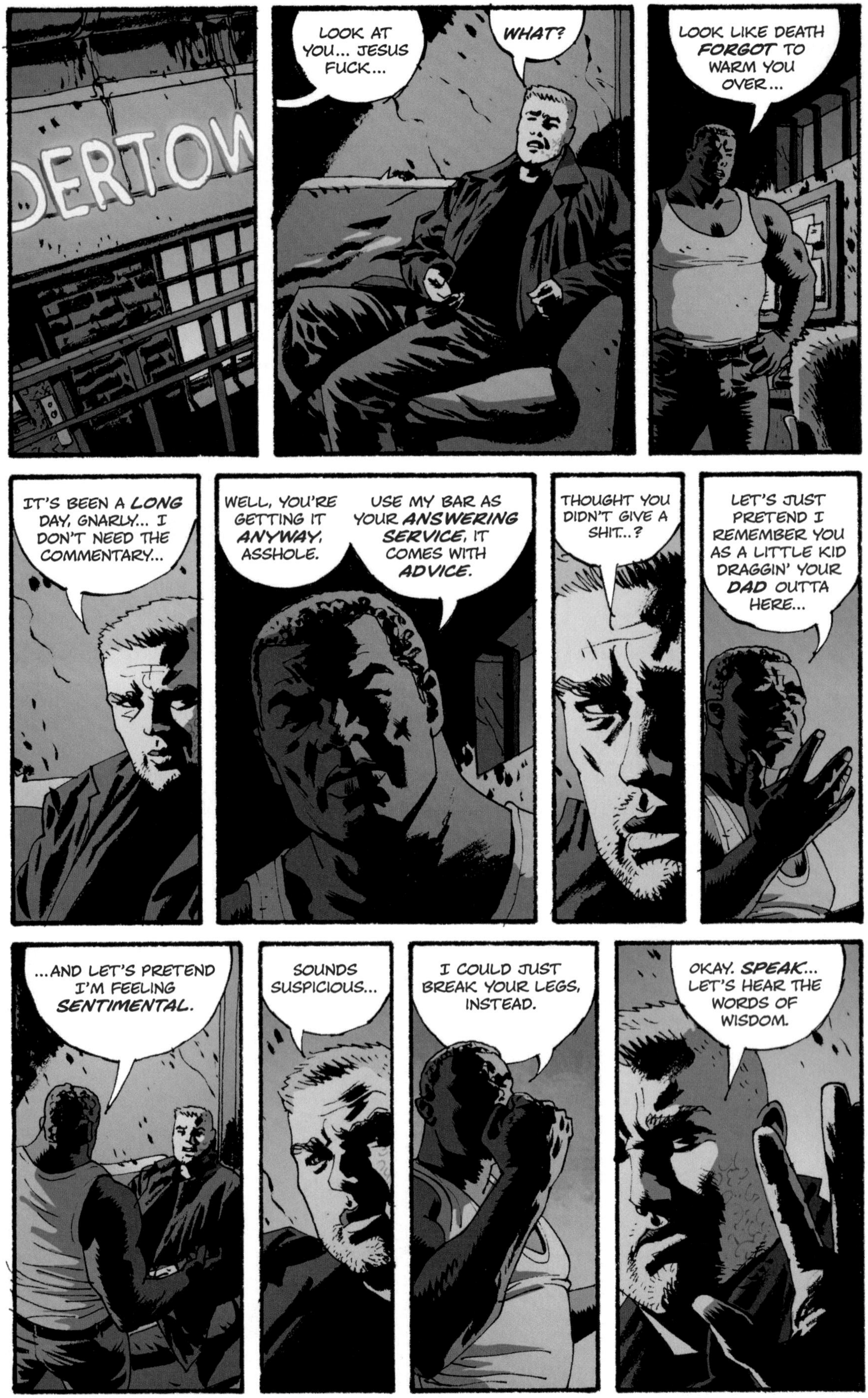
DERTOW
LOOK AT YOU... JESUS FUCK...
WHAT?
LOOK LIKE DEATH FORGOT TO WARM YOU OVER...
IT'S BEEN A LONG DAY, GNARLY... I DON'T NEED THE COMMENTARY...
WELL, YOU'RE GETTING IT ANYWAY, ASSHOLE.
USE MY BAR AS YOUR ANSWERING SERVICE, IT COMES WITH ADVICE.
THOUGHT YOU DIDN'T GIVE A SHIT...?
LET'S JUST PRETEND I REMEMBER YOU AS A LITTLE KID DRAGGIN' YOUR DAD OUTTA HERE...
...AND LET'S PRETEND I'M FEELING SENTIMENTAL.
SOUNDS SUSPICIOUS...
I COULD JUST BREAK YOUR LEGS, INSTEAD.
OKAY. SPEAK... LET'S HEAR THE WORDS OF WISDOM.

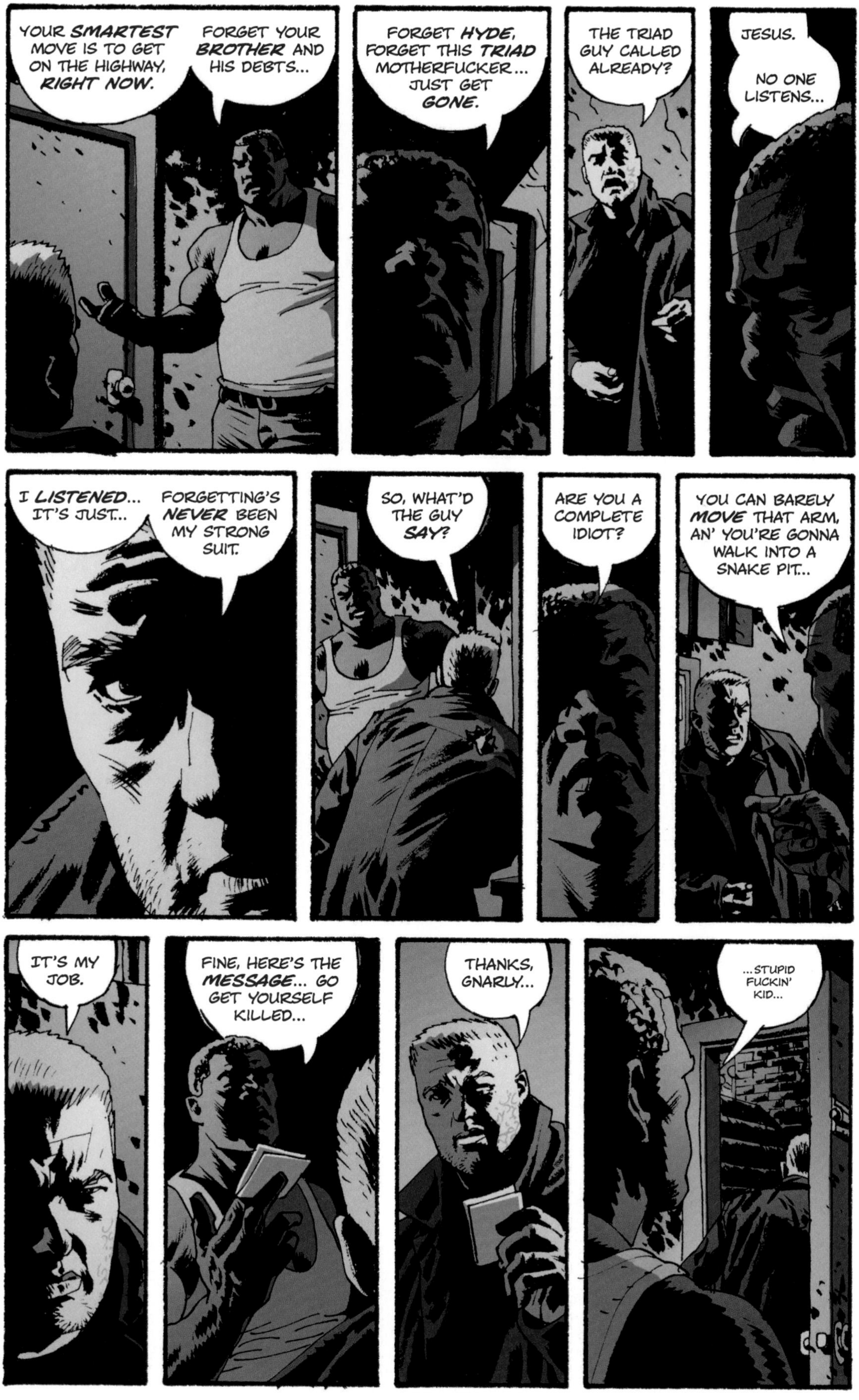
YOUR SMARTEST MOVE IS TO GET ON THE HIGHWAY, RIGHT NOW.
FORGET YOUR BROTHER AND HIS DEBTS...
FORGET HYDE, FORGET THIS TRIAD MOTHERFUCKER... JUST GET GONE.
THE TRIAD GUY CALLED ALREADY?
JESUS.
NO ONE LISTENS...
I LISTENED... IT'S JUST...
FORGETTING'S NEVER BEEN MY STRONG SUIT.
SO, WHAT'D THE GUY SAY?
ARE YOU A COMPLETE IDIOT?
YOU CAN BARELY MOVE THAT ARM, AN' YOU'RE GONNA WALK INTO A SNAKE PIT...
IT'S MY JOB.
FINE, HERE'S THE MESSAGE... GO GET YOURSELF KILLED...
THANKS, GNARLY...
...STUPID FUCKIN' KID...

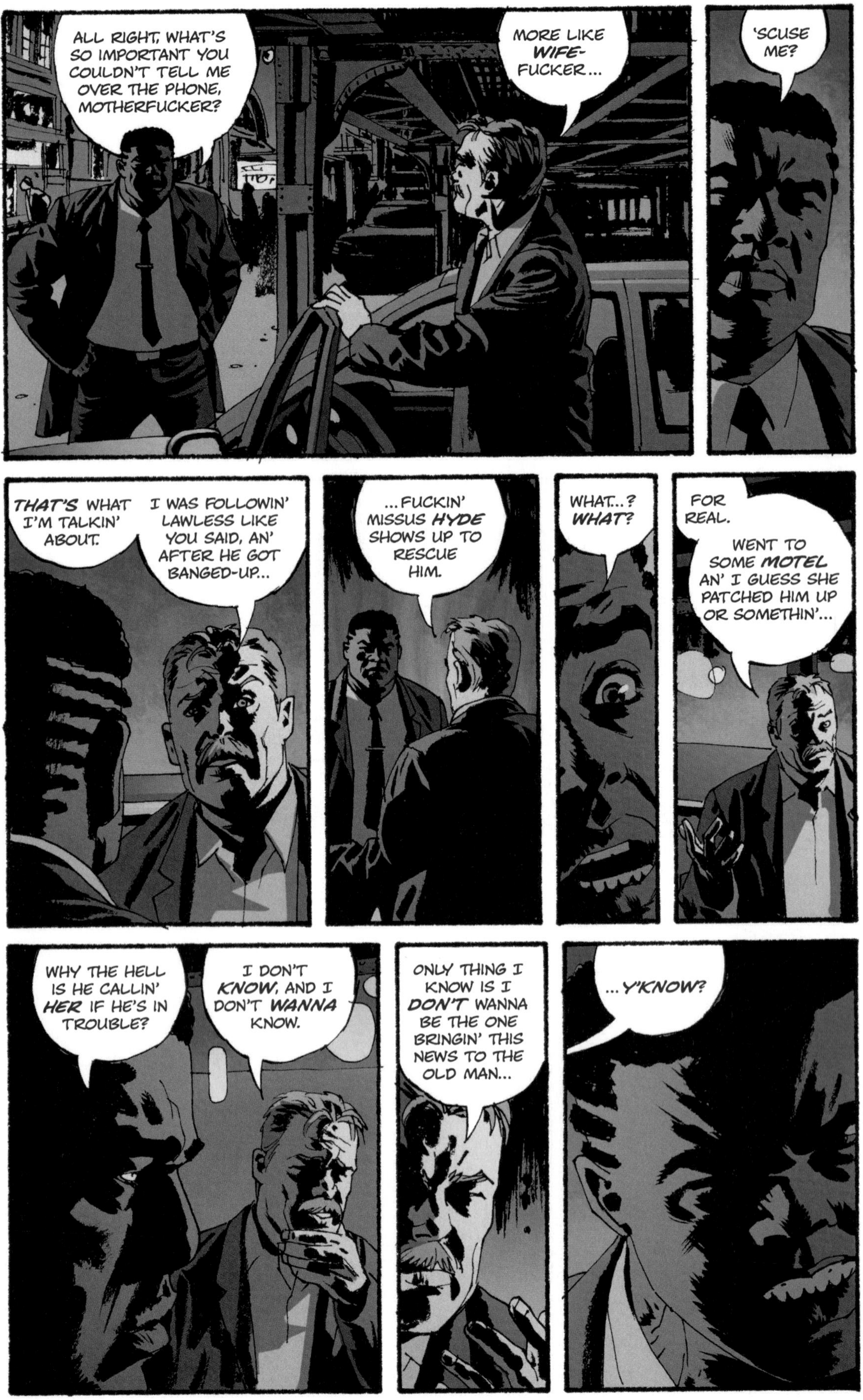
ALL RIGHT, WHAT'S SO IMPORTANT YOU COULDN'T TELL ME OVER THE PHONE, MOTHERFUCKER?
MORE LIKE WIFE-FUCKER...
'SCUSE ME?
THAT'S WHAT I'M TALKIN' ABOUT.
I WAS FOLLOWIN' LAWLESS LIKE YOU SAID, AN' AFTER HE GOT BANGED-UP...
...FUCKIN' MISSUS HYDE SHOWS UP TO RESCUE HIM.
WHAT...? WHAT?
FOR REAL.
WENT TO SOME MOTEL AN' I GUESS SHE PATCHED HIM UP OR SOMETHIN'...
WHY THE HELL IS HE CALLIN' HER IF HE'S IN TROUBLE?
I DON'T KNOW, AND I DON'T WANNA KNOW.
ONLY THING I KNOW IS I DON'T WANNA BE THE ONE BRINGIN' THIS NEWS TO THE OLD MAN...
...Y'KNOW?

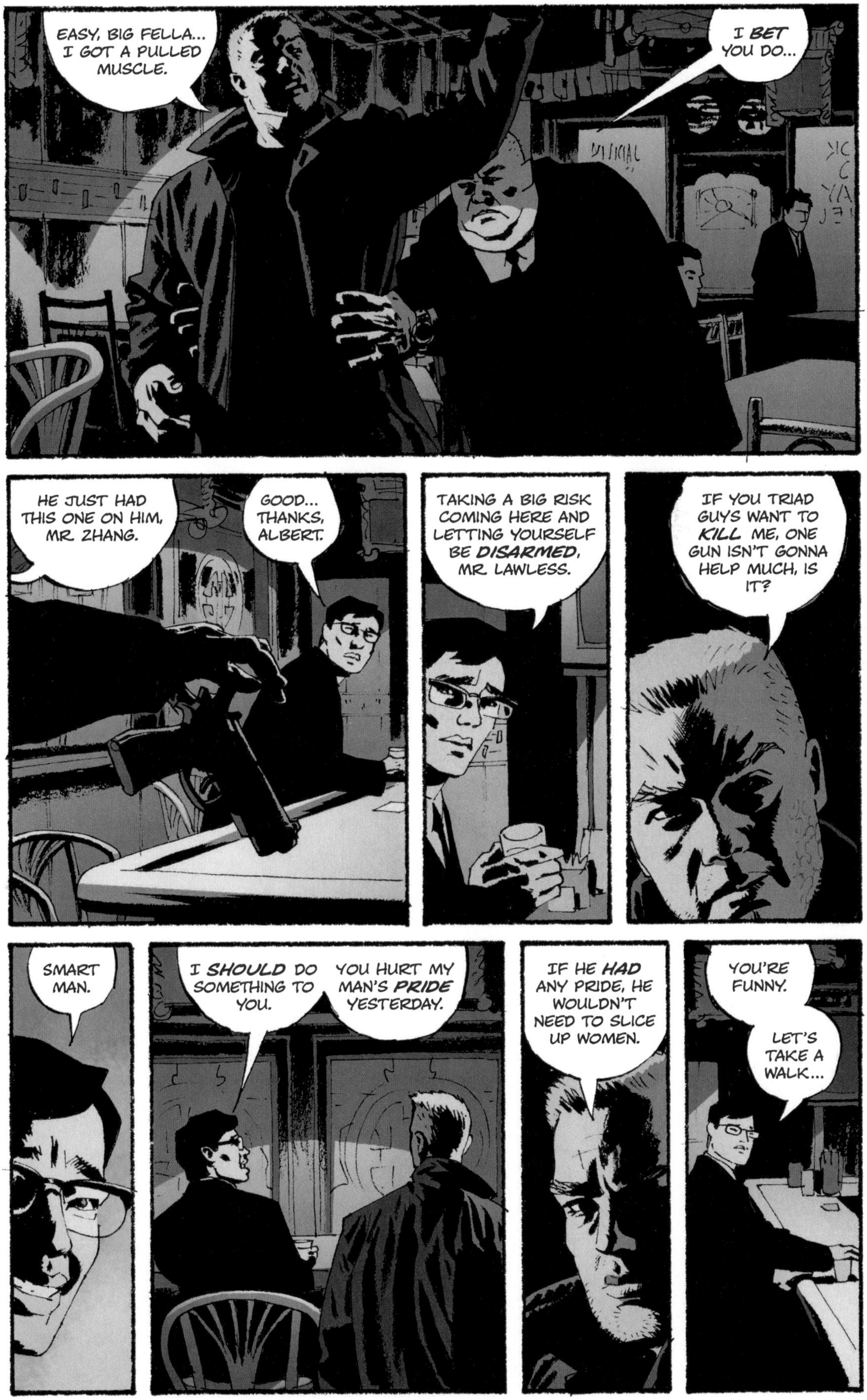
EASY, BIG FELLA... I GOT A PULLED MUSCLE.
I BET YOU DO...
HE JUST HAD THIS ONE ON HIM, MR. ZHANG.
GOOD... THANKS, ALBERT.
TAKING A BIG RISK COMING HERE AND LETTING YOURSELF BE DISARMED, MR. LAWLESS.
IF YOU TRIAD GUYS WANT TO KILL ME, ONE GUN ISN'T GONNA HELP MUCH, IS IT?
SMART MAN.
YOU HURT MY MAN'S PRIDE YESTERDAY.
I SHOULD DO SOMETHING TO YOU.
IF HE HAD ANY PRIDE, HE WOULDN'T NEED TO SLICE UP WOMEN.
YOU'RE FUNNY.
LET'S TAKE A WALK...

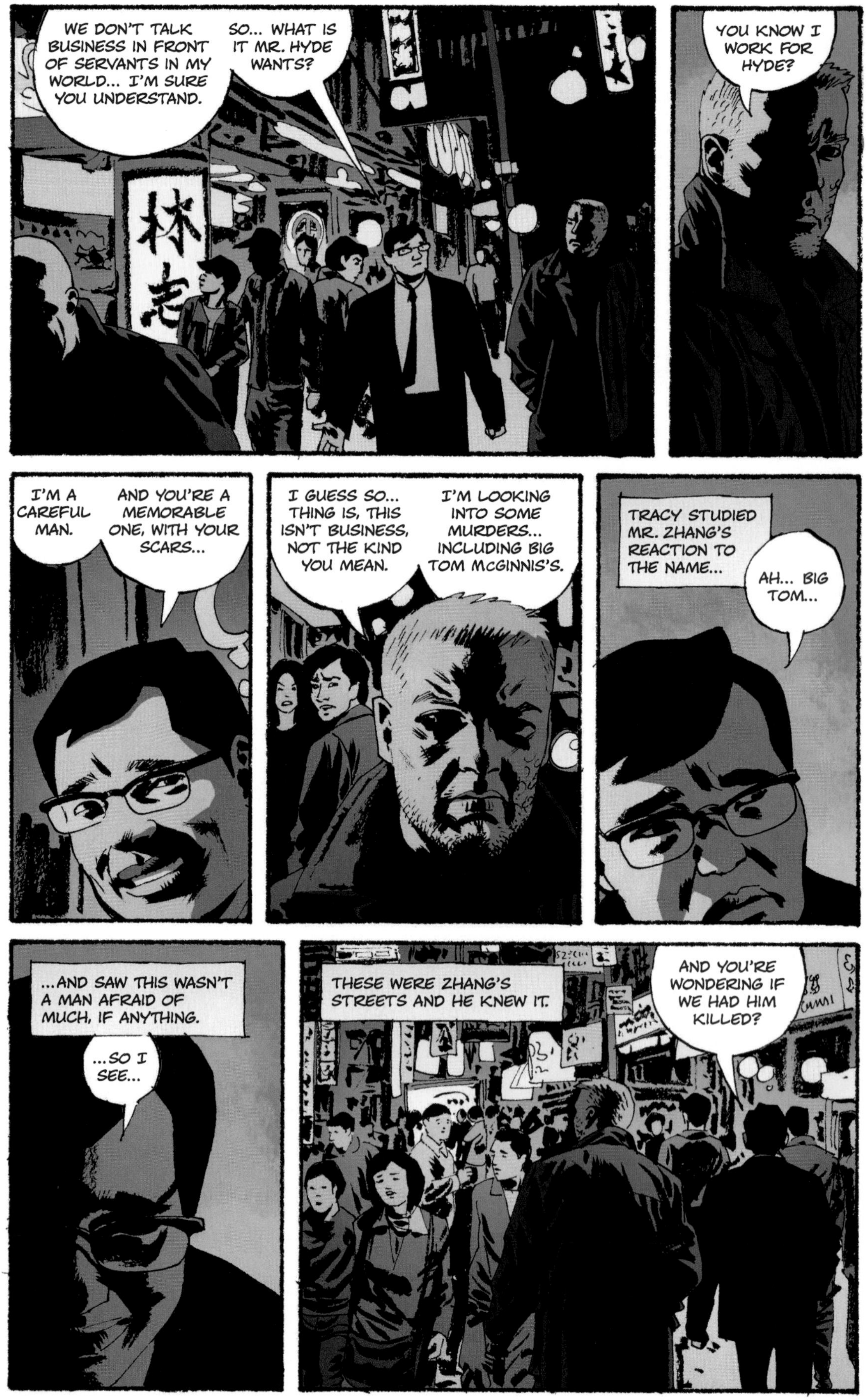
WE DON'T TALK BUSINESS IN FRONT OF SERVANTS IN MY WORLD... I'M SURE YOU UNDERSTAND.
SO... WHAT IS IT MR. HYDE WANTS?
YOU KNOW I WORK FOR HYDE?
I'M A CAREFUL MAN.
AND YOU'RE A MEMORABLE ONE, WITH YOUR SCARS...
I GUESS SO... THING IS, THIS ISN'T BUSINESS, NOT THE KIND YOU MEAN.
I'M LOOKING INTO SOME MURDERS... INCLUDING BIG TOM McGINNIS'S.
TRACY STUDIED MR. ZHANG'S REACTION TO THE NAME...
AH... BIG TOM...
...AND SAW THIS WASN'T A MAN AFRAID OF MUCH, IF ANYTHING.
...SO I SEE...
THESE WERE ZHANG'S STREETS AND HE KNEW IT.
AND YOU'RE WONDERING IF WE HAD HIM KILLED?

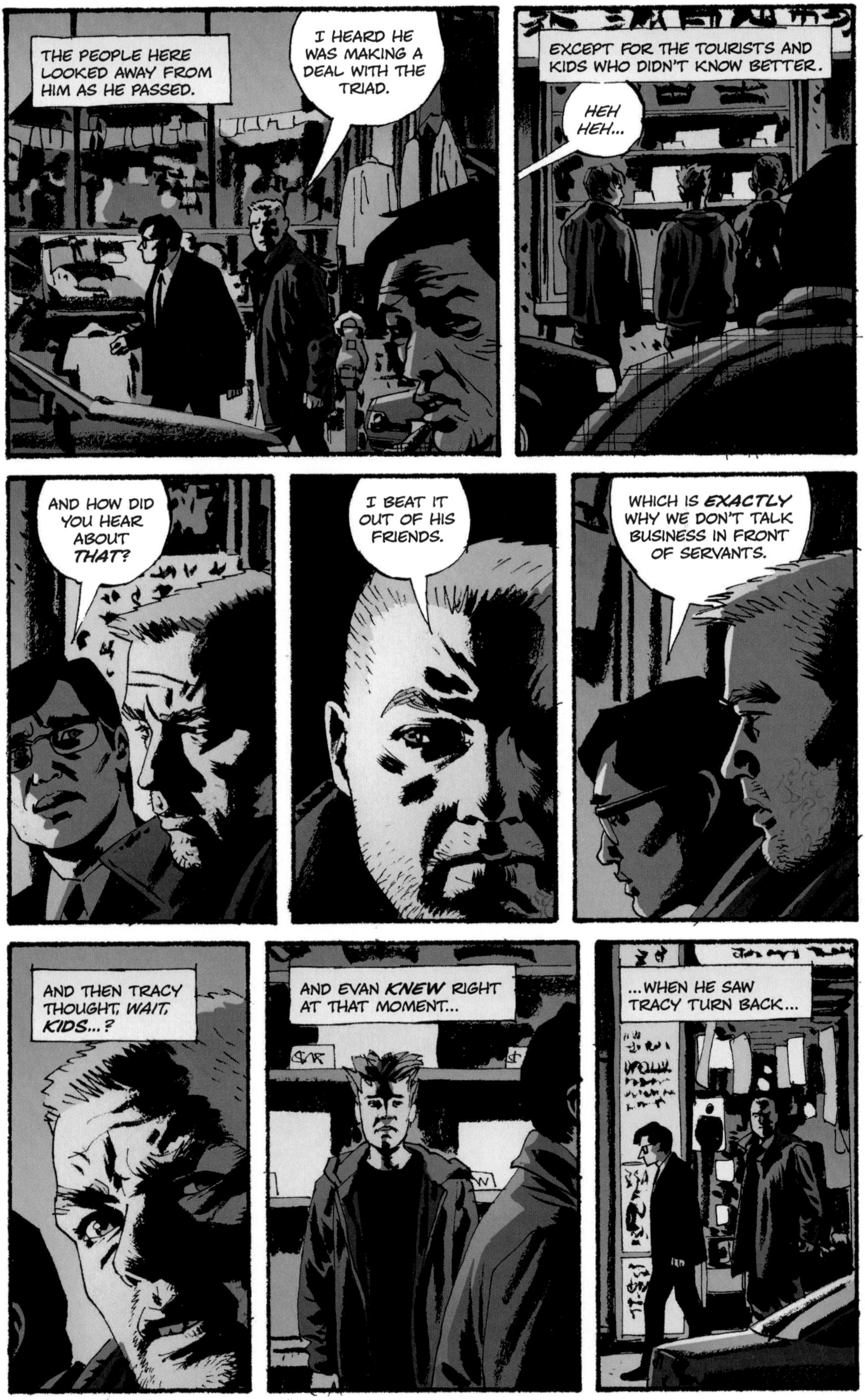

THE PEOPLE HERE LOOKED AWAY FROM HIM AS HE PASSED.
I HEARD HE WAS MAKING A DEAL WITH THE TRIAD.
EXCEPT FOR THE TOURISTS AND KIDS WHO DIDN'T KNOW BETTER.
HEH HEH...
AND HOW DID YOU HEAR ABOUT *THAT*?
I BEAT IT OUT OF HIS FRIENDS.
WHICH IS *EXACTLY* WHY WE DON'T TALK BUSINESS IN FRONT OF SERVANTS.
AND THEN TRACY THOUGHT, *WAIT, KIDS...?*
AND EVAN *KNEW* RIGHT AT THAT MOMENT...
...WHEN HE SAW TRACY TURN BACK...

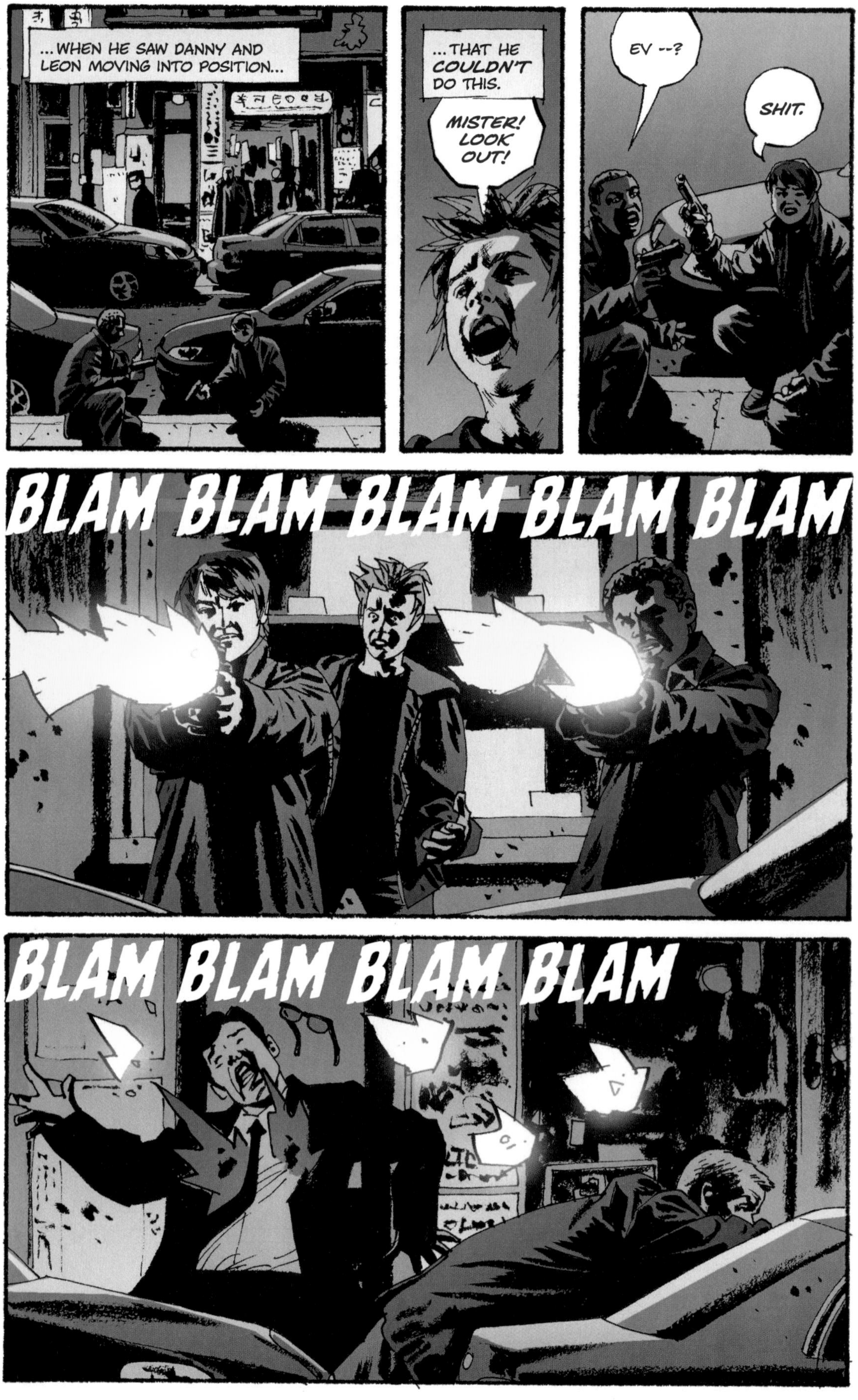
...WHEN HE SAW DANNY AND LEON MOVING INTO POSITION...
...THAT HE COULDN'T DO THIS.
MISTER! LOOK OUT!
EV --?
SHIT.
BLAM BLAM BLAM BLAM BLAM
BLAM BLAM BLAM BLAM

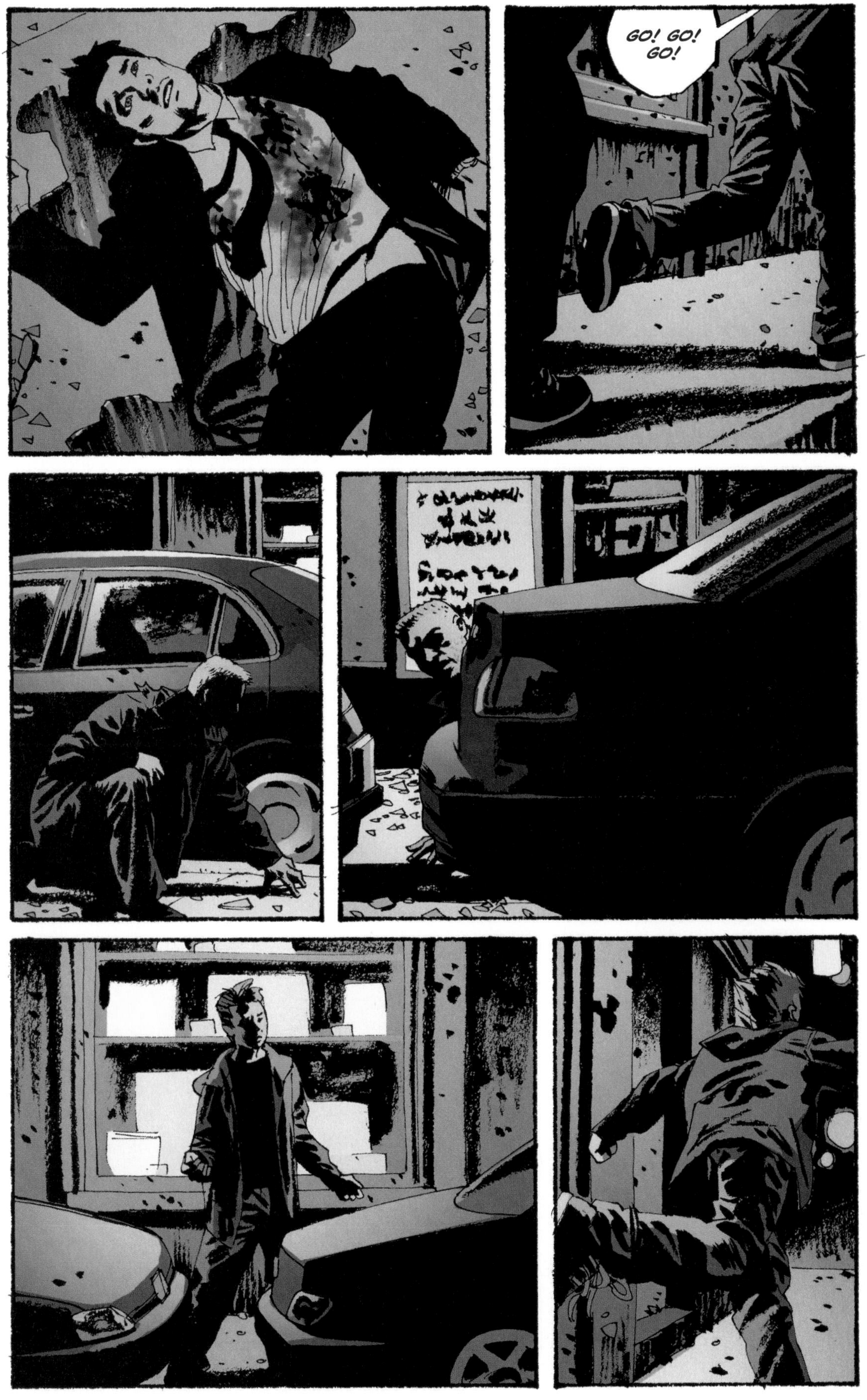
GO! GO! GO!

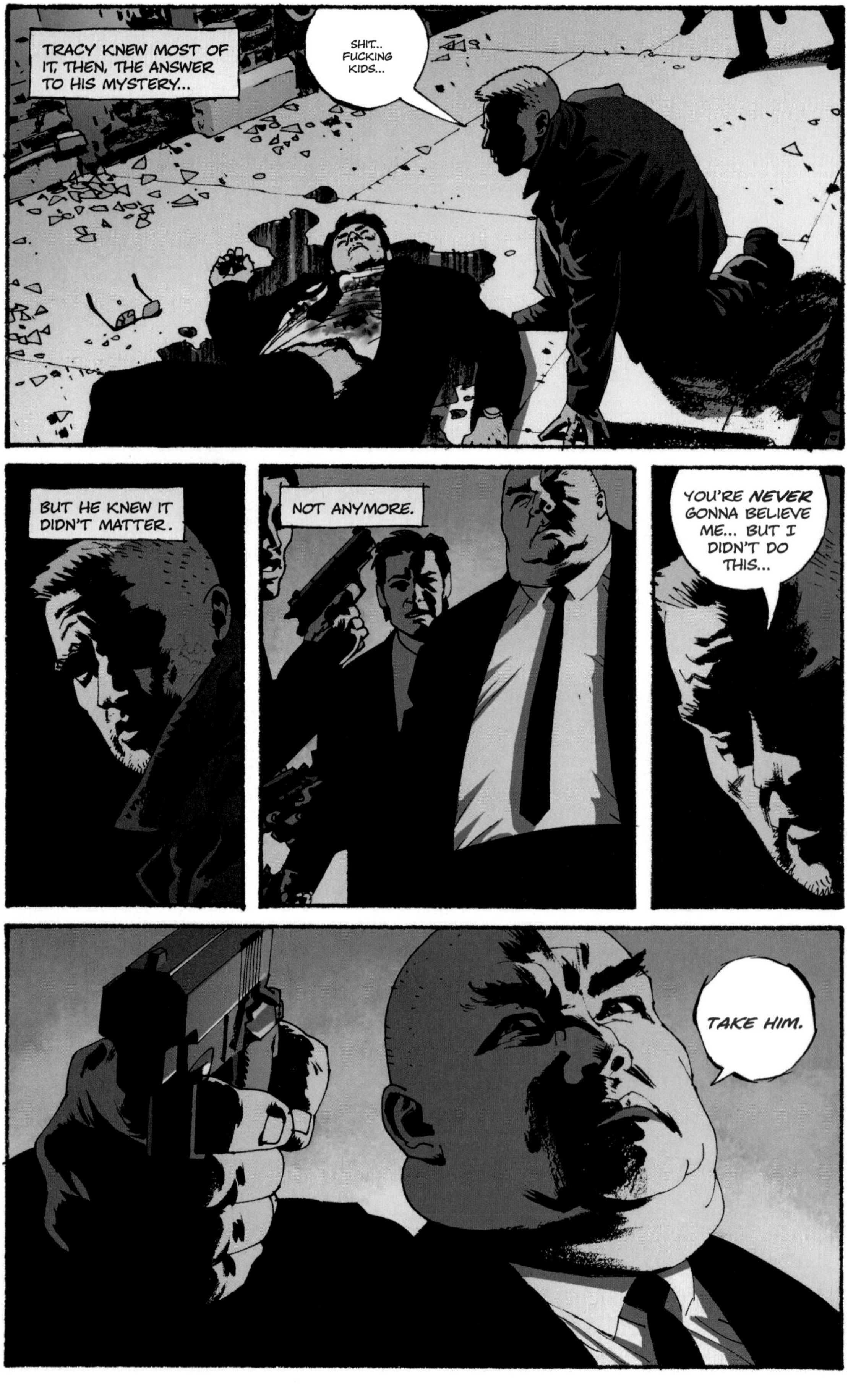
TRACY KNEW MOST OF IT, THEN, THE ANSWER TO HIS MYSTERY...
SHIT... FUCKING KIDS...
BUT HE KNEW IT DIDN'T MATTER.
NOT ANYMORE.
YOU'RE *NEVER* GONNA BELIEVE ME... BUT I DIDN'T DO THIS...
TAKE HIM.

The Sinners Part Five

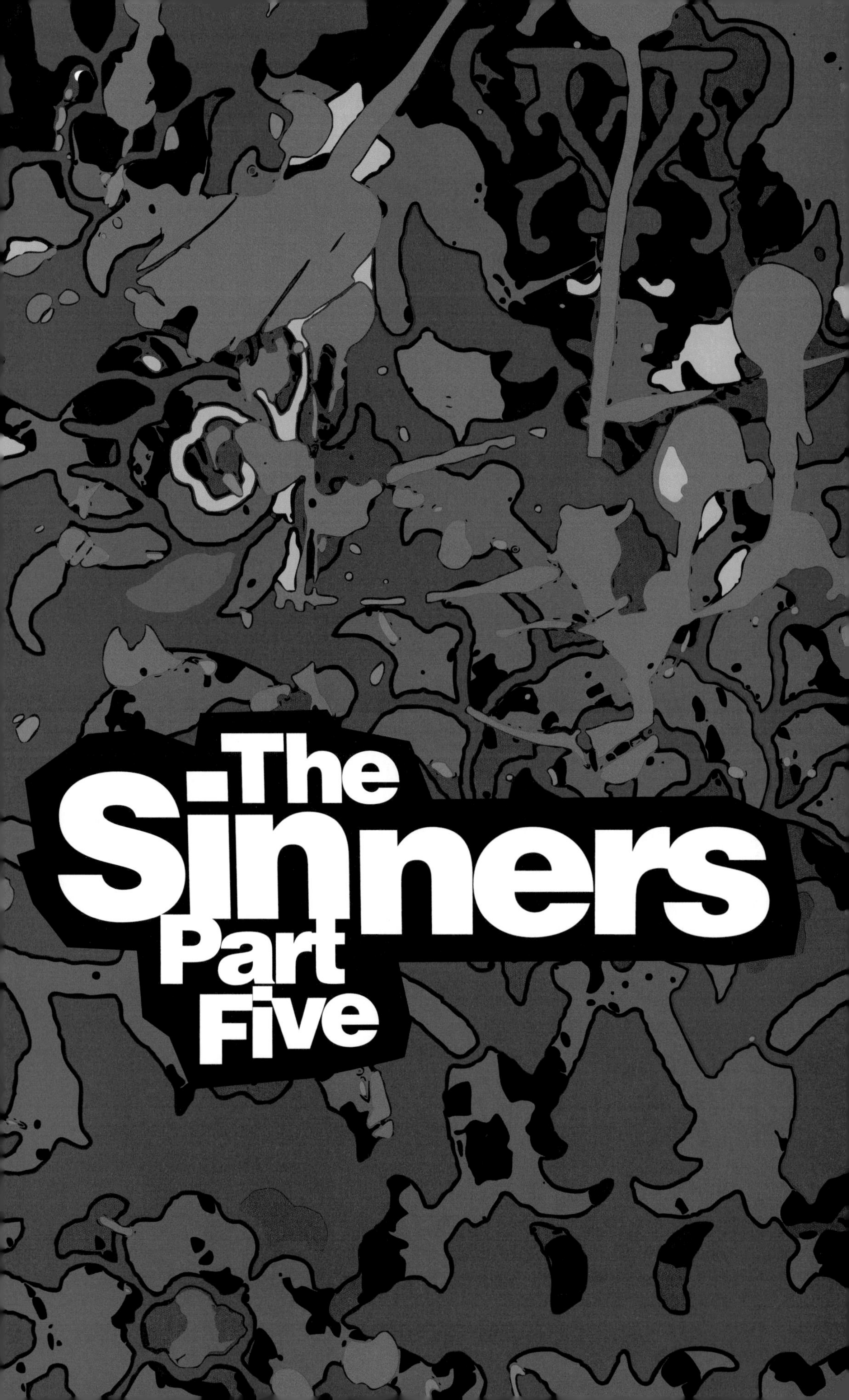

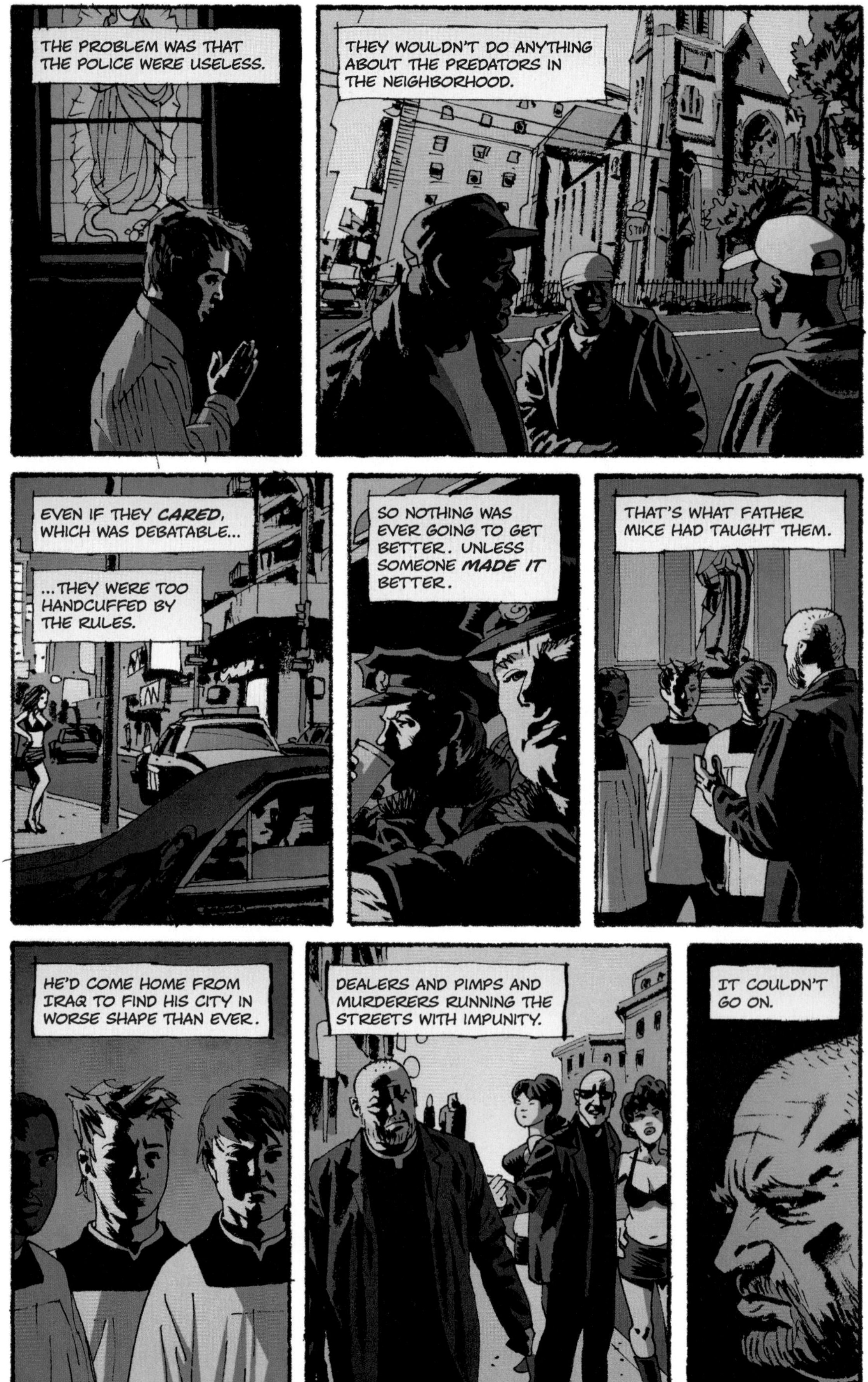
THE PROBLEM WAS THAT THE POLICE WERE USELESS.
THEY WOULDN'T DO ANYTHING ABOUT THE PREDATORS IN THE NEIGHBORHOOD.
EVEN IF THEY *CARED*, WHICH WAS DEBATABLE...
...THEY WERE TOO HANDCUFFED BY THE RULES.
SO NOTHING WAS EVER GOING TO GET BETTER. UNLESS SOMEONE ***MADE IT*** BETTER.
THAT'S WHAT FATHER MIKE HAD TAUGHT THEM.
HE'D COME HOME FROM IRAQ TO FIND HIS CITY IN WORSE SHAPE THAN EVER.
DEALERS AND PIMPS AND MURDERERS RUNNING THE STREETS WITH IMPUNITY.
IT COULDN'T GO ON.

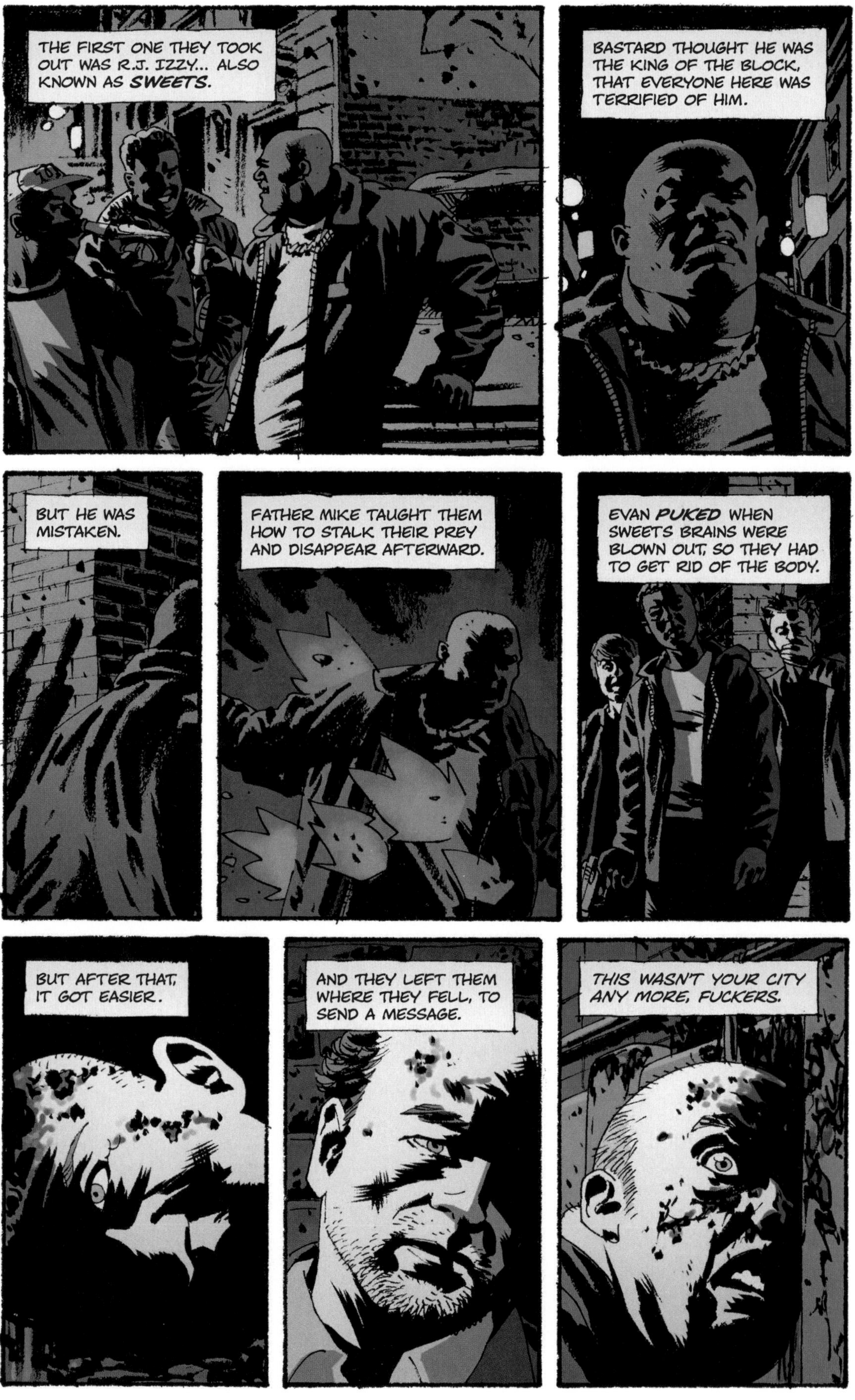
THE FIRST ONE THEY TOOK OUT WAS R.J. IZZY... ALSO KNOWN AS SWEETS.
BASTARD THOUGHT HE WAS THE KING OF THE BLOCK, THAT EVERYONE HERE WAS TERRIFIED OF HIM.
BUT HE WAS MISTAKEN.
FATHER MIKE TAUGHT THEM HOW TO STALK THEIR PREY AND DISAPPEAR AFTERWARD.
EVAN PUKED WHEN SWEETS BRAINS WERE BLOWN OUT, SO THEY HAD TO GET RID OF THE BODY.
BUT AFTER THAT, IT GOT EASIER.
AND THEY LEFT THEM WHERE THEY FELL, TO SEND A MESSAGE.
THIS WASN'T YOUR CITY ANY MORE, FUCKERS.

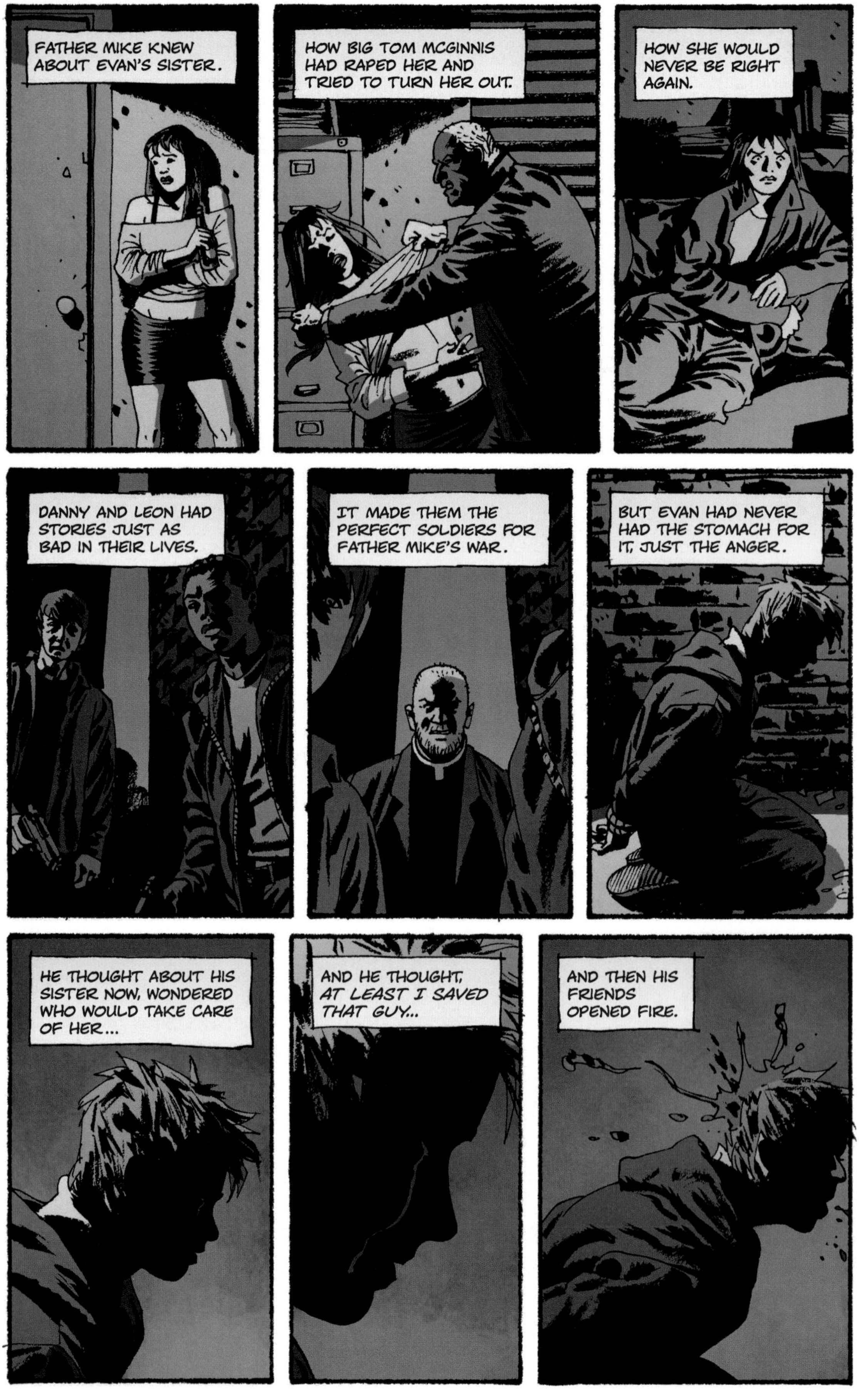
FATHER MIKE KNEW ABOUT EVAN'S SISTER.
HOW BIG TOM MCGINNIS HAD RAPED HER AND TRIED TO TURN HER OUT.
HOW SHE WOULD NEVER BE RIGHT AGAIN.
DANNY AND LEON HAD STORIES JUST AS BAD IN THEIR LIVES.
IT MADE THEM THE PERFECT SOLDIERS FOR FATHER MIKE'S WAR.
BUT EVAN HAD NEVER HAD THE STOMACH FOR IT, JUST THE ANGER.
HE THOUGHT ABOUT HIS SISTER NOW, WONDERED WHO WOULD TAKE CARE OF HER...
AND HE THOUGHT, *AT LEAST I SAVED THAT GUY...*
AND THEN HIS FRIENDS OPENED FIRE.

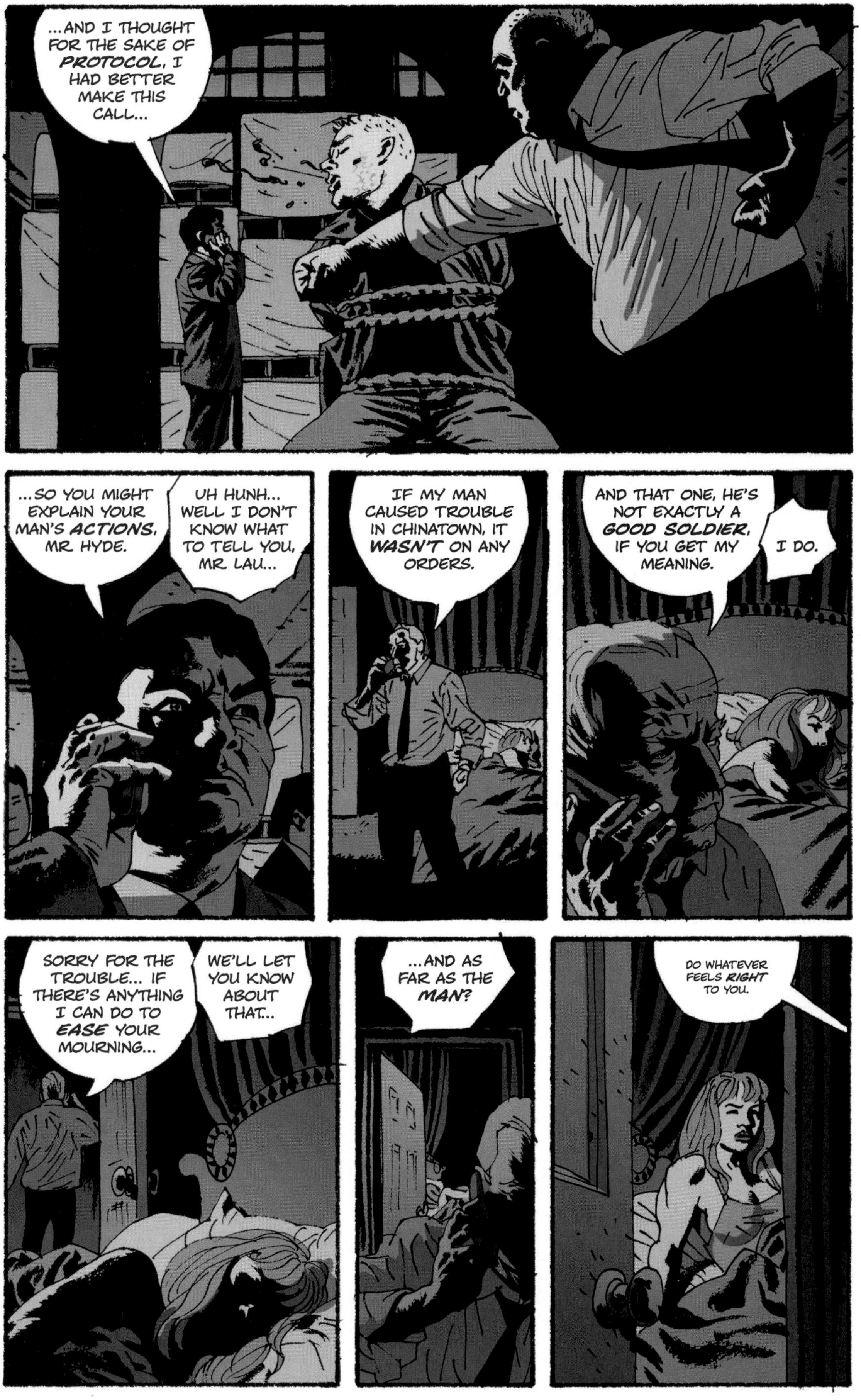
...AND I THOUGHT FOR THE SAKE OF PROTOCOL, I HAD BETTER MAKE THIS CALL...
...SO YOU MIGHT EXPLAIN YOUR MAN'S ACTIONS, MR HYDE.
UH HUNH... WELL I DON'T KNOW WHAT TO TELL YOU, MR LAU...
IF MY MAN CAUSED TROUBLE IN CHINATOWN, IT WASN'T ON ANY ORDERS.
AND THAT ONE, HE'S NOT EXACTLY A GOOD SOLDIER, IF YOU GET MY MEANING.
I DO.
SORRY FOR THE TROUBLE... IF THERE'S ANYTHING I CAN DO TO EASE YOUR MOURNING...
WE'LL LET YOU KNOW ABOUT THAT...
...AND AS FAR AS THE MAN?
DO WHATEVER FEELS RIGHT TO YOU.

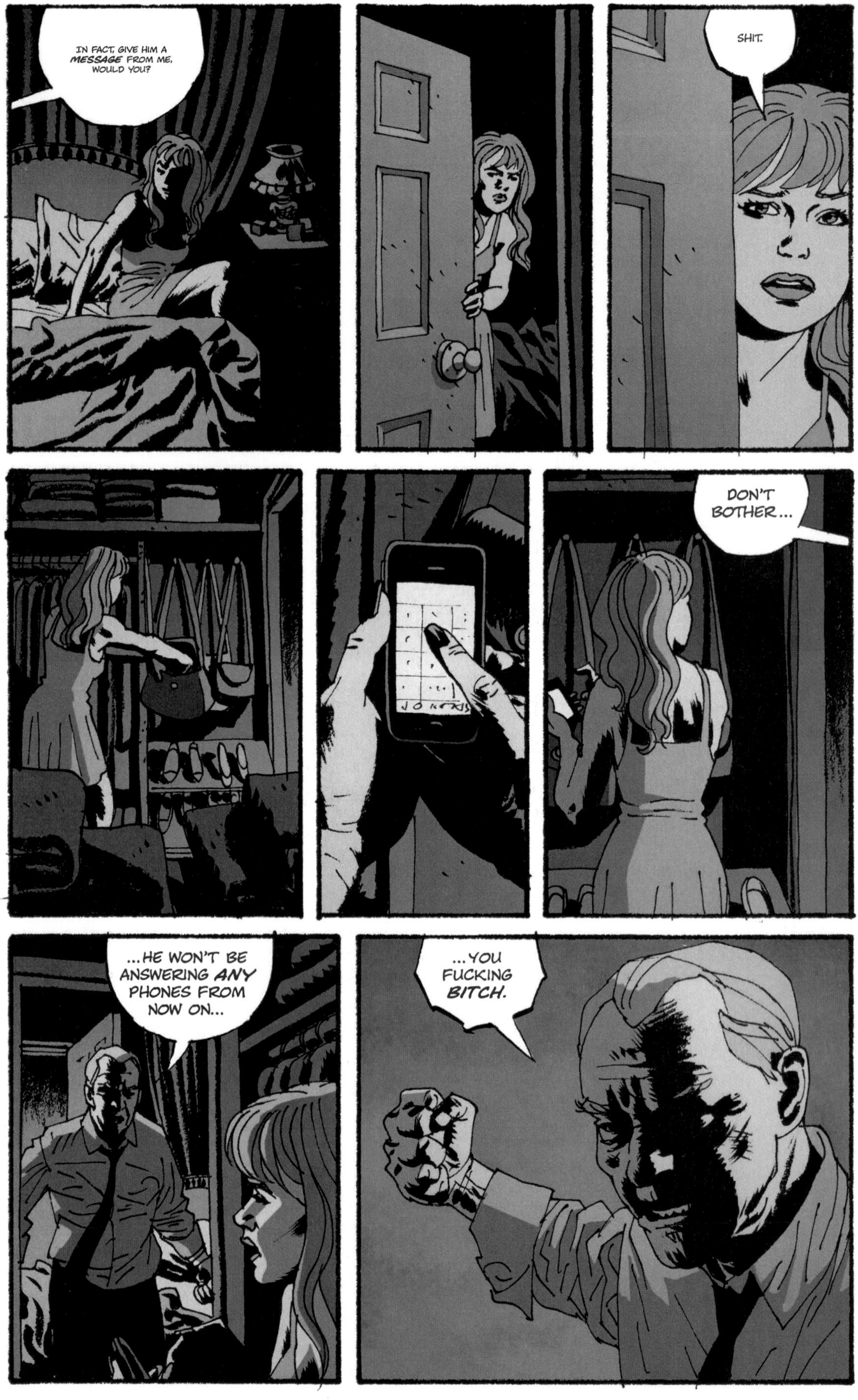
IN FACT, GIVE HIM A MESSAGE FROM ME, WOULD YOU?
SHIT.
DON'T BOTHER...
...HE WON'T BE ANSWERING ANY PHONES FROM NOW ON...
...YOU FUCKING BITCH.

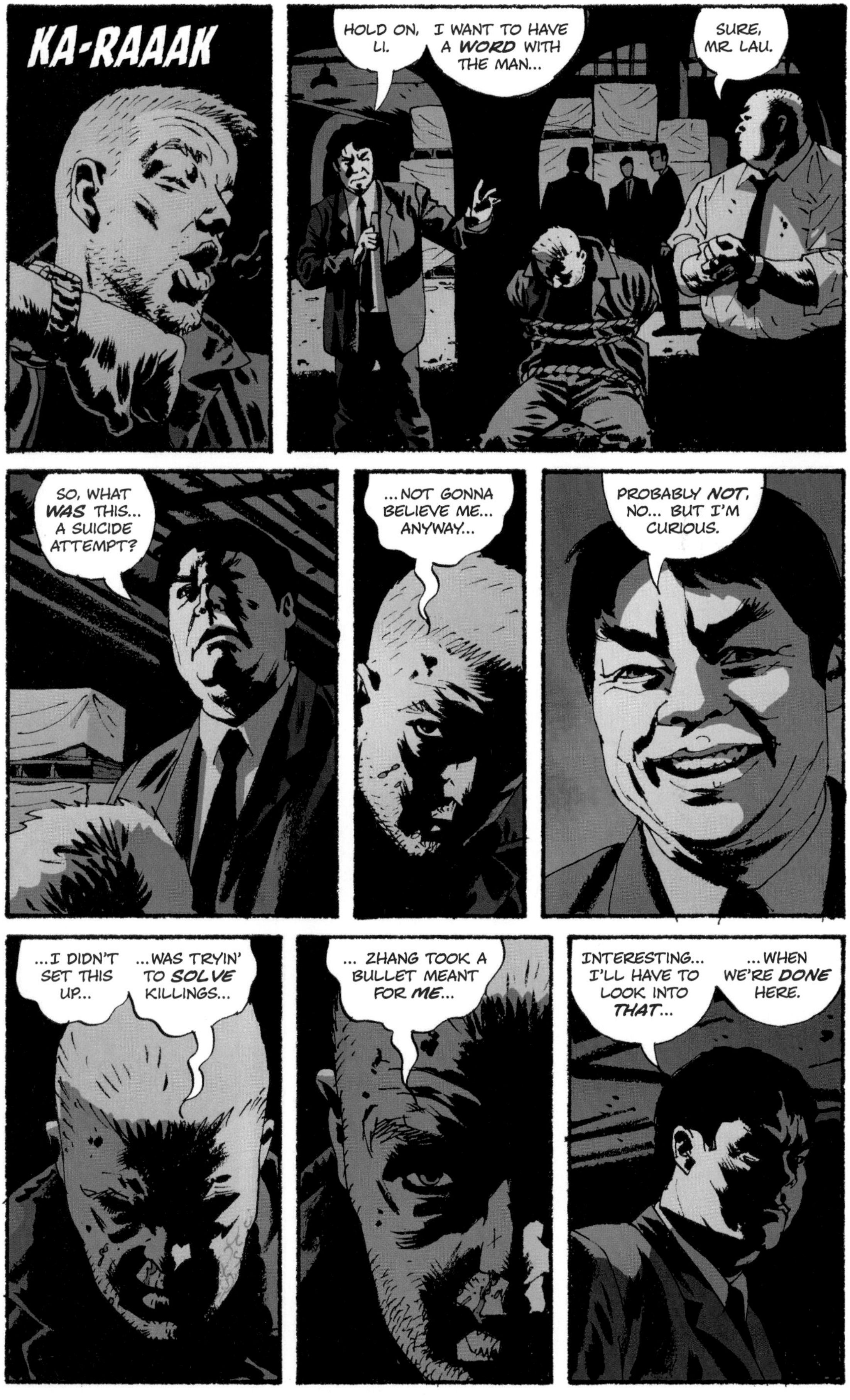
KA-RAAAK
HOLD ON, LI.
I WANT TO HAVE A WORD WITH THE MAN...
SURE, MR LAU.
SO, WHAT WAS THIS... A SUICIDE ATTEMPT?
...NOT GONNA BELIEVE ME... ANYWAY...
PROBABLY NOT, NO... BUT I'M CURIOUS.
...I DIDN'T SET THIS UP...
...WAS TRYIN' TO SOLVE KILLINGS...
... ZHANG TOOK A BULLET MEANT FOR ME...
INTERESTING... I'LL HAVE TO LOOK INTO THAT...
...WHEN WE'RE DONE HERE.

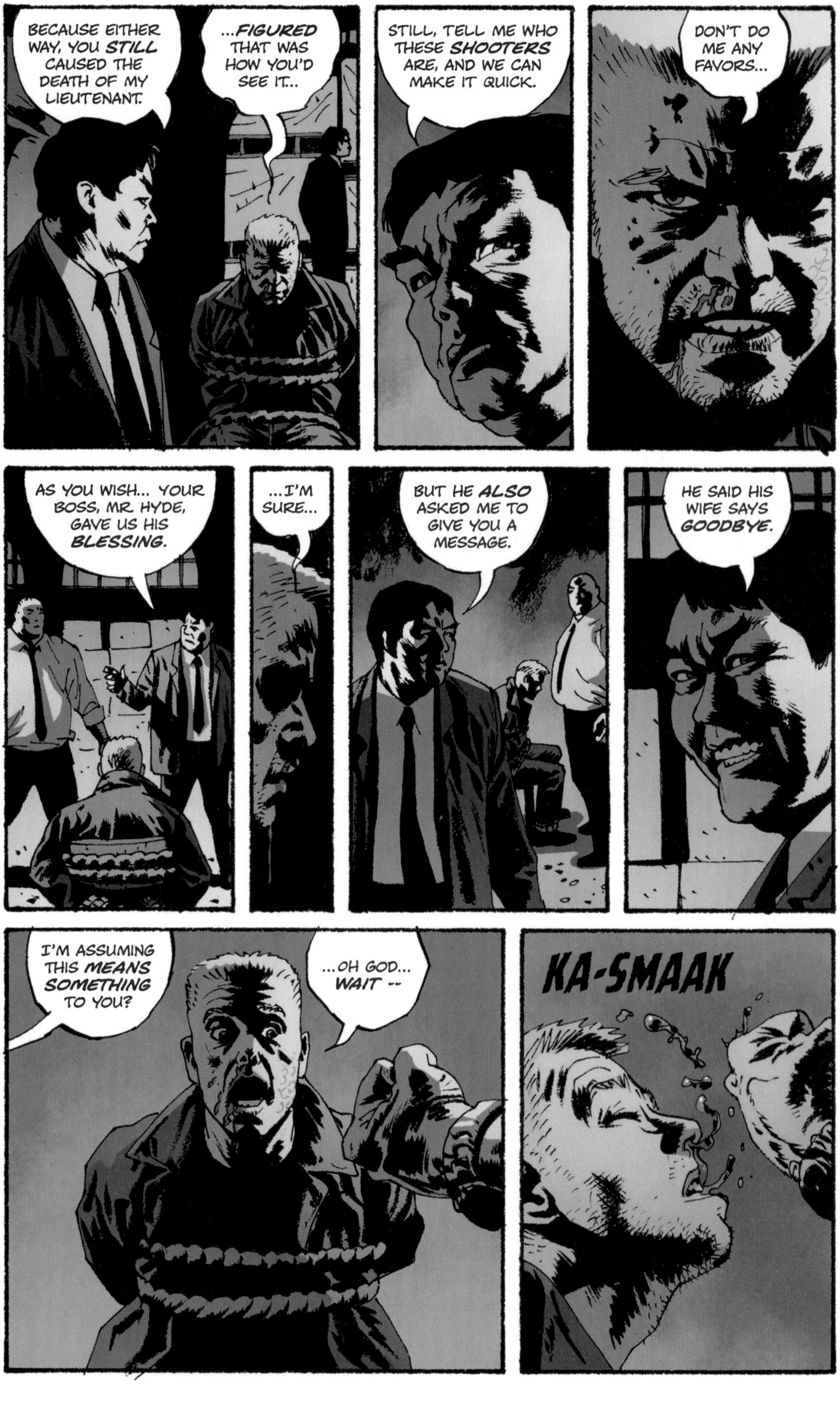
BECAUSE EITHER WAY, YOU STILL CAUSED THE DEATH OF MY LIEUTENANT.
...FIGURED THAT WAS HOW YOU'D SEE IT...
STILL, TELL ME WHO THESE SHOOTERS ARE, AND WE CAN MAKE IT QUICK.
DON'T DO ME ANY FAVORS...
AS YOU WISH... YOUR BOSS, MR. HYDE, GAVE US HIS BLESSING.
...I'M SURE...
BUT HE ALSO ASKED ME TO GIVE YOU A MESSAGE.
HE SAID HIS WIFE SAYS GOODBYE.
I'M ASSUMING THIS MEANS SOMETHING TO YOU?
...OH GOD... WAIT --
KA-SMAAK

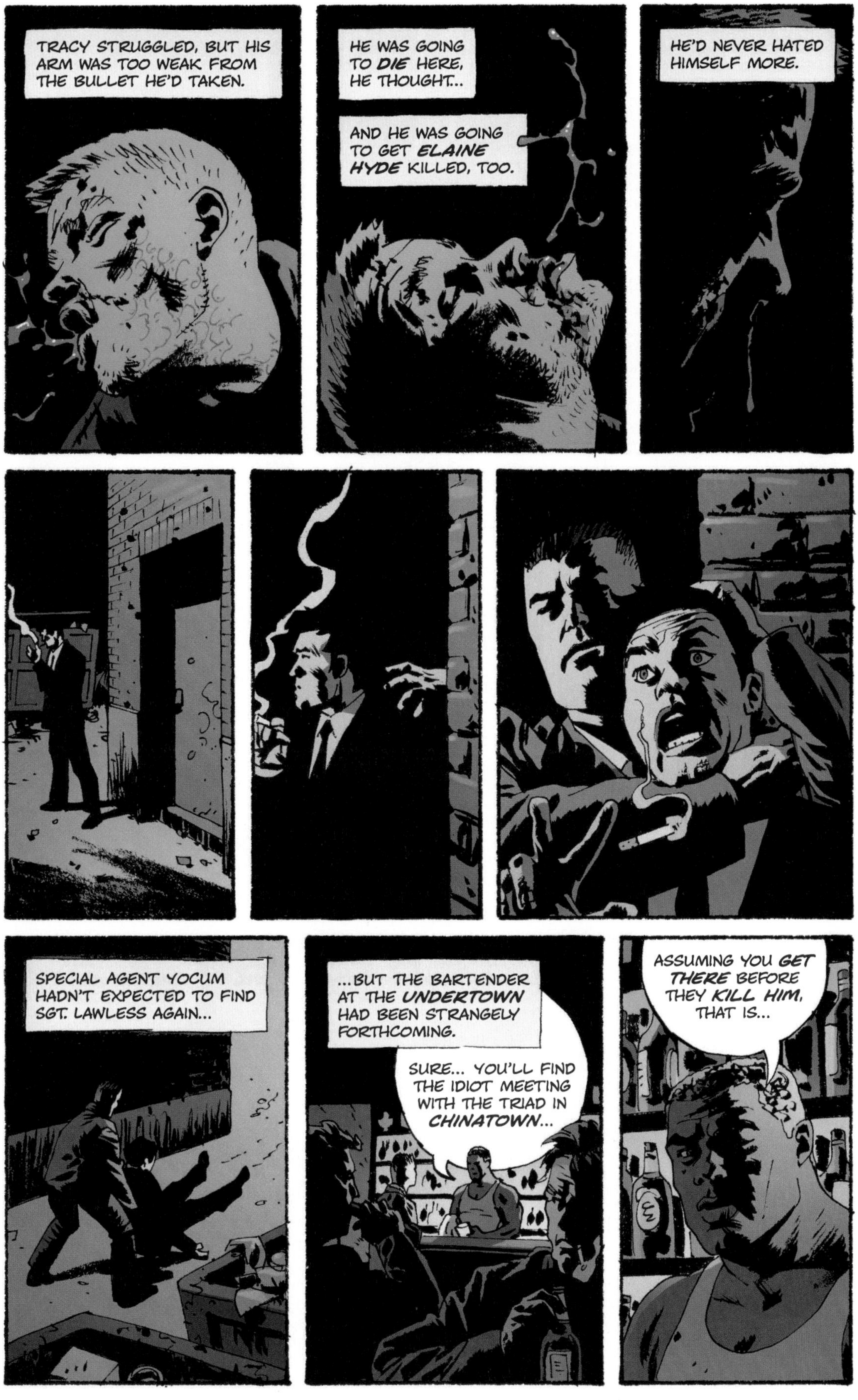
TRACY STRUGGLED, BUT HIS ARM WAS TOO WEAK FROM THE BULLET HE'D TAKEN.
HE WAS GOING TO *DIE* HERE, HE THOUGHT...
AND HE WAS GOING TO GET *ELAINE HYDE* KILLED, TOO.
HE'D NEVER HATED HIMSELF MORE.
SPECIAL AGENT YOCUM HADN'T EXPECTED TO FIND SGT. LAWLESS AGAIN...
...BUT THE BARTENDER AT THE *UNDERTOWN* HAD BEEN STRANGELY FORTHCOMING.
SURE... YOU'LL FIND THE IDIOT MEETING WITH THE TRIAD IN *CHINATOWN*...
ASSUMING YOU *GET THERE* BEFORE THEY *KILL HIM*, THAT IS...

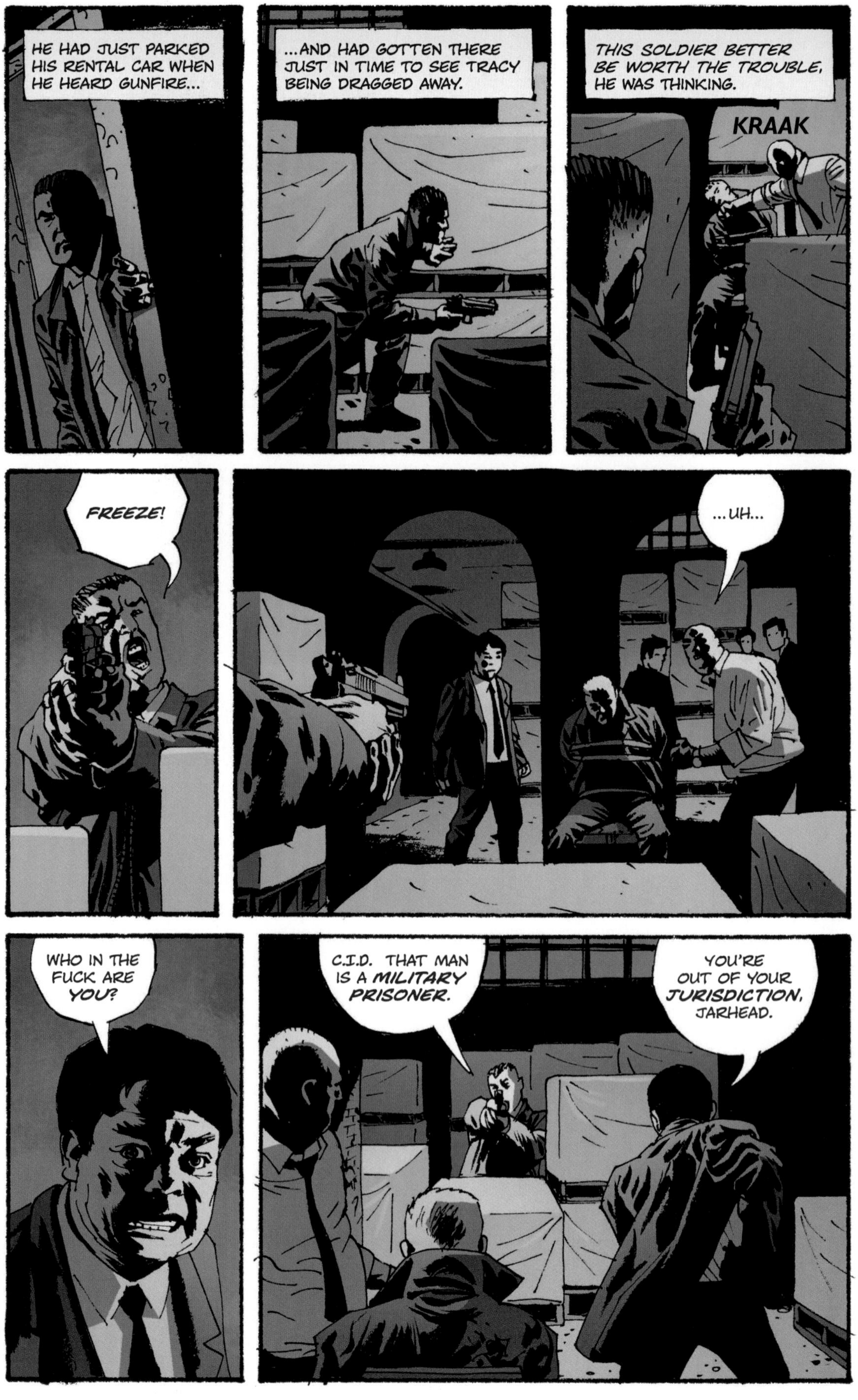
HE HAD JUST PARKED HIS RENTAL CAR WHEN HE HEARD GUNFIRE...
...AND HAD GOTTEN THERE JUST IN TIME TO SEE TRACY BEING DRAGGED AWAY.
THIS SOLDIER BETTER BE WORTH THE TROUBLE, HE WAS THINKING.
KRAAK
FREEZE!
...UH...
WHO IN THE FUCK ARE YOU?
C.I.D. THAT MAN IS A MILITARY PRISONER.
YOU'RE OUT OF YOUR JURISDICTION, JARHEAD.

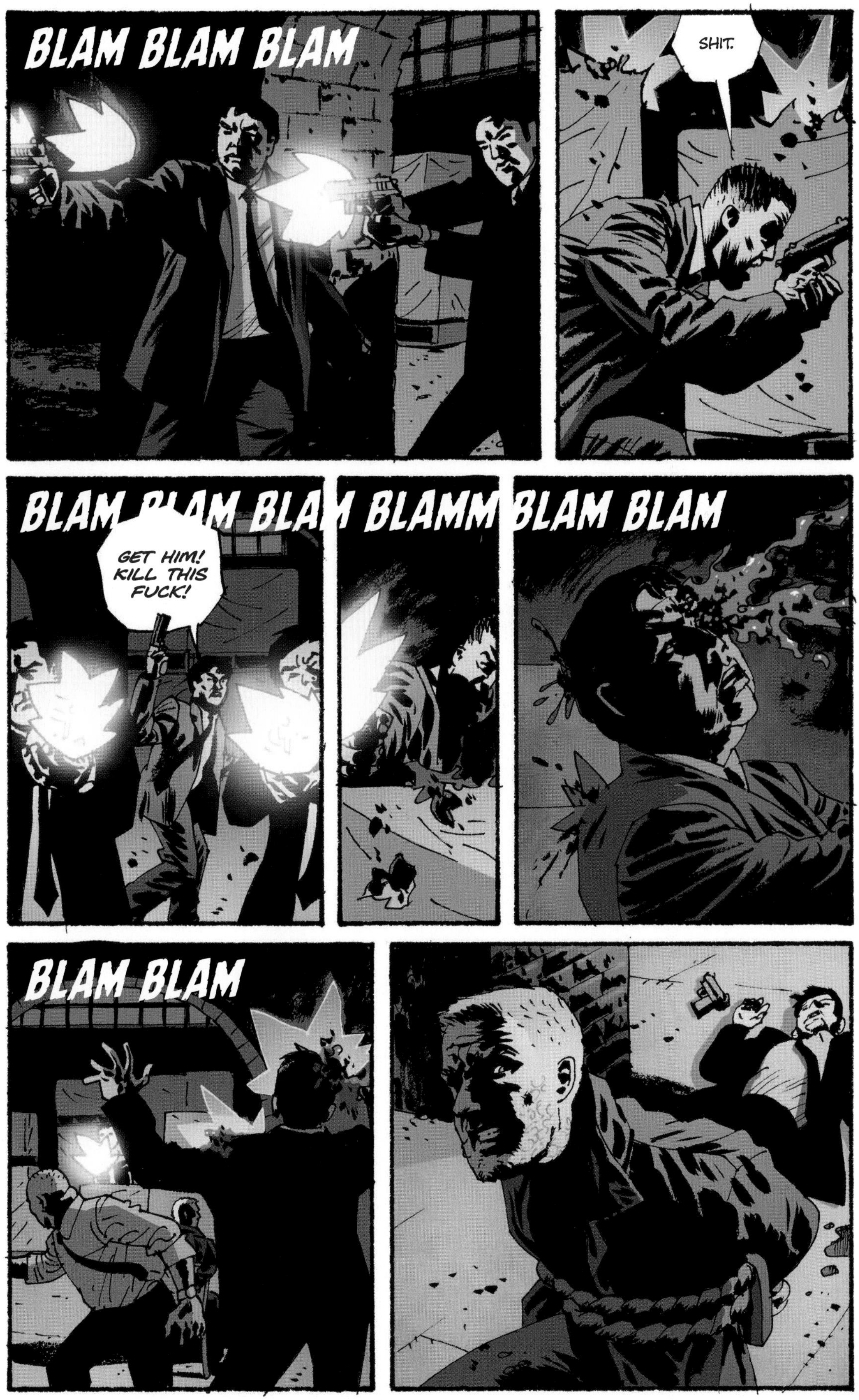
BLAM BLAM BLAM
SHIT.
BLAM BLAM BLAM BLAMM BLAM BLAM
GET HIM! KILL THIS FUCK!
BLAM BLAM

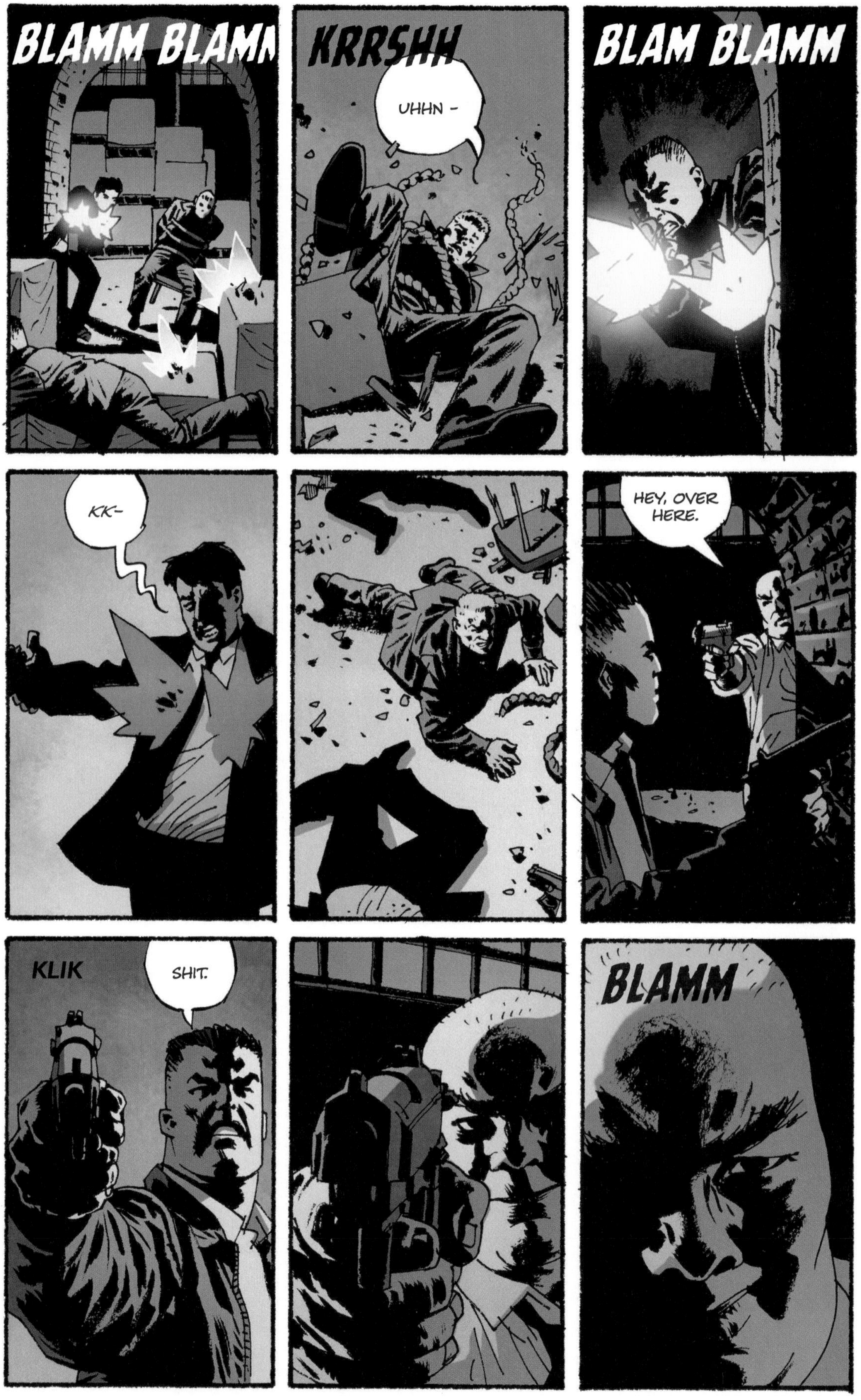
BLAMM BLAMM
KRRSHH
UHHN -
BLAM BLAMM
KK-
HEY, OVER HERE.
KLIK
SHIT.
BLAMM

...YOU'RE WELCOME...

AND YOU'RE UNDER ARREST...

NO... NOT RIGHT NOW, I'M NOT...

I DON'T THINK YOU COULD PULL THAT TRIGGER AGAIN EVEN IF YOU **WANTED TO**, LAWLESS.

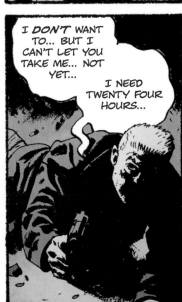

I **DON'T** WANT TO... BUT I CAN'T LET YOU TAKE ME... NOT YET...

I NEED TWENTY FOUR HOURS...

WHAT? NO WAY IN HELL.

TWENTY FOUR HOURS... **THEN** YOU CAN ARREST ME.

C'MON... DON'T BE A **DICK**, SOLDIER...

...THERE'S A WOMAN'S **LIFE** AT STAKE...

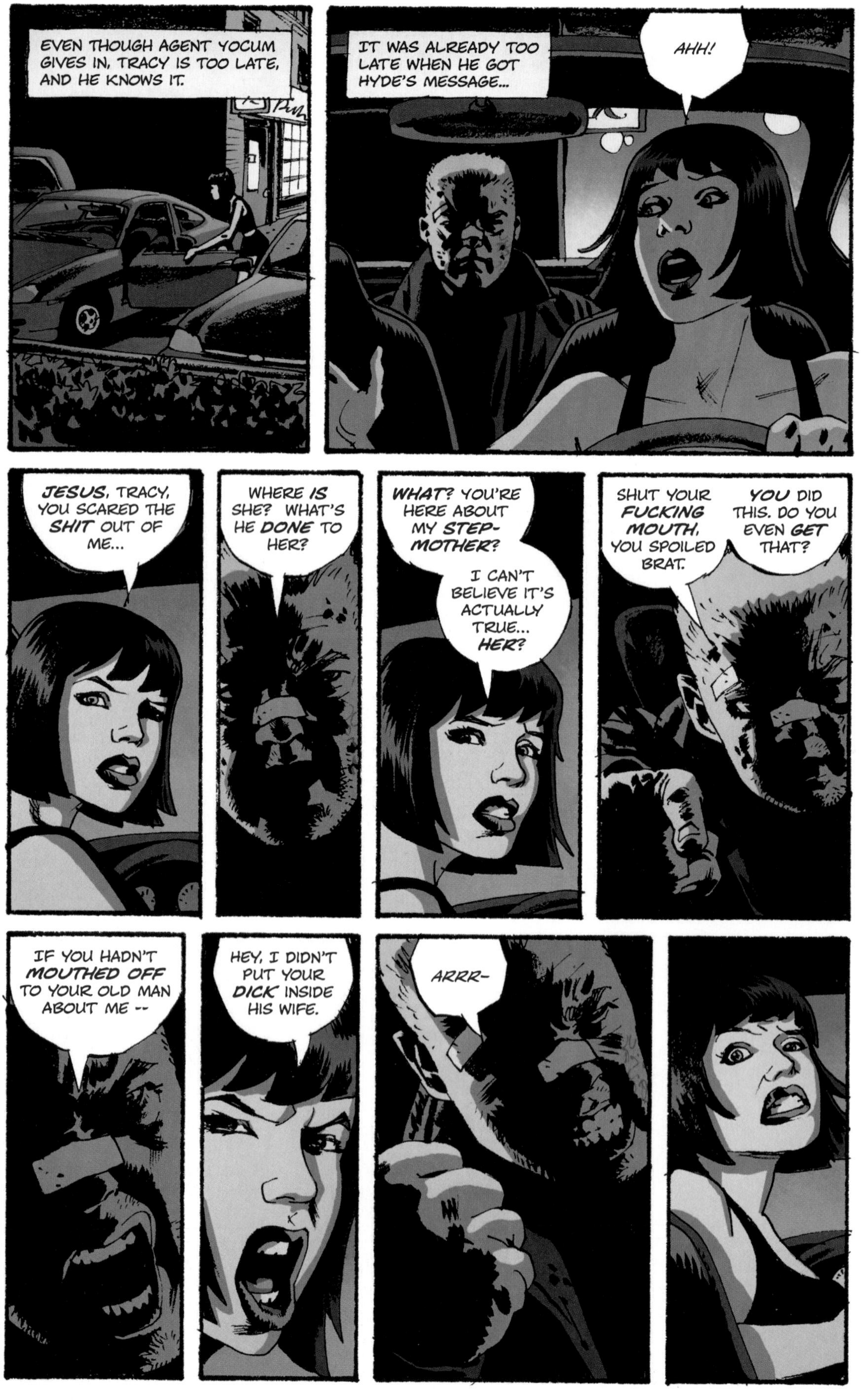
EVEN THOUGH AGENT YOCUM GIVES IN, TRACY IS TOO LATE, AND HE KNOWS IT.
IT WAS ALREADY TOO LATE WHEN HE GOT HYDE'S MESSAGE...
AHH!
JESUS, TRACY, YOU SCARED THE SHIT OUT OF ME...
WHERE IS SHE? WHAT'S HE DONE TO HER?
WHAT? YOU'RE HERE ABOUT MY STEP-MOTHER?
I CAN'T BELIEVE IT'S ACTUALLY TRUE... HER?
SHUT YOUR FUCKING MOUTH, YOU SPOILED BRAT.
YOU DID THIS. DO YOU EVEN GET THAT?
IF YOU HADN'T MOUTHED OFF TO YOUR OLD MAN ABOUT ME --
HEY, I DIDN'T PUT YOUR DICK INSIDE HIS WIFE.
ARRR-

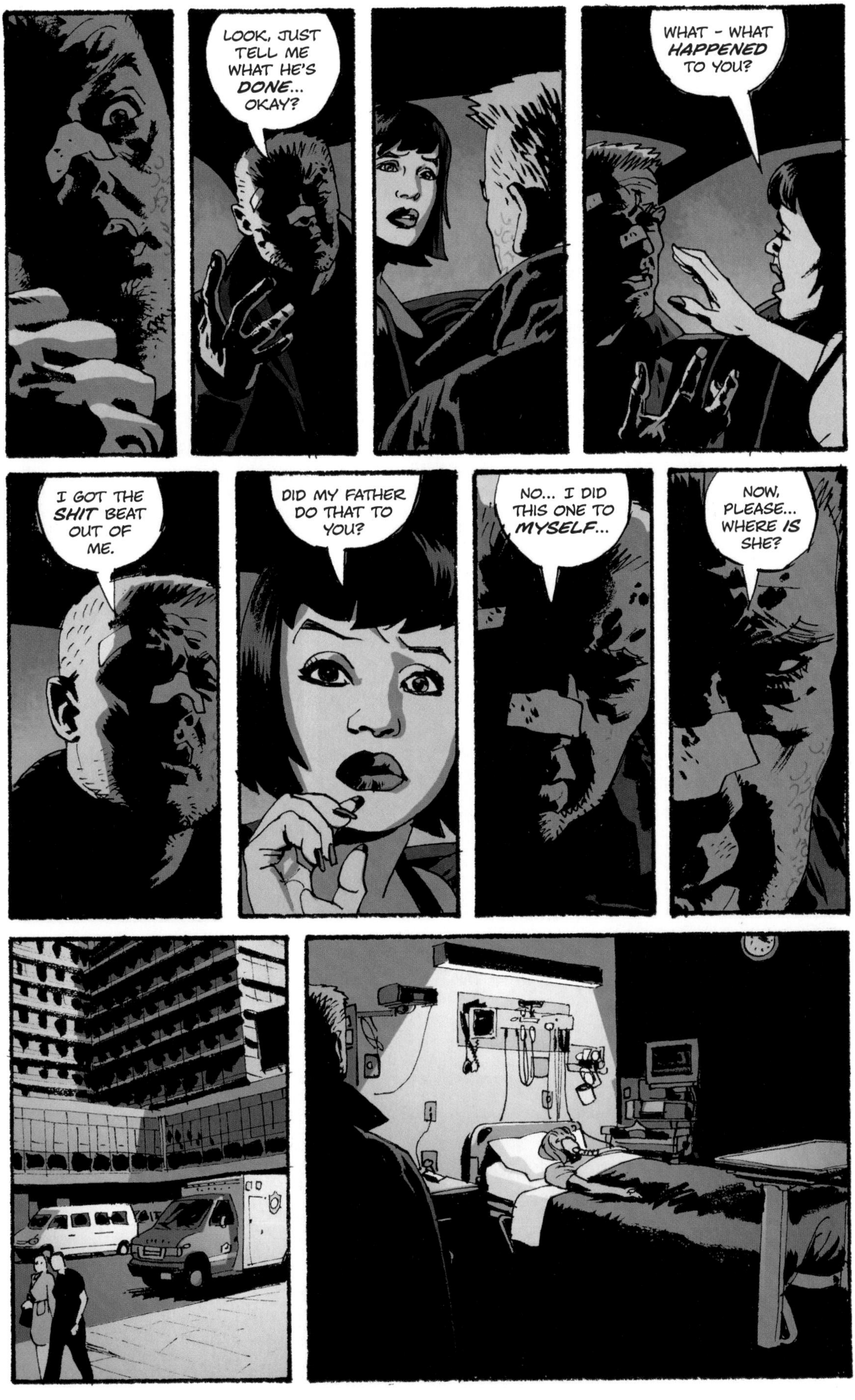

LOOK, JUST TELL ME WHAT HE'S DONE... OKAY?
WHAT - WHAT HAPPENED TO YOU?
I GOT THE SHIT BEAT OUT OF ME.
DID MY FATHER DO THAT TO YOU?
NO... I DID THIS ONE TO MYSELF...
NOW, PLEASE... WHERE IS SHE?

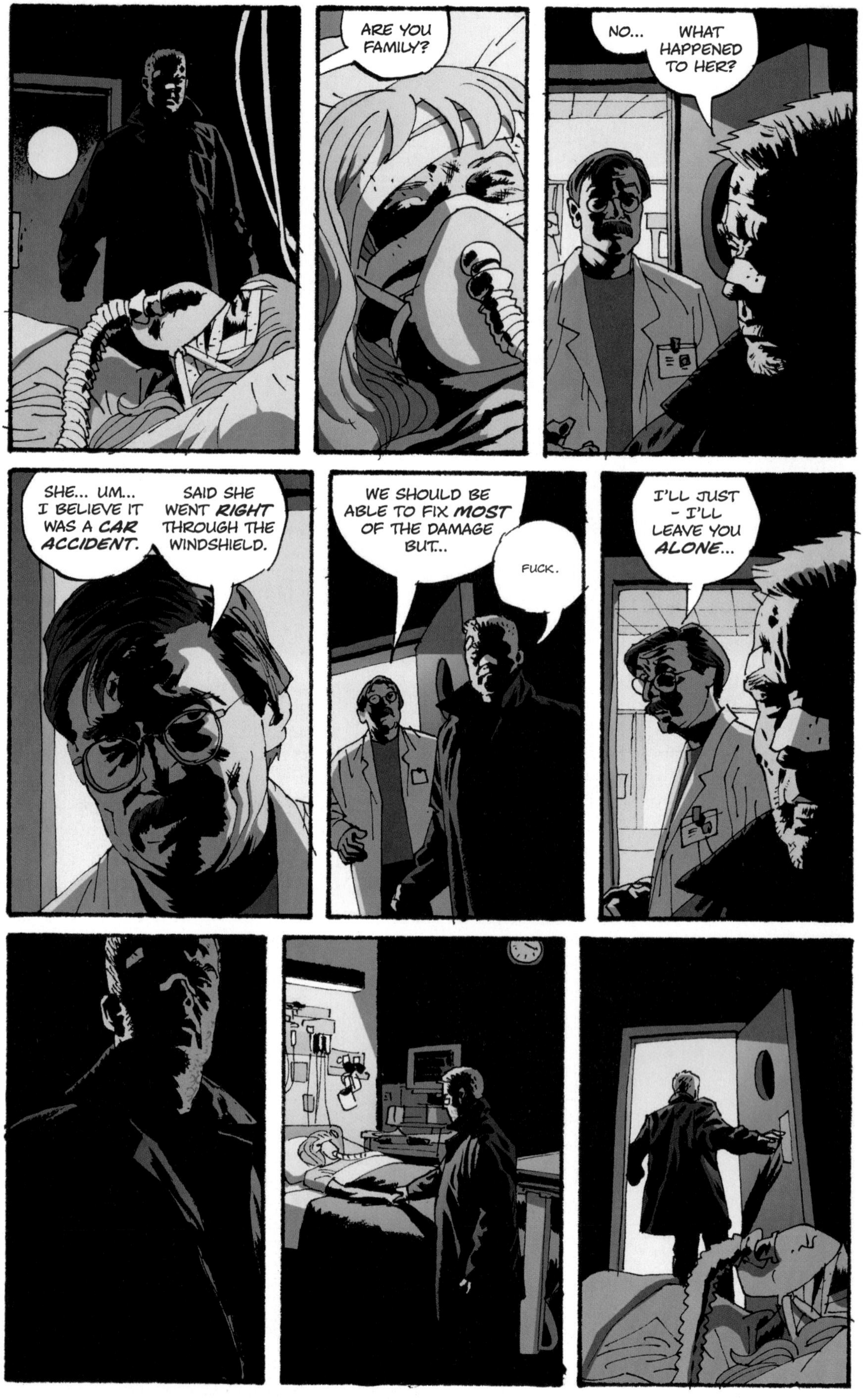
ARE YOU FAMILY?
NO...
WHAT HAPPENED TO HER?
SHE... UM... I BELIEVE IT WAS A CAR ACCIDENT.
SAID SHE WENT RIGHT THROUGH THE WINDSHIELD.
WE SHOULD BE ABLE TO FIX MOST OF THE DAMAGE BUT...
FUCK.
I'LL JUST - I'LL LEAVE YOU ALONE...

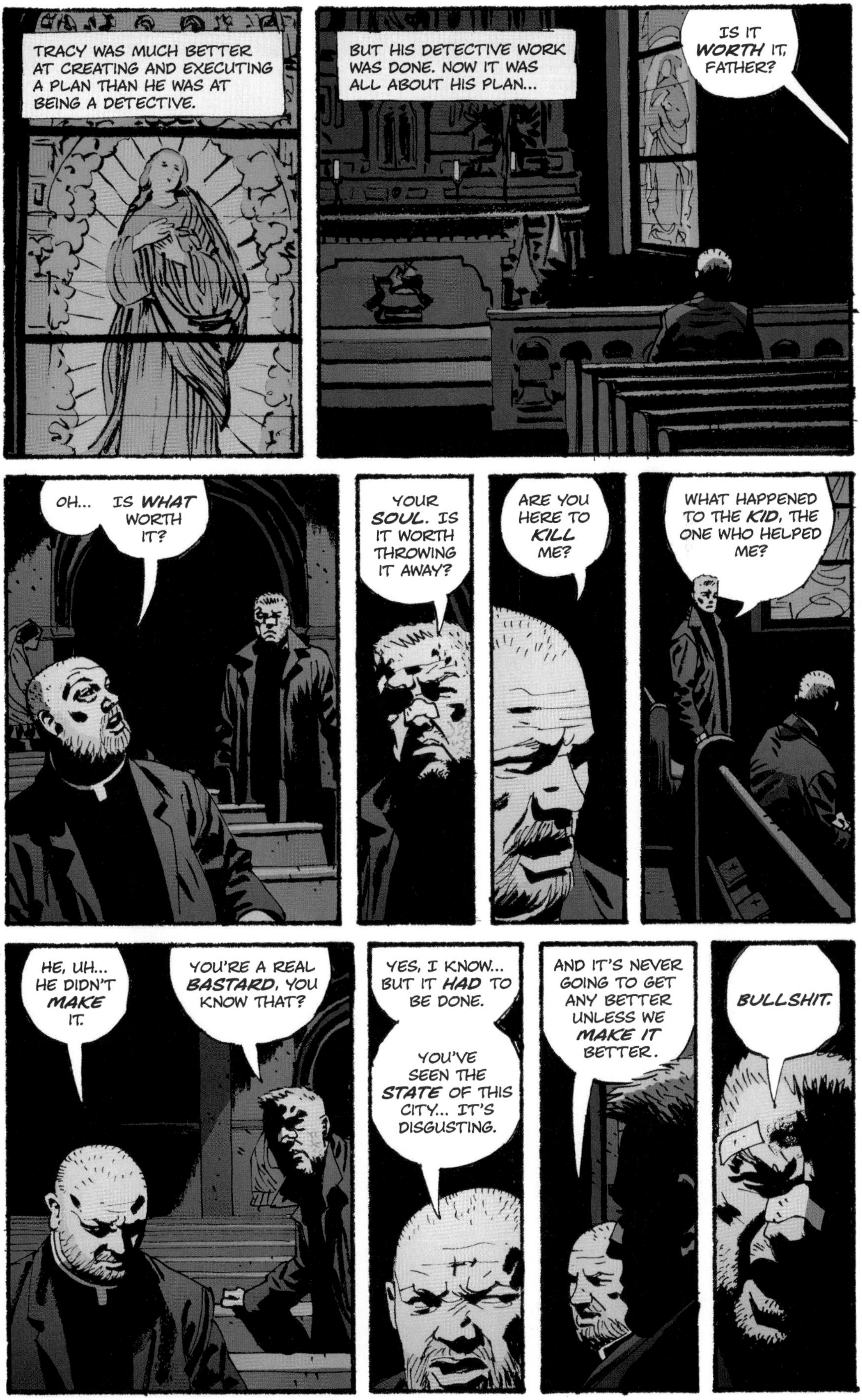
TRACY WAS MUCH BETTER AT CREATING AND EXECUTING A PLAN THAN HE WAS AT BEING A DETECTIVE.
BUT HIS DETECTIVE WORK WAS DONE. NOW IT WAS ALL ABOUT HIS PLAN...
IS IT WORTH IT, FATHER?
OH... IS WHAT WORTH IT?
YOUR SOUL. IS IT WORTH THROWING IT AWAY?
ARE YOU HERE TO KILL ME?
WHAT HAPPENED TO THE KID, THE ONE WHO HELPED ME?
HE, UH... HE DIDN'T MAKE IT.
YOU'RE A REAL BASTARD, YOU KNOW THAT?
YES, I KNOW... BUT IT HAD TO BE DONE.
YOU'VE SEEN THE STATE OF THIS CITY... IT'S DISGUSTING.
AND IT'S NEVER GOING TO GET ANY BETTER UNLESS WE MAKE IT BETTER.
BULLSHIT.

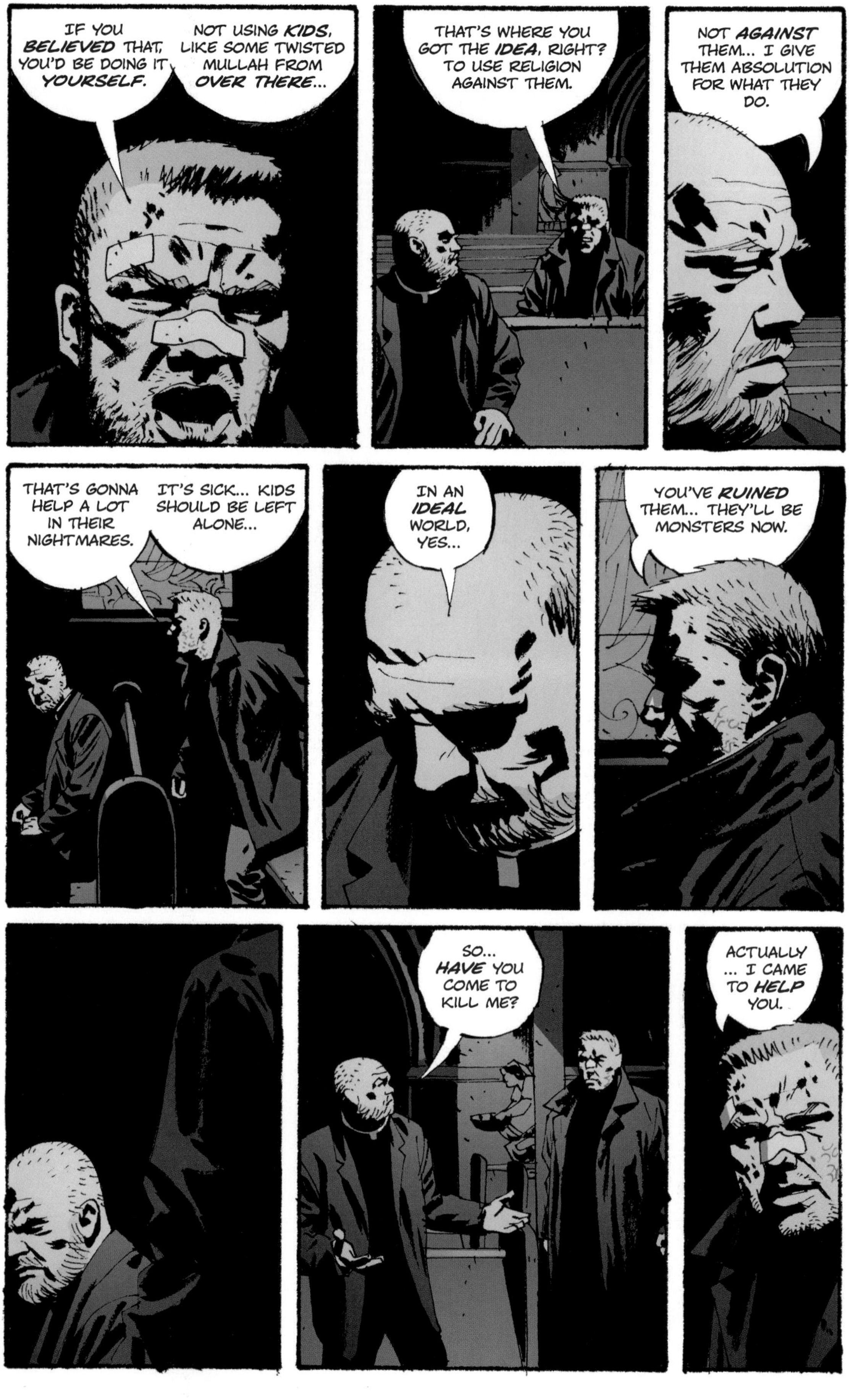
IF YOU BELIEVED THAT, YOU'D BE DOING IT YOURSELF.
NOT USING KIDS, LIKE SOME TWISTED MULLAH FROM OVER THERE...
THAT'S WHERE YOU GOT THE IDEA, RIGHT? TO USE RELIGION AGAINST THEM.
NOT AGAINST THEM... I GIVE THEM ABSOLUTION FOR WHAT THEY DO.
THAT'S GONNA HELP A LOT IN THEIR NIGHTMARES.
IT'S SICK... KIDS SHOULD BE LEFT ALONE...
IN AN IDEAL WORLD, YES...
YOU'VE RUINED THEM... THEY'LL BE MONSTERS NOW.
SO... HAVE YOU COME TO KILL ME?
ACTUALLY ... I CAME TO HELP YOU.

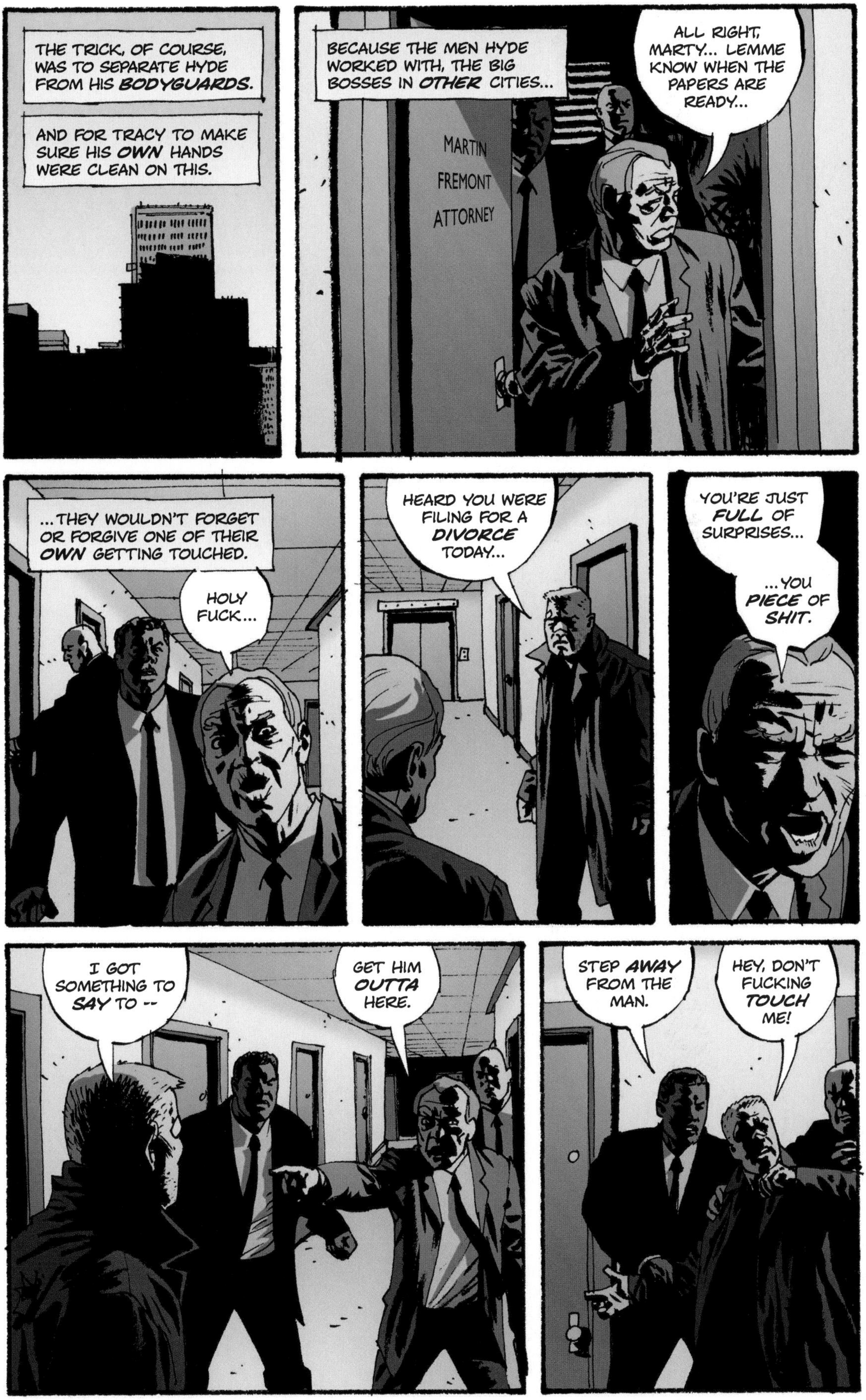
THE TRICK, OF COURSE, WAS TO SEPARATE HYDE FROM HIS BODYGUARDS.
AND FOR TRACY TO MAKE SURE HIS OWN HANDS WERE CLEAN ON THIS.
BECAUSE THE MEN HYDE WORKED WITH, THE BIG BOSSES IN OTHER CITIES...
MARTIN FREMONT ATTORNEY
ALL RIGHT, MARTY... LEMME KNOW WHEN THE PAPERS ARE READY...
...THEY WOULDN'T FORGET OR FORGIVE ONE OF THEIR OWN GETTING TOUCHED.
HOLY FUCK...
HEARD YOU WERE FILING FOR A DIVORCE TODAY...
YOU'RE JUST FULL OF SURPRISES...
...YOU PIECE OF SHIT.
I GOT SOMETHING TO SAY TO --
GET HIM OUTTA HERE.
STEP AWAY FROM THE MAN.
HEY, DON'T FUCKING TOUCH ME!

UHN!

IS THERE A PROB-

IT'S *FINE*, JUST AN ACCIDENT.

YOU'RE LUCKY WE'RE IN *PUBLIC*, LAWLESS...

I'M TRYING TO *TELL YOU* SOMETHING...

Y'KNOW, I LIKED YOU, BUT I SHOULD'VE *KNOWN* BETTER...

FIRST TIME I WANTED TO SHOOT YOUR *DAD* WAS OVER A WOMAN, TOO...

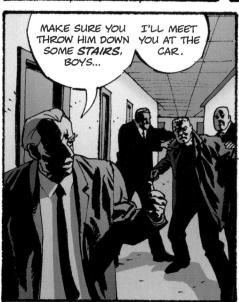

MAKE SURE YOU THROW HIM DOWN SOME *STAIRS*, BOYS...

I'LL MEET YOU AT THE CAR.

C'MON, ASSHOLE...

HOLD ON!

DON'T YOU WANNA KNOW WHO THE *KILLERS* ARE?

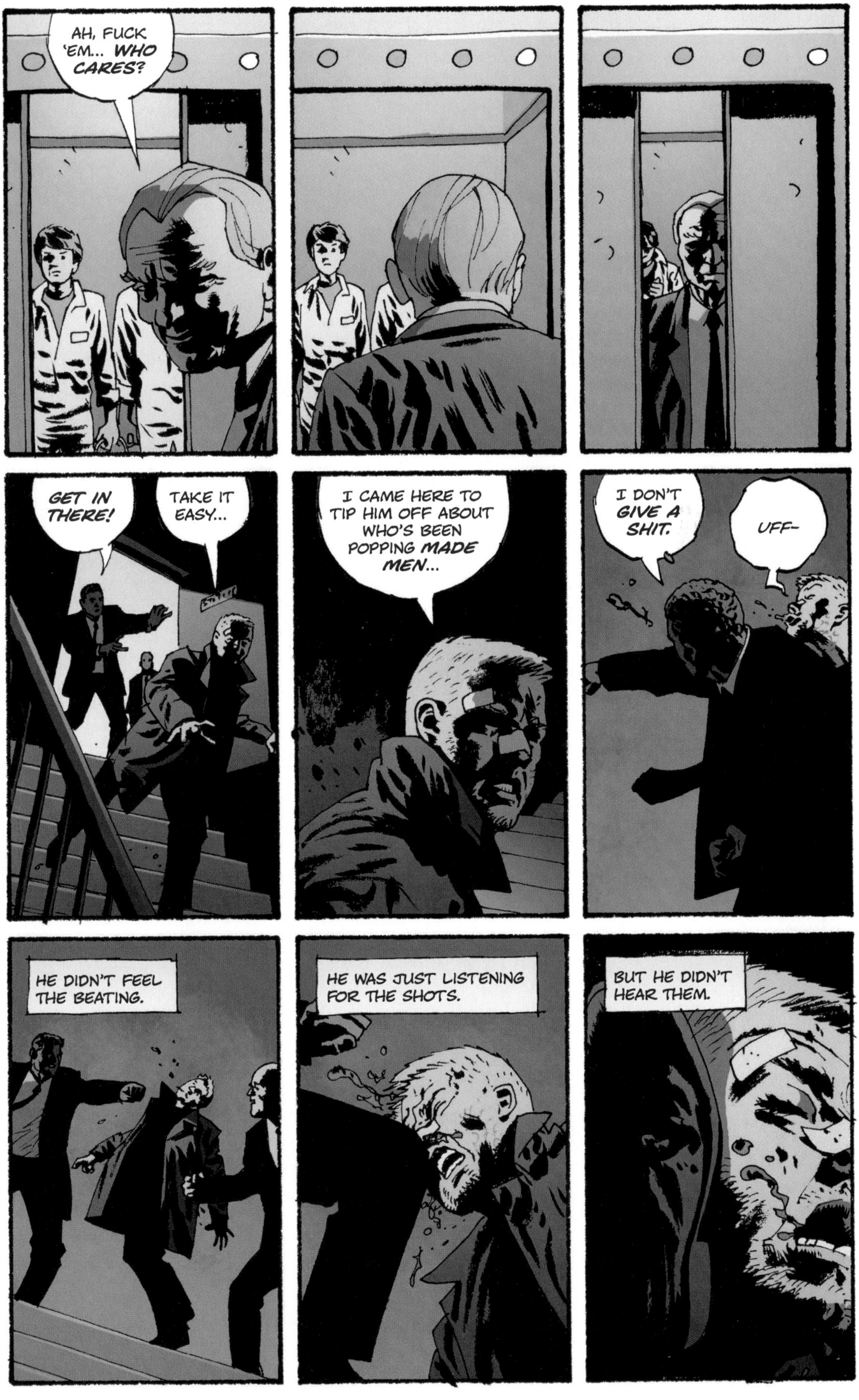
AH, FUCK 'EM... WHO CARES?
GET IN THERE!
TAKE IT EASY...
I CAME HERE TO TIP HIM OFF ABOUT WHO'S BEEN POPPING MADE MEN...
I DON'T GIVE A SHIT.
UFF-
HE DIDN'T FEEL THE BEATING.
HE WAS JUST LISTENING FOR THE SHOTS.
BUT HE DIDN'T HEAR THEM.

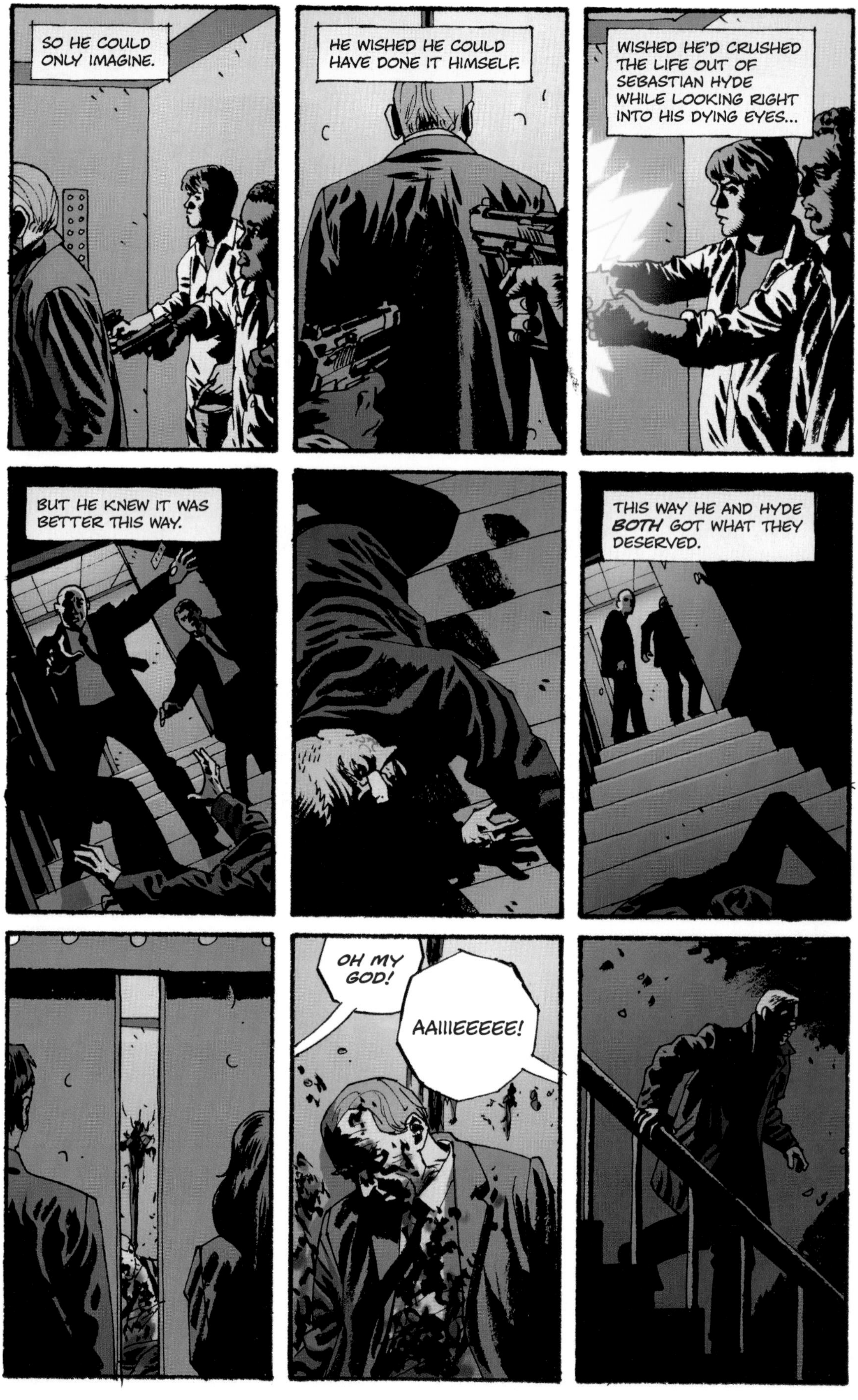
SO HE COULD ONLY IMAGINE.
HE WISHED HE COULD HAVE DONE IT HIMSELF.
WISHED HE'D CRUSHED THE LIFE OUT OF SEBASTIAN HYDE WHILE LOOKING RIGHT INTO HIS DYING EYES...
BUT HE KNEW IT WAS BETTER THIS WAY.
THIS WAY HE AND HYDE *BOTH* GOT WHAT THEY DESERVED.
OH MY GOD!
AAIIIEEEEE!

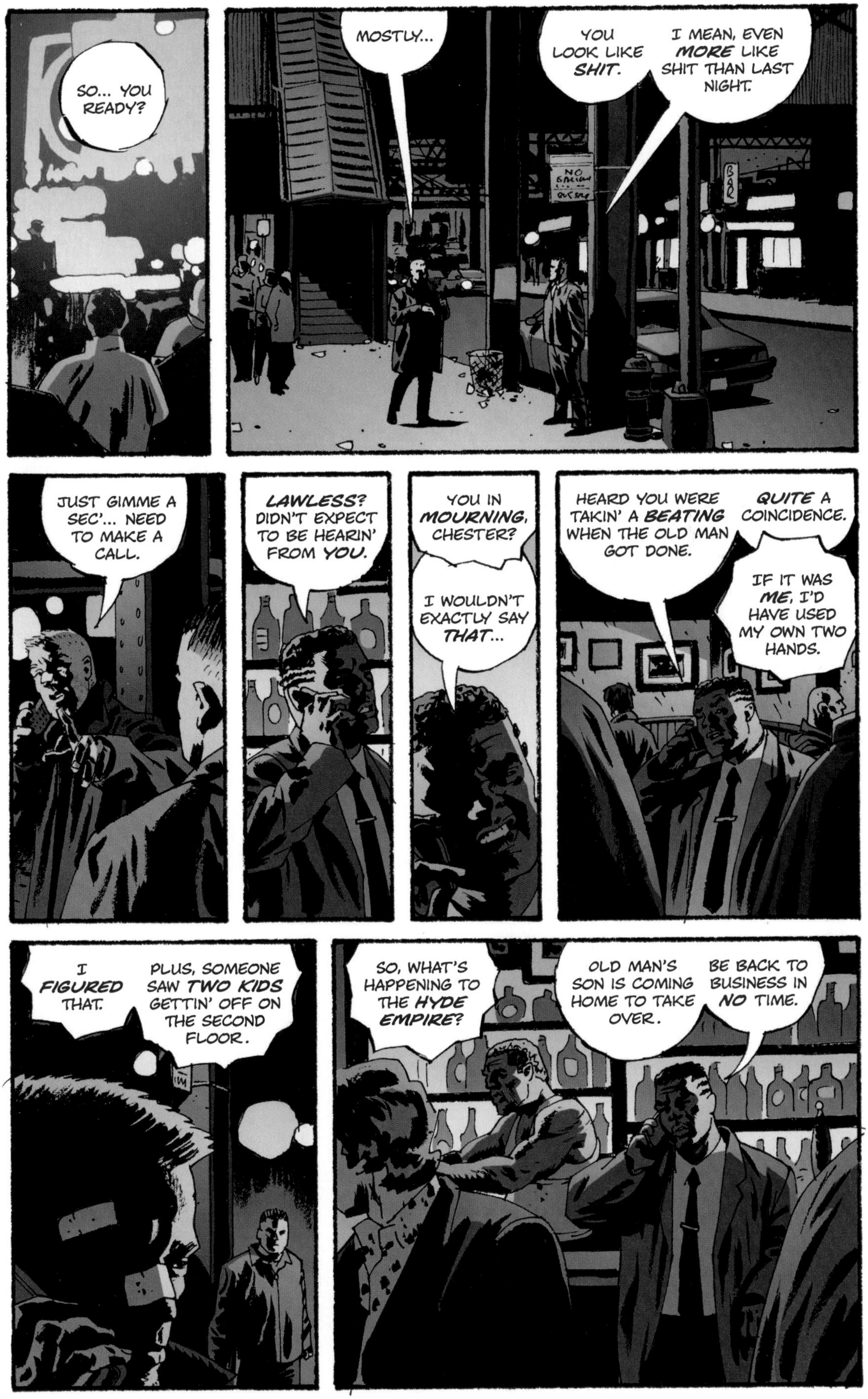
SO... YOU READY?
MOSTLY...
YOU LOOK LIKE SHIT.
I MEAN, EVEN MORE LIKE SHIT THAN LAST NIGHT.
BAR
JUST GIMME A SEC'... NEED TO MAKE A CALL.
LAWLESS? DIDN'T EXPECT TO BE HEARIN' FROM YOU.
YOU IN MOURNING, CHESTER?
I WOULDN'T EXACTLY SAY THAT...
HEARD YOU WERE TAKIN' A BEATING WHEN THE OLD MAN GOT DONE.
QUITE A COINCIDENCE.
IF IT WAS ME, I'D HAVE USED MY OWN TWO HANDS.
I FIGURED THAT.
PLUS, SOMEONE SAW TWO KIDS GETTIN' OFF ON THE SECOND FLOOR.
SO, WHAT'S HAPPENING TO THE HYDE EMPIRE?
OLD MAN'S SON IS COMING HOME TO TAKE OVER.
BE BACK TO BUSINESS IN NO TIME.

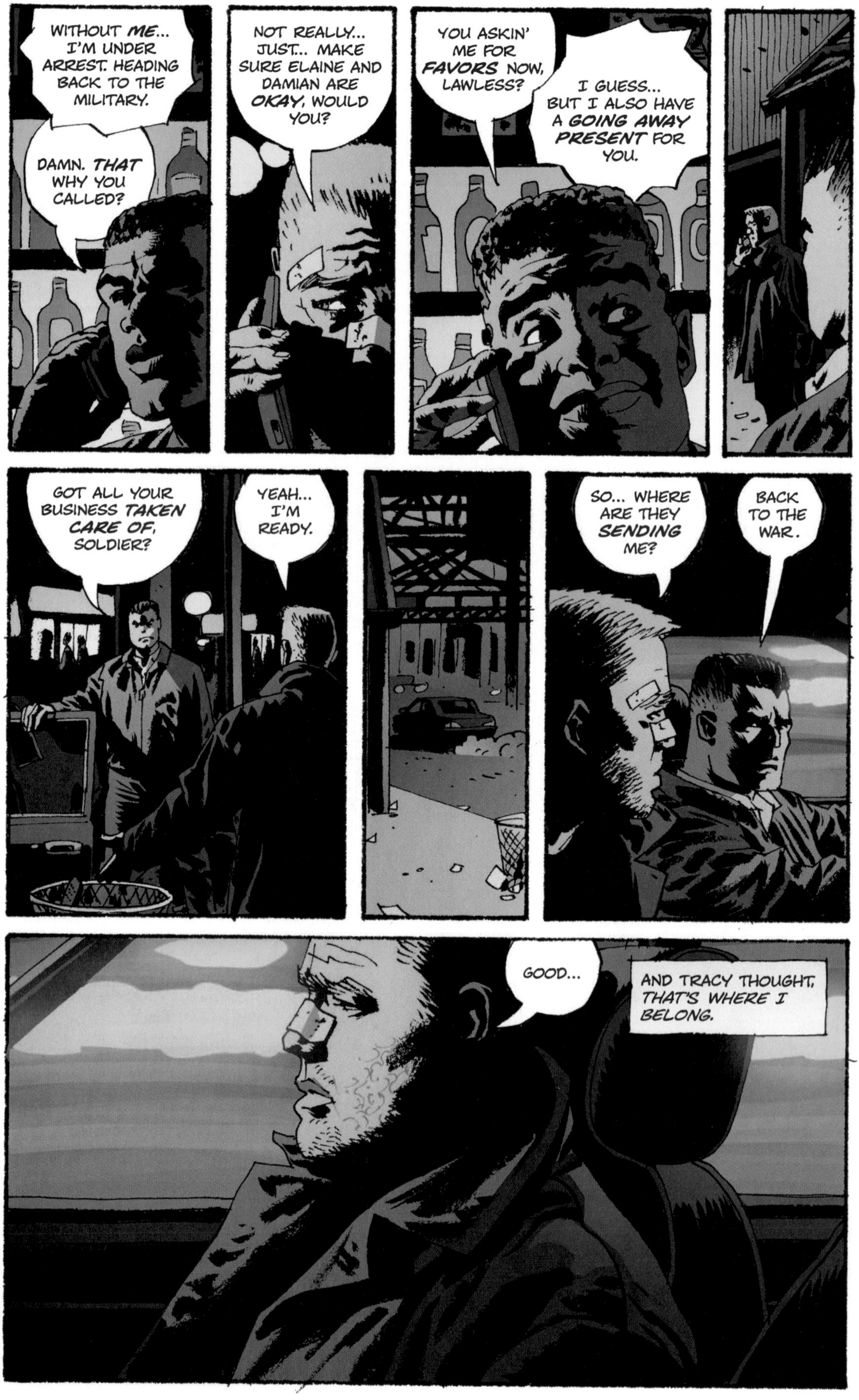
WITHOUT ME... I'M UNDER ARREST. HEADING BACK TO THE MILITARY.
DAMN. THAT WHY YOU CALLED?
NOT REALLY... JUST... MAKE SURE ELAINE AND DAMIAN ARE OKAY, WOULD YOU?
YOU ASKIN' ME FOR FAVORS NOW, LAWLESS?
I GUESS... BUT I ALSO HAVE A GOING AWAY PRESENT FOR YOU.
GOT ALL YOUR BUSINESS TAKEN CARE OF, SOLDIER?
YEAH... I'M READY.
SO... WHERE ARE THEY SENDING ME?
BACK TO THE WAR.
GOOD...
AND TRACY THOUGHT, THAT'S WHERE I BELONG.

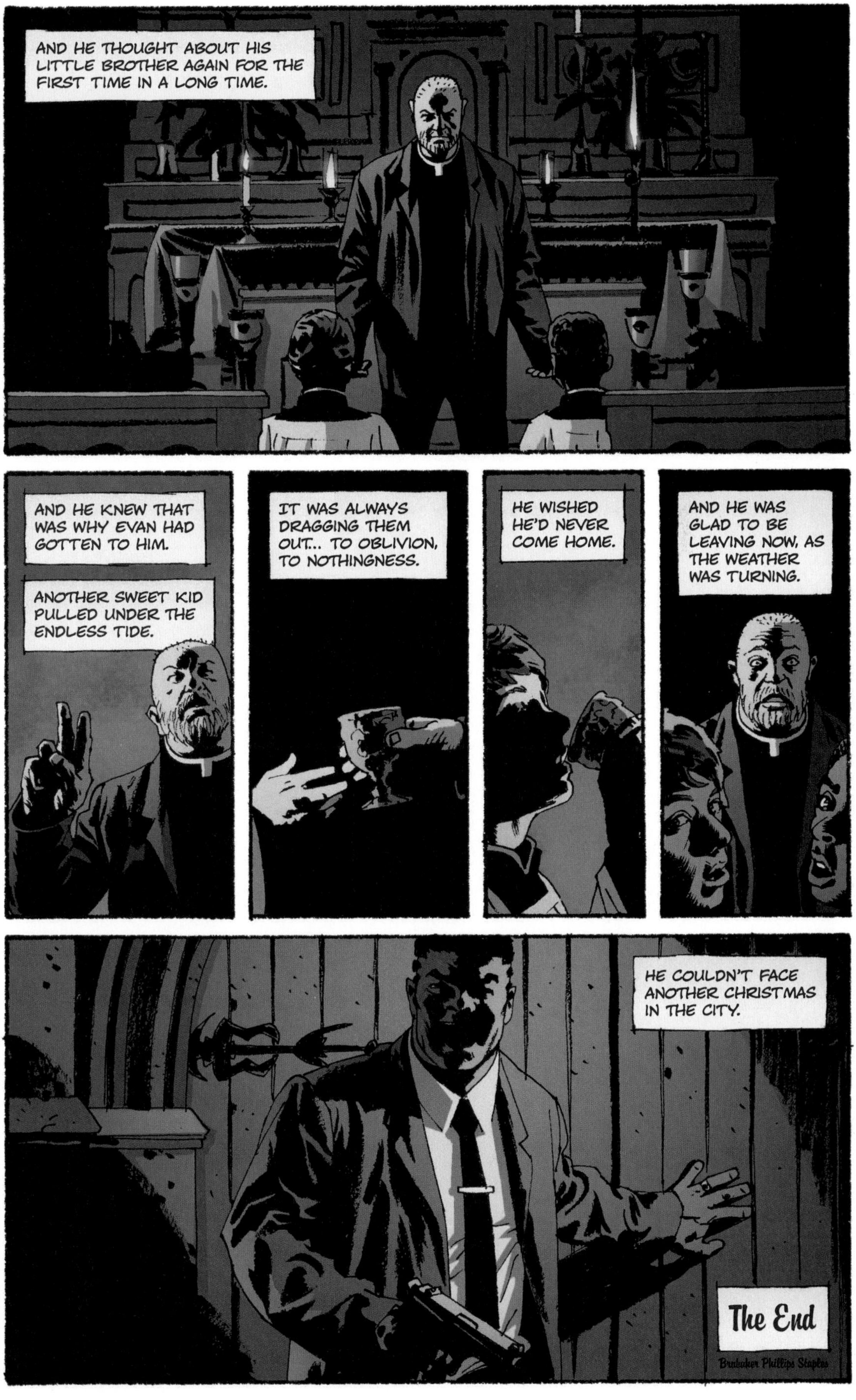
AND HE THOUGHT ABOUT HIS LITTLE BROTHER AGAIN FOR THE FIRST TIME IN A LONG TIME.
AND HE KNEW THAT WAS WHY EVAN HAD GOTTEN TO HIM.
ANOTHER SWEET KID PULLED UNDER THE ENDLESS TIDE.
IT WAS ALWAYS DRAGGING THEM OUT... TO OBLIVION, TO NOTHINGNESS.
HE WISHED HE'D NEVER COME HOME.
AND HE WAS GLAD TO BE LEAVING NOW, AS THE WEATHER WAS TURNING.
HE COULDN'T FACE ANOTHER CHRISTMAS IN THE CITY.
The End
Brubaker Phillips Staples

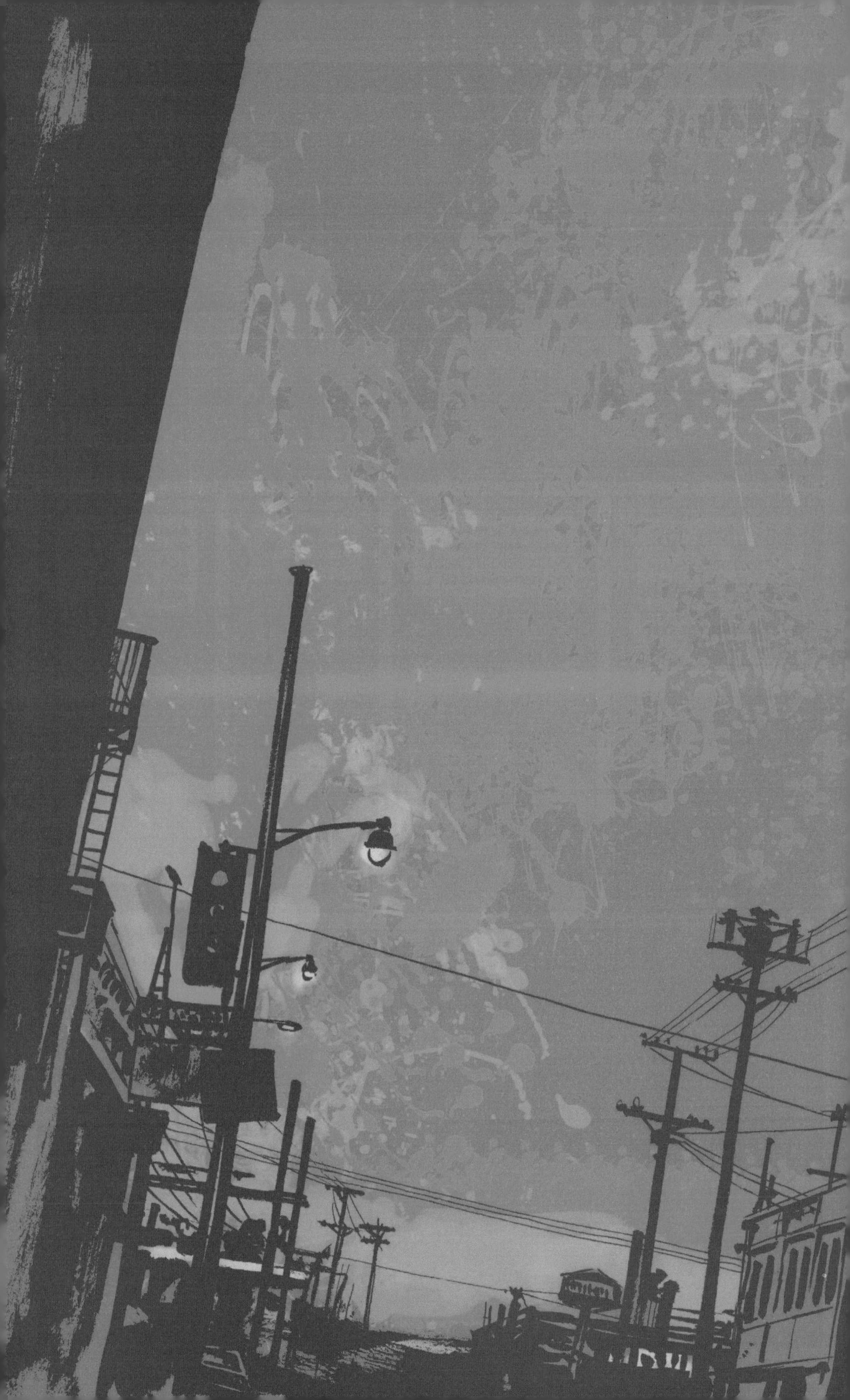

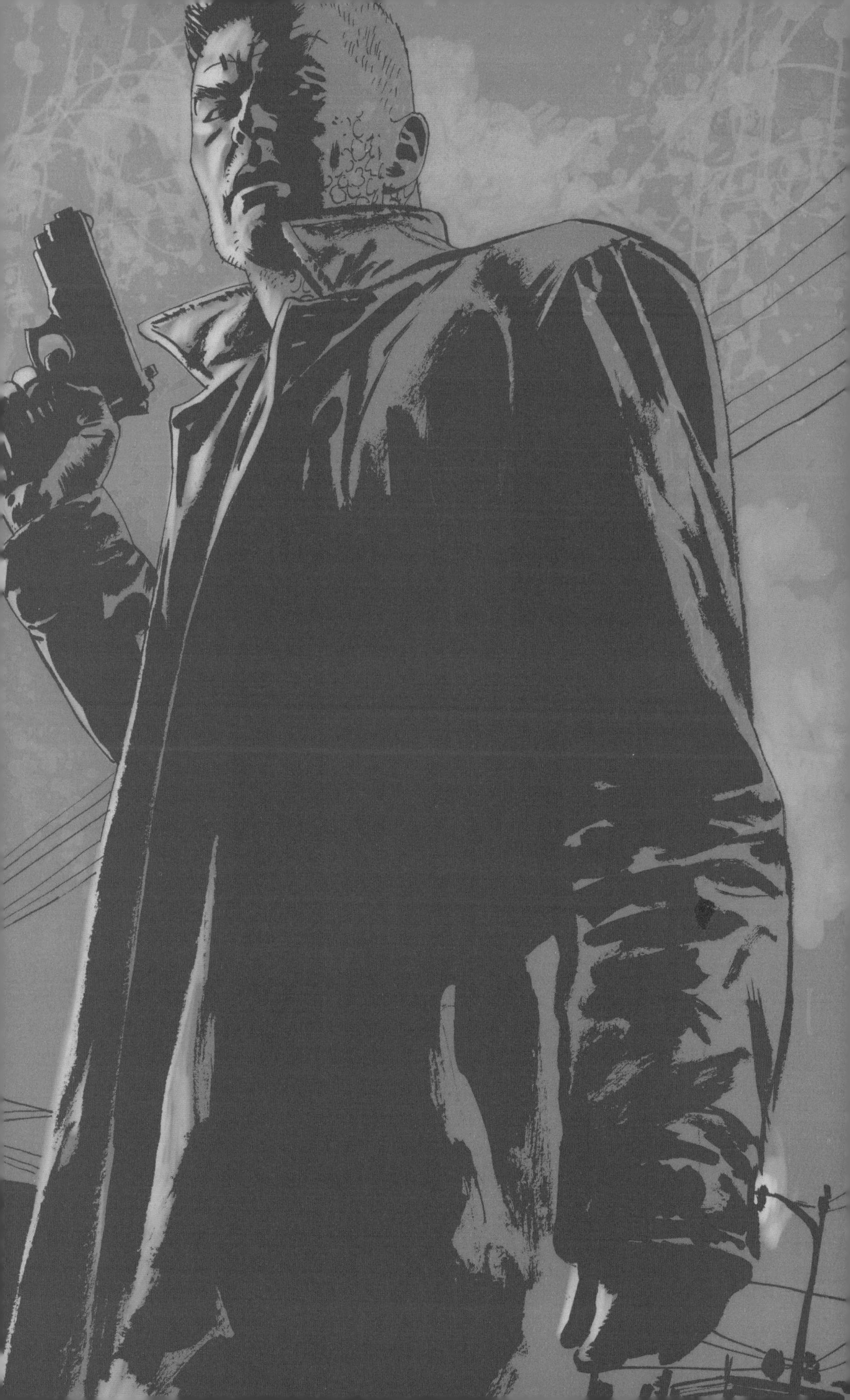

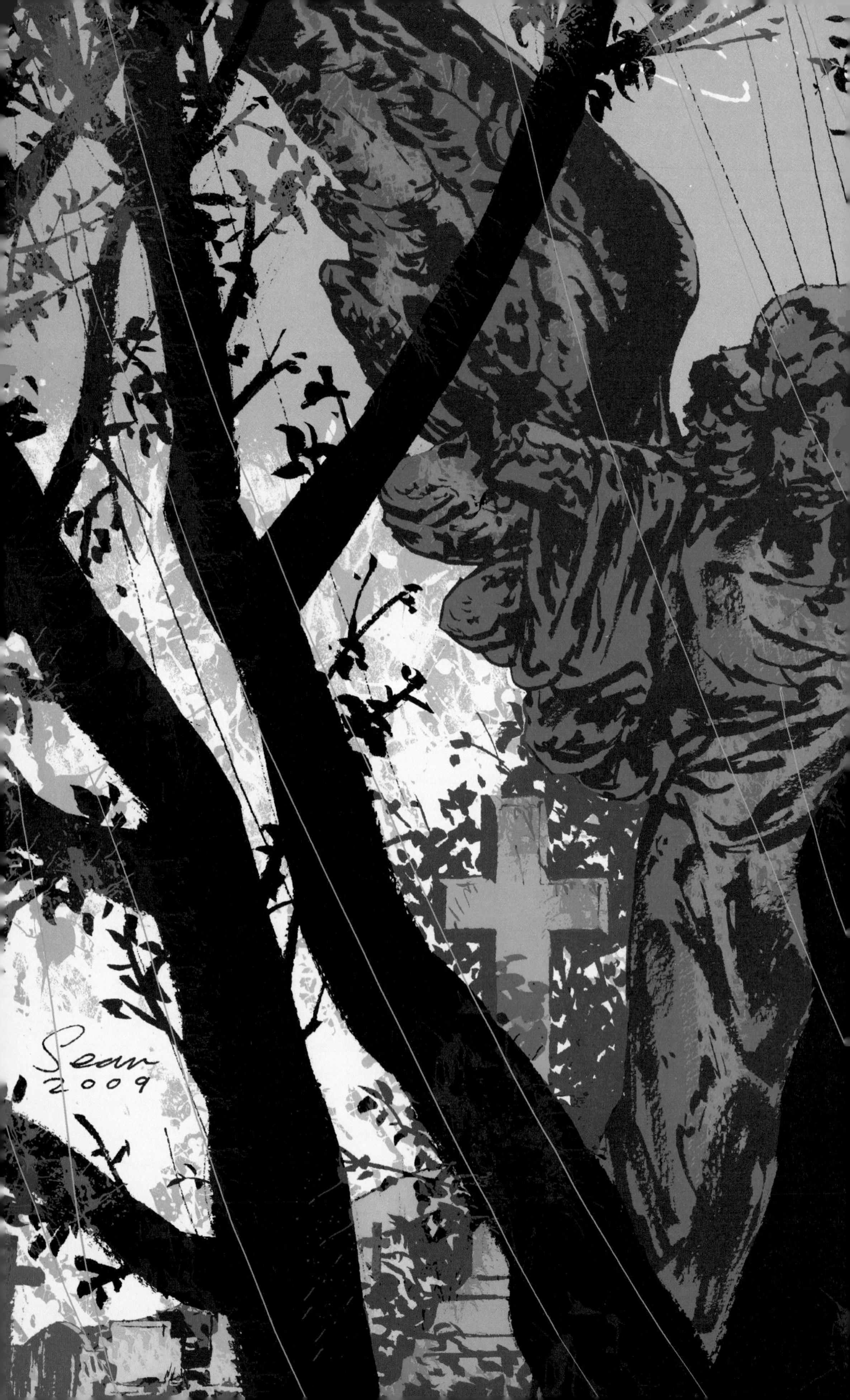
Sean
2009

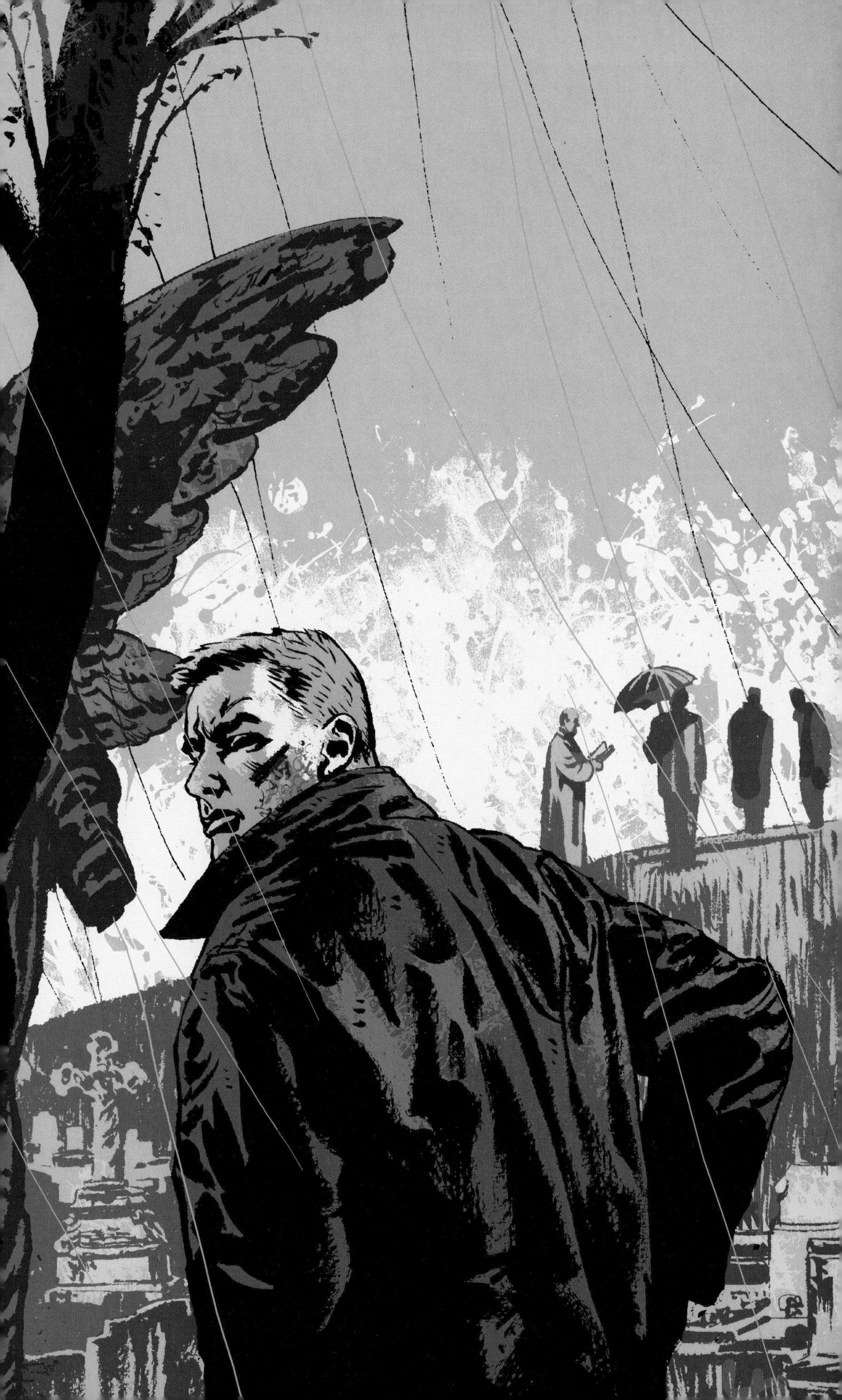

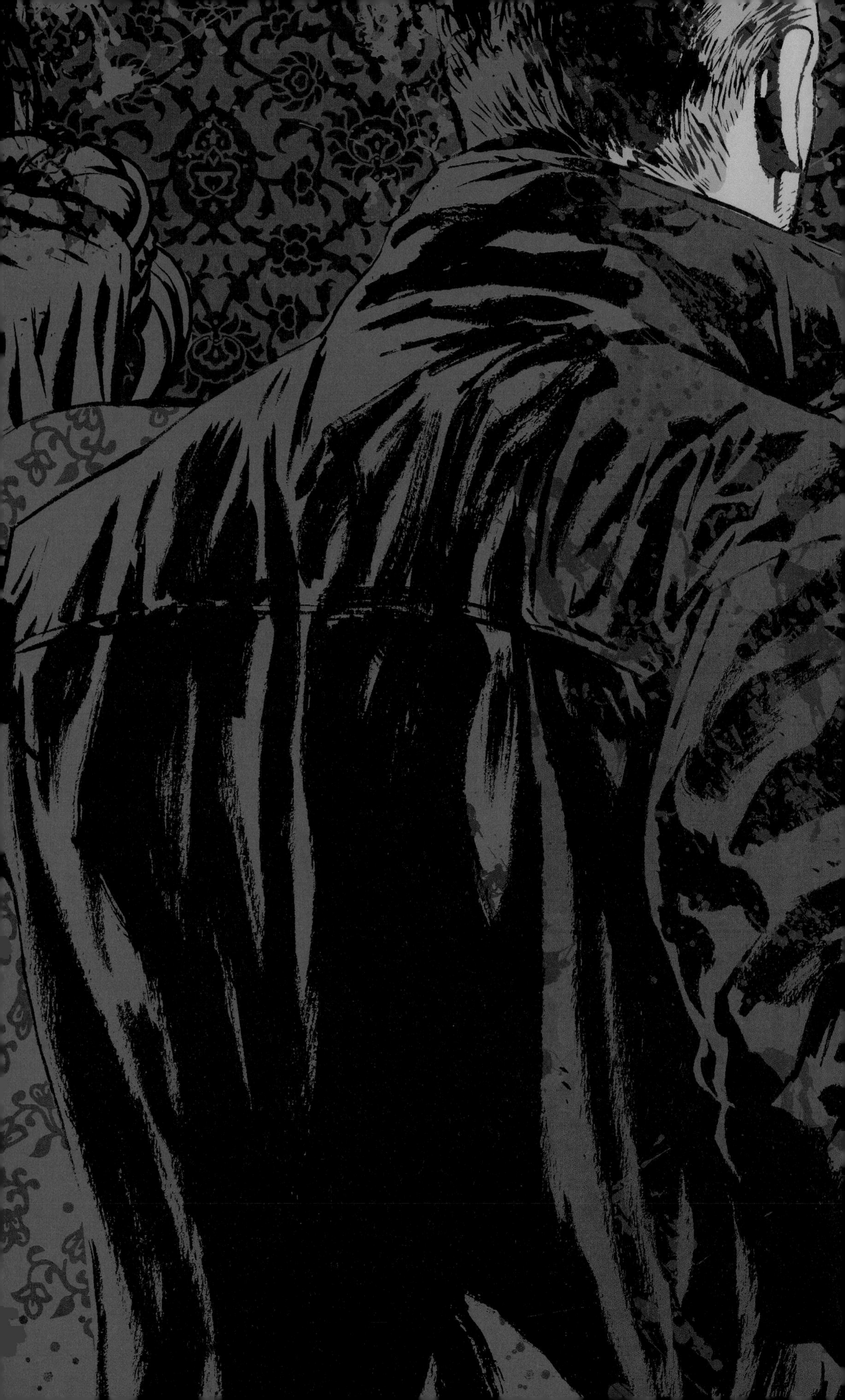

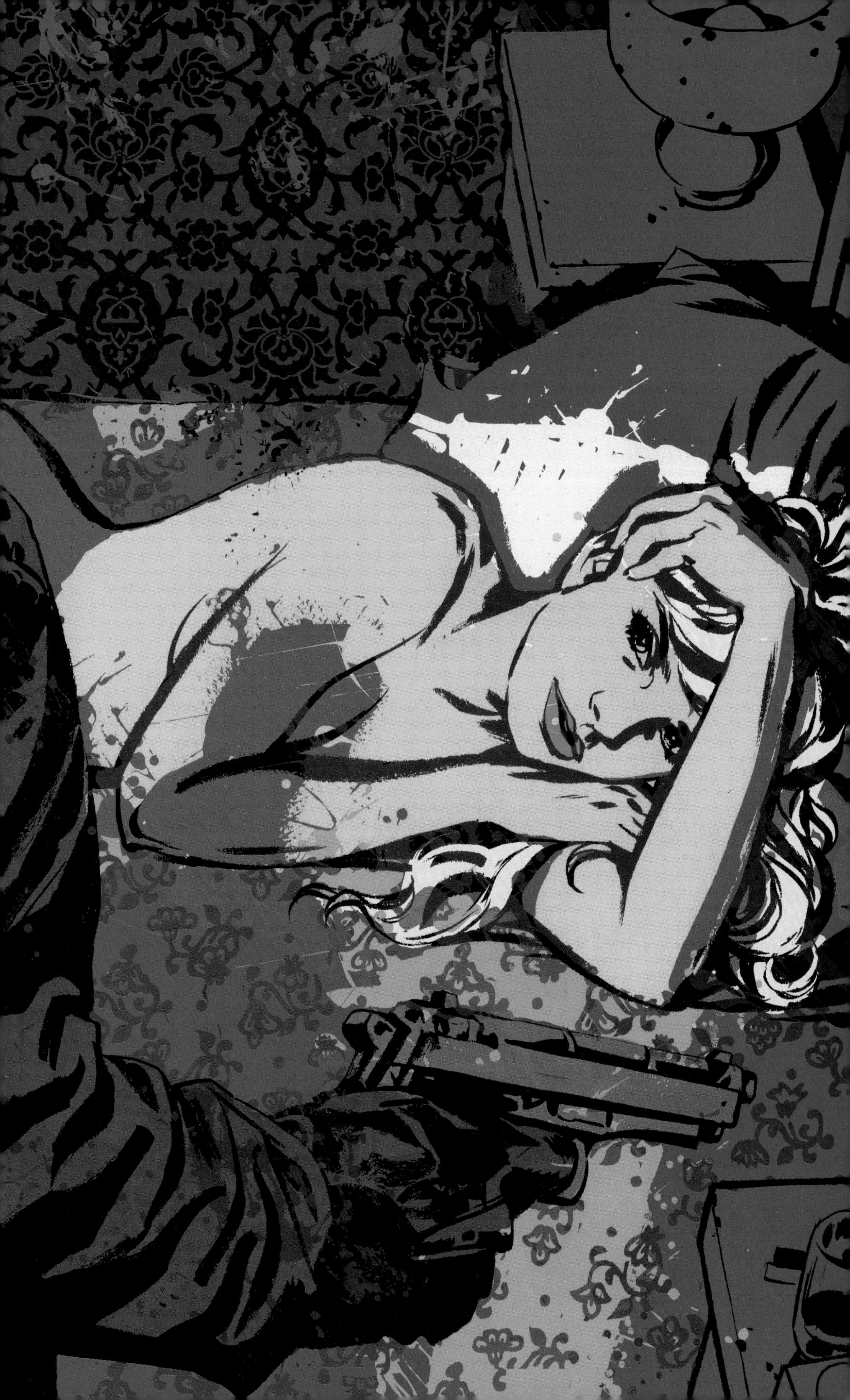

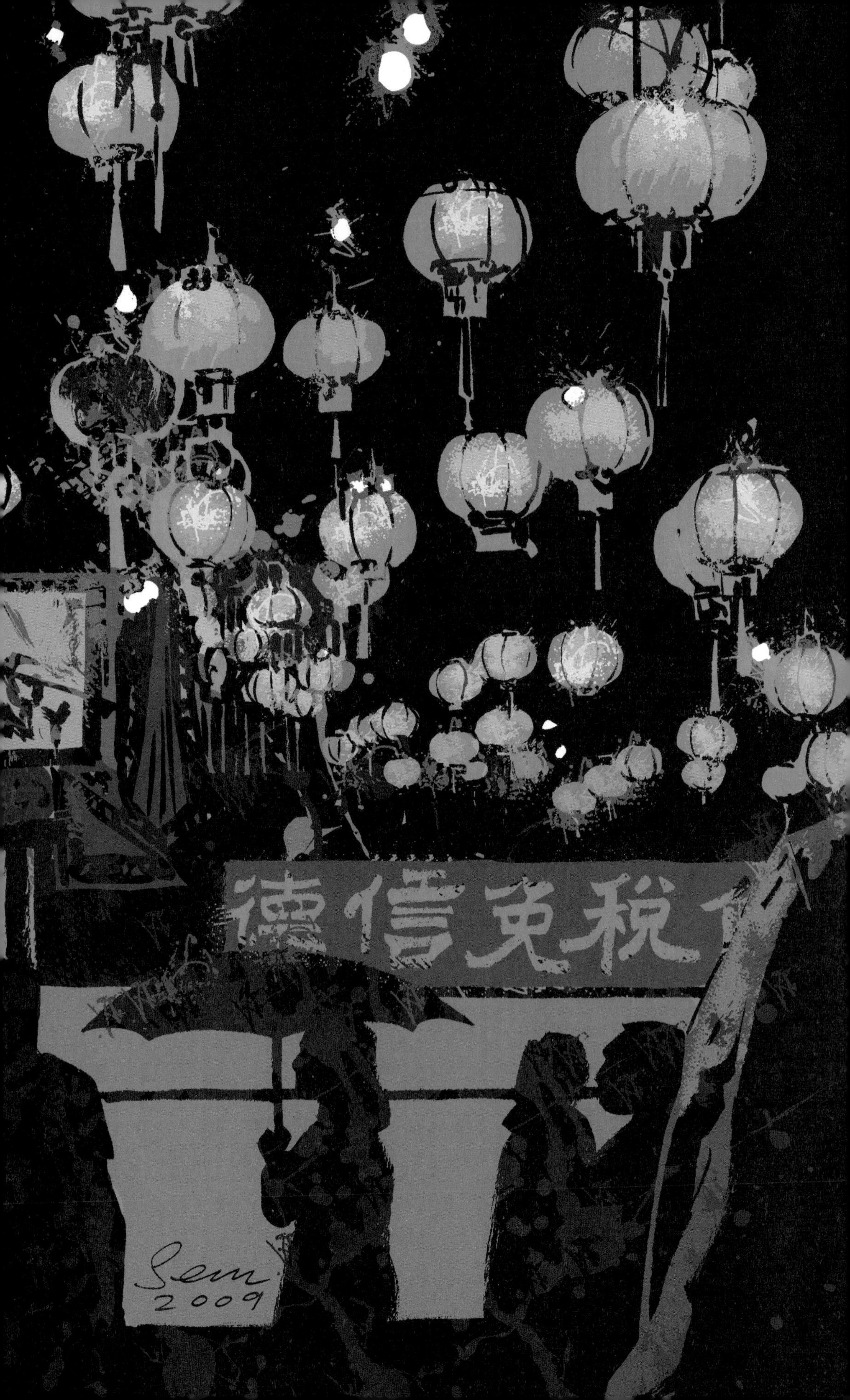
德信免税

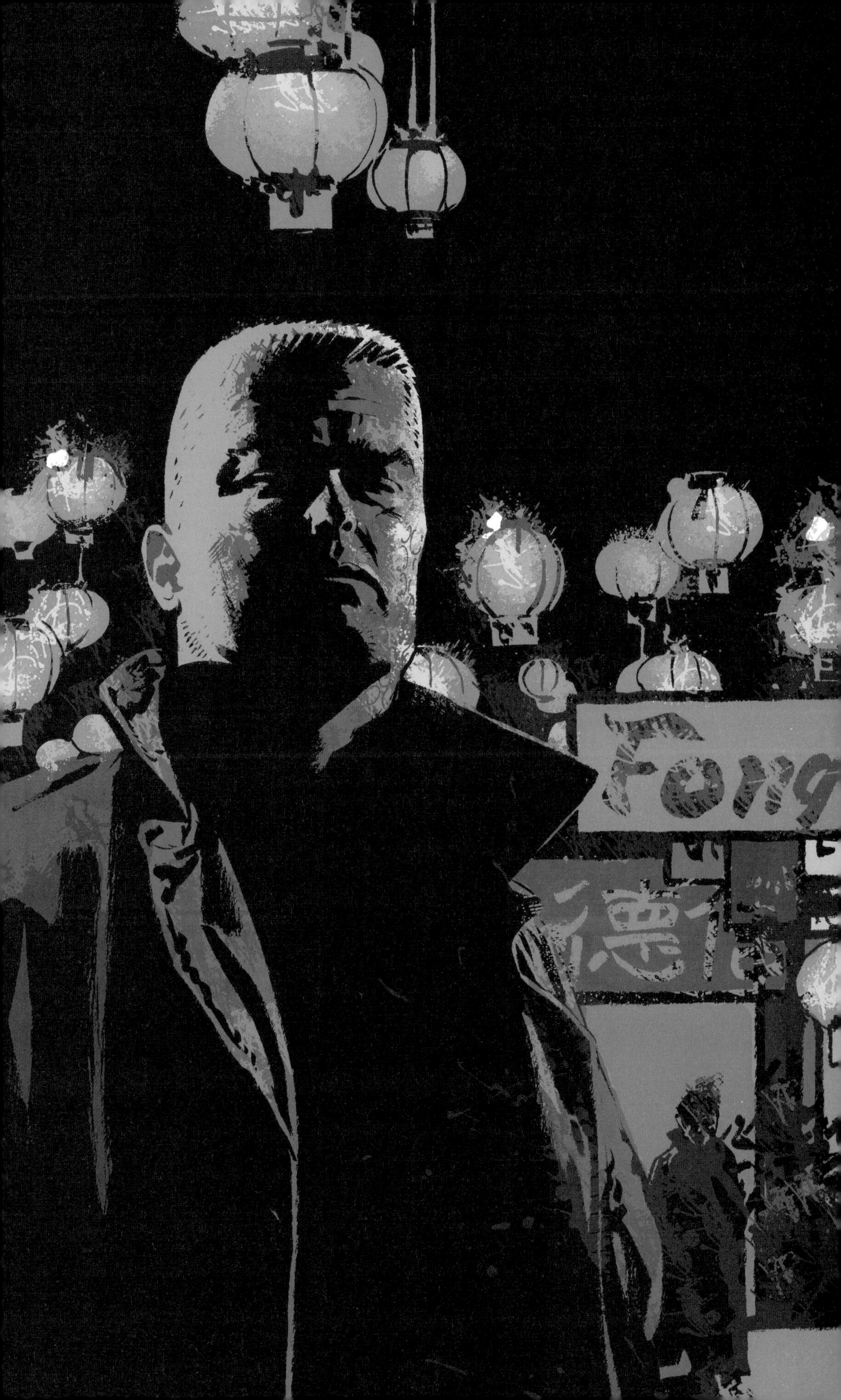
德

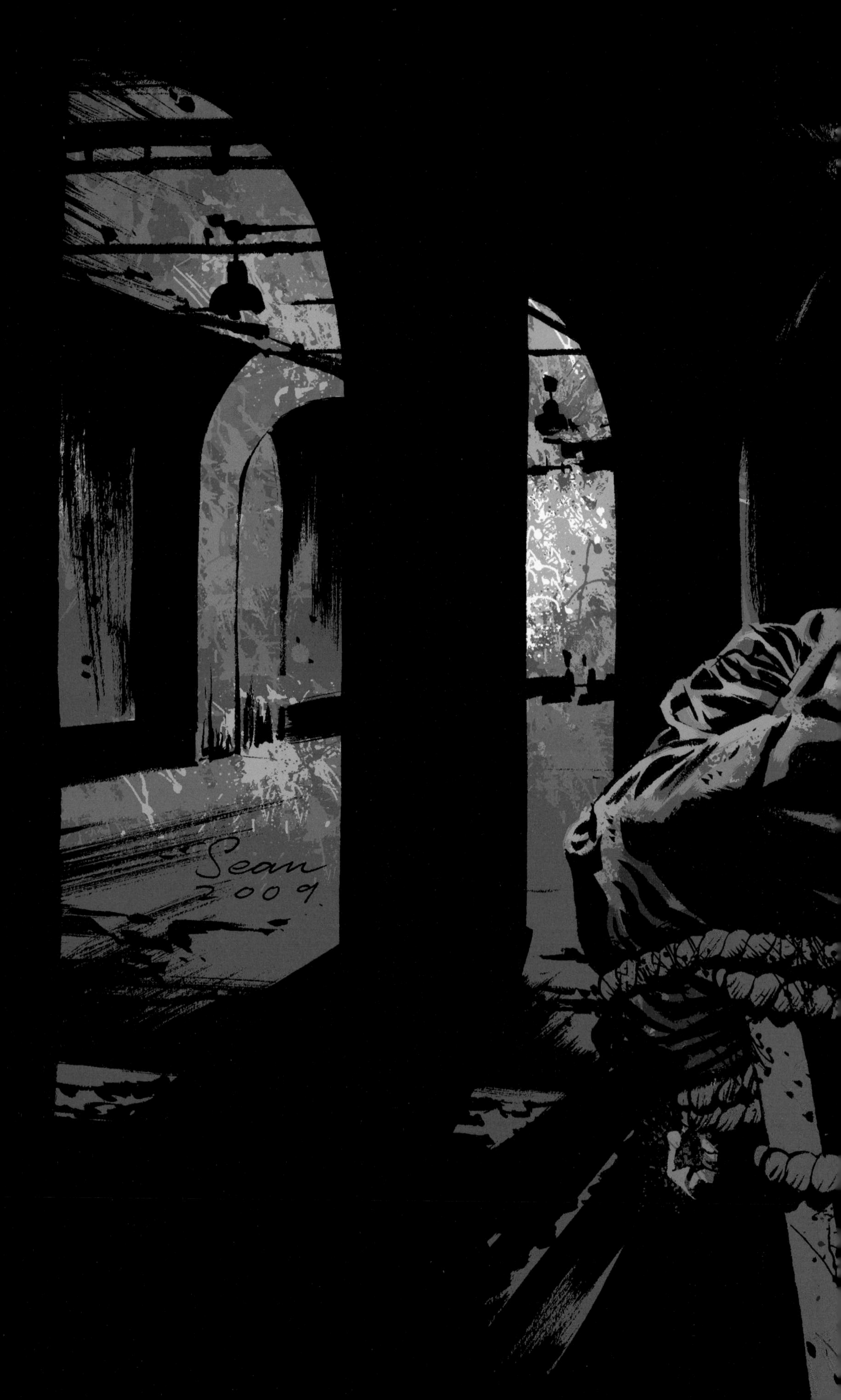
Sean
2009

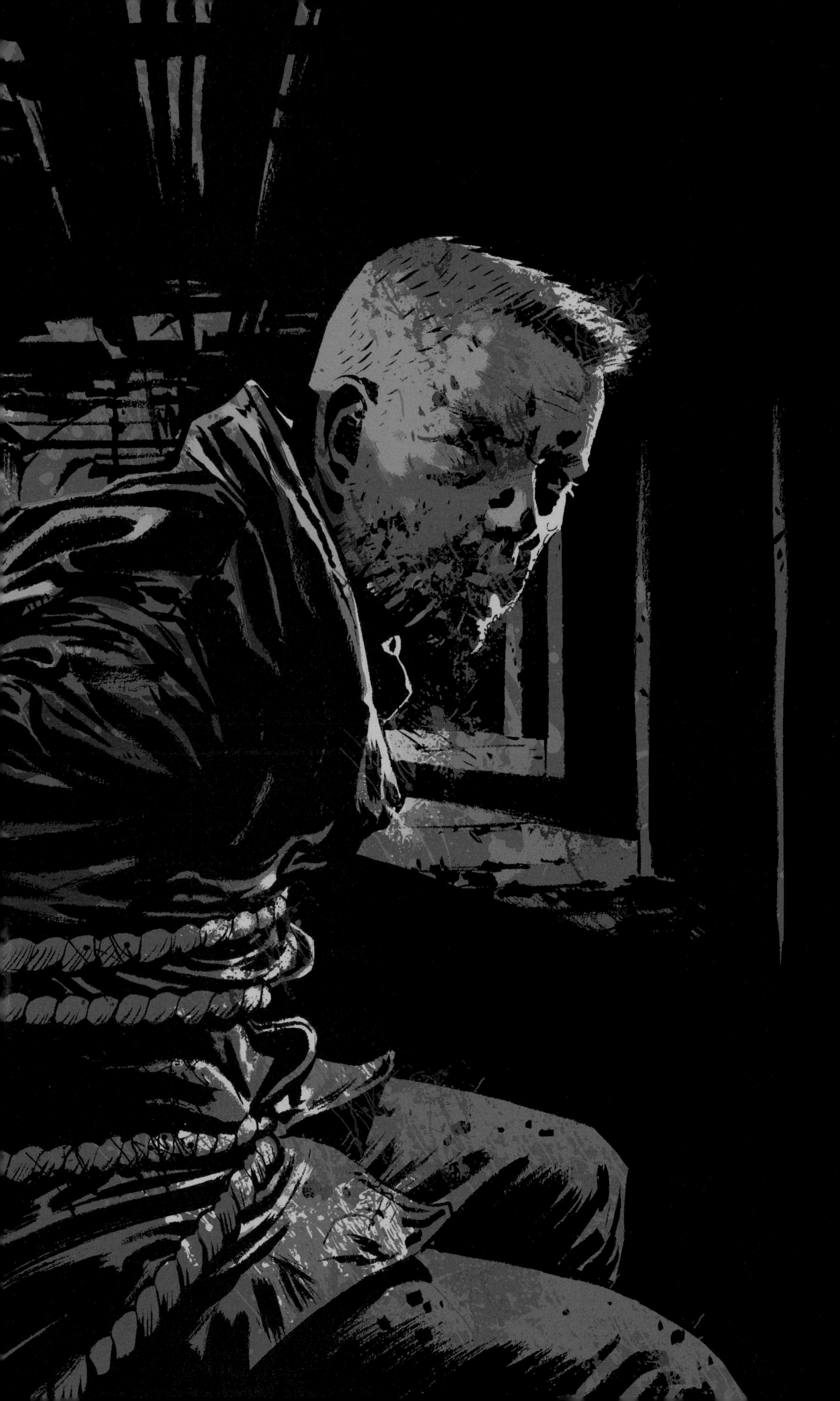

DESCEND INTO THE WORLD OF

A CRIMINAL edition by Ed Brubaker and Sean Phillips
Coward
Introduction by Tom Fontana

A CRIMINAL edition by Ed Brubaker and Sean Phillips
Lawless
Introduction by Frank Miller

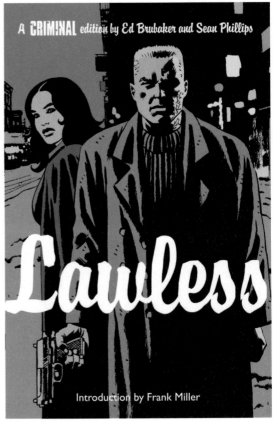

Meet Leo, who can plan the perfect heist... but only if he can be convinced the job is safe enough. See, Leo is not a shoot-first think-later guy; Leo is a professional. But to some criminals, even professionals, the right payout is worth almost any risk. So when an old friend and a crooked cop approach with a plan to seize millions of dollars in contraband from an evidence transport van, Leo must make tough choices, knowing there's nothing you can trust less in this world than a cop on the take.

CRIMINAL Vol. 1 COWARD ISBN: 0-7851-2439-X

Tracy Lawless has come home for his first Christmas in the city in nearly twenty years. But the only kind of family reunion he'll find is in a graveyard, because his last living relative, his little brother Ricky, was killed almost a year earlier. Now Tracy is back to find out who did it, and why, and to do that he'll have to immerse himself back into the criminal world that he once ran away from. The question is, even if he finds the answers he seeks, will he survive the experience?

CRIMINAL Vol. 2 LAWLESS ISBN: 978-0-7851-2816-8

FOUR MORE AWARD-WINNING

CRIMINAL

The third collection of Ed Brubaker and Sean Phillips' critically-acclaimed noir series follows a different twist of the knife this time -- telling three interlinking stories that take place during the early 1970s and swirl around the fate of a hard-luck Femme Fatale, a boxer and a thief and killer just home from Vietnam. Each story is told from a different narrative point-of-view, so we can see the varied secrets and hidden desires that ultimately lead to a lot of murder and mayhem.

Years ago, Jacob Kurtz was a happy family man, long-retired from the life of crime he was raised in. Then the police made him the prime suspect in a horrible crime and ripped his life apart. Now Jacob is less than a shadow of his former self, an insomniac who roams the city at night, looking for anything to distract him from his empty bed. Until he walks into the wrong place at the right time, and one bad night starts Jacob down a twisted path to kidnapping, robbery, murder… and just maybe the answer to the mystery buried in his past.

CRIMINAL Vol. 3 THE DEAD AND THE DYING ISBN: 978-0-7851-3227-1   CRIMINAL Vol. 4 BAD NIGHT ISBN: 978-0-7851-3228-8

VOLUMES CURRENTLY AVAILABLE